THERE IS A TIDE ...

RuthAnn K. Harper

Pollock and Son, Publisher

Post Office Box 2854
St. Petersburg, Florida 33731

727 322 0840
pollockson@tampabay.rr.com

Cover Design by Rebecca Jane Sankner ©

ISBN: 0-9761216-1-1

FIRST PRINTING
Printed in the United States of America

In memory of Doug Christiansen, who was
not able to visit *i Gatti Felici* in Italy but who
made her journey there possible.

ACKNOWLEDGEMENTS

I owe a debt of thanks to several people who have helped to make this book a reality. Not one had any thought of personal reward, but gave what they did solely for love of me.

Three Ph.D's lent their professional expertise despite other demands on their time. My sister, Ingrid L. Kohler, volunteered her scant free time as a professional editor to edit my manuscript. My childhood neighbor and lifetime friend, Rebecca Sankner, took out time from her professorial duties to undertake the awesome task of illustrating places she has not yet had the opportunity to visit. Léon Danco, and his dear wife Katie, took me in as a foster child, so to speak. Having already published a number of prestigious books of his own, Léon laid out a plan of publication and heel-nipping. He motivated me to pursue a goal I had never hoped to attain.

We also appreciate the good work by BookPublishingWorld.com for so capably fitting all the pieces together for publication.

Our children, Charles and Nicole Harper, helped in handling affairs in the United States that were difficult for us to manage smoothly from abroad. They have never wavered in their support of and enthusiasm for our somewhat unorthodox lifestyles.

And, finally, I thank my captain and photographer, William Pollock Harper, who has voyaged with me for many decades to places new and unexpected but always exciting and wonderful.

RuthAnn K. Harper
December, 2006

TABLE OF CONTENTS

TABLE OF CONTENTS

INTRODUCTION

This is the story of an old wooden Chris-Craft motor yacht and the people who love her. It is the story of a love affair with Italy. It is the story of a couple facing life changes as their working careers come to a successful conclusion. These elements meld between these covers to catalogue a story of resolve, adjustment, freedom, toil, expanding horizons, simplicity and joy in life. If you are a yachtsman with immutable ideas of what the proper yacht should be, chances are good that you will not enjoy this book. It will frustrate and annoy you, and you will scoff. It would be best that you read no further.

Bill and I were each raised in homes where we were expected to be seen and not heard. They were good, caring homes, and we were good, filial children. But beneath the placid surface bubbled seditious thoughts. We were never rebels as that word is generally understood, but we marched to a different drummer. When we met as teenagers, the sparks of kindred spirits discovered ignited in both of us. We married young to "escape" home, but we continued in college, earned our degrees, became steady and successful, bought houses and raised two children. But we never quite fit in. We seemed to always be liberals in a conservative environment. We compromised in necessary areas for the sake of our occupations but, frankly, we were gadflies who often nipped and annoyed (but sometimes actually initiated change). We refused to live in neighborhoods recommended as proper for executives, preferring to remodel old farmhouses and surround ourselves with land and animals. Our idea of a great vacation was exploring the back roads of Mexico in a beat-up pickup truck. Professionally we advanced nicely and were respected in our fields despite our frustrating lack of conformity.

We worked hard and we worked well, but we did not live to work. It was probably no surprise that we fell in love with Italy on our first visit in 1989. We experienced a sense of freedom, an appreciation of beauty and leisure, a social awareness that suited our natures. For a couple years we looked into buying property there – everything from *rusticos* to *villas* to apartments in *palazzos*. The problems were many. Most importantly, all 20 regions of Italy have their own irresistible appeal, and we were torn among the history and cosmopolitan atmosphere of Rome, the waterways of Venice, the wide beaches of Rimini, the fruitful Tuscan hills, and the towering Dolomites, to name only a few of the intriguing locations. The prices in Rome were not affordable, and the red tape everywhere discouraged us. We were, after all, trying to escape a world of silly and confining rules and officious people. In our late 40s, the idea of living on a boat occurred to us and no sooner was the thought conceived than we became actively involved in its gestation and birth. In our early 50s we were ready to sail away on a full and beckoning tide.

What you hold in your hands is an account of a couple facing "retirement" who purchase a boat nearly as old as they are, refurbish her, and move with her to the Mediterranean coast of Italy. We are not wealthy yachtsmen, nor are we "cruisers" who travel full time in the waters of the world. We maintain a home in the United States and fly the American flag at the stern of our U.S. documented vessel. We are not world class sailors nor are we neophytes. This is the story that describes how we found and appropriately outfitted a 1952 Chris-Craft and went about settling on the Italian coast. It is a tale of doors opening to a new world; the discovery of fascinating people from many cultures; the growth of nautical competence; and a few inevitable disappointments.

In our retirement we have found a whole new focus – discovering Europe, learning foreign languages and ways, pushing ourselves to become better and more knowledgeable in a number of fields. We have discovered kindred spirits in unexpected and wonderful ways and we hope we are avoiding the cynicism and self-centeredness that often accompany the senior years. Prior to Bill's leaving the workplace, his company had sent us to a lovely town near Seattle for a relaxed weekend and retirement seminar. One of the "funny" anecdotes told concerned the disenfranchised husband who invades his wife's kitchen with the intent of reorganizing. His own turf being gone, he seeks a new niche and purpose. This little story made our blood run cold. There was no way we were going to "re-divvy up" existing turf. Our decision was made to find a whole new geography to explore. While this was exactly the opposite of what the well-intentioned seminar had meant to suggest, it has worked out well for us. Like most people, we have done some smart things and many stupid things, but in the end can look back on our adventures as good fun. While ignorance is in no way bliss, overcoming it is a delightful way to spend one's life.

THERE IS A TIDE ...

'There is a tide in the affairs of men,
Which, taken at the flood, leads on to fortune;
Omitted, all the voyage of their life
Is bound in shallows and in miseries.
On such a full sea are we now afloat,
And we must take the current when it serves
Or lose our ventures.'
William Shakespeare, *Julius Caesar*

CHAPTER I

TIDE AND TIME

'People wish to be settled: only as far as they are unsettled is there any hope for them.'

Ralph Waldo Emerson, *Circles*

Swept in on the great flood that gives us life, we gasp for our first lungful of air, shake off the water that has protected and sustained us in our dependence, and begin our search for meaning and our individual self. We know that soon or late a great ebb tide – sometimes expected and awaited, sometimes awesomely sudden – will carry us back whence we came. Between these great events are the average ups and downs of life, some of the waves rocking us comfortably, others tossing us about fearfully. One of the most tumultuous of these tides is retirement.

The very word "retirement" has its own peculiarly American connotations. In many other countries "on pension" is the more relevant term used. "Retirement" smacks of withdrawal or taking yourself to bed leaving fun, frolic and society to the young. Today's retirees may not be young in the conventional sense, but we are certainly still a strong force. Generally fit, healthy, benefiting from medicines our generation did much to develop, we feel beautiful, financially comfortable and ready to enjoy life unfettered by the Puritan work ethic. And yet many of us in this category leave the work force so ill-prepared for that new life that we spend it dejected, frustrated and unhappy. Somehow, throwing off that old mooring line seems suicidal rather than liberating.

My husband Bill and I found ourselves in our early 50s having worked hard at our jobs for 31 years. Our two children had completed their educations and had been successfully launched to follow their own stars. We set about listing some of the things we had always wanted to do but hadn't the time. Travel, learn a new language, read all the plays of Shakespeare, educate ourselves about the world's great religions, spend time practicing classical guitar, learn to play chess, appreciate opera…. Our list seemed endless, and the longer it grew, the more excited we became. We were eligible for retirement and ready to explore the many exciting currents running outside our little pond of daily routine.

We had fallen in love with Italy 13 years earlier and had visited regularly and frequently. I had been teaching Latin since I was 21 and was currently being tutored in Italian. The idea of relocating to a country that had been part of me for so long – if only scholastically – had a strong attraction. First we seriously pursued buying an apartment in Rome. We had rented apartments and houses throughout the country. We had read all the books about villas being restored in Tuscany and Umbria and expatriates making their way in Rome and other large cities. Acquaintances had bought a medieval house in Todi in central Italy.

While we read enthusiastically about these delightful undertakings, they did not seem right for us. We did not want to live in a big city, at least not yet. We had spent our lives maintaining old houses and big yards and wanted a break from that kind of commitment. If we desired neither a noisy urban life nor a rustic country one, what did we want? It is one thing to displace oneself from familiar things, but could we really expect to fit into a foreign culture without feeling a bit of an outsider, i.e. one in retirement? We sat down and listed our requirements. We did not want to spend our time on maintenance. We needed to own and not rent. We needed our personal things around us and our own bed. We needed to have the ability to move about and feel a part of the flow of life. What we needed was – a boat in Italy.

The notion was not that farfetched for us. We had both been raised in Florida and had owned boats. Close proximity to water was in our blood. When we married as starry-eyed youngsters, we dreamed of sailing around the world in a sailboat and working odd jobs in exotic ports. But that dream required the physical strength of youth and the financial resources accrued with age. While we had the former, we were woefully lacking in the latter. Now our situation was reversed and a sailing craft would no longer suit our plans. We did not want to share our home with crew, and we did not possess the physical ability or knowledge and experience to handle a sailboat by ourselves. So it became clear that what we needed was – a power yacht in Italy.

In over 30 years of married life we had owned a few boats, one a 30-foot cabin cruiser, so we had some pretty definite ideas of what we did and did not want. Both of our families had a wealth of antique furnishings, and we had spent many a dreamy hour admiring the beautiful wooden Riva runabouts in Italy, both in Venice, on the Adriatic coast, and in Portofino, on the Ligurian coast. We could not envision ourselves in a modern fiberglass boat. What we needed was a classic wooden yacht. In July 1997 we purchased a 32-foot wooden Chris-Craft, vintage 1964, in Newport Beach, Calif., and began spending our weekends on her. *Leone Felice* was a stout bark with a soul that sighed vague ideas of Mediterranean adventure. Vague ideas metamorphosed into strong longings. But *Leone Felice*, while fostering and focusing the dream, was not capable of fulfilling it.

The vision came into sudden clear focus in December 1997 in Huntington Beach. Rocking gently at dock was a 42-foot Chris-Craft Commander Express Cruiser. A master craftsman had toiled daily in a work shed for three years to restore and perfect her. His aim had been to create a modern wooden classic motor yacht. Her stainless steel gleamed and her tall sides rose from the water, as dazzling white and slick as wet paint. The burnished luster of her mahogany trim glowed warmly in the sun. Every plug of her unsoiled spacious teak decks lined up to grain.

We sat on the elegantly upholstered settee in her mahogany paneled saloon and watched the sunbeams sparkle through the clear and emerald cut-glass design that comprised the companionway door. Two little pink marble-topped tables and two fine upholstered mahogany chairs completed the lavish furnishings of the cabin. The two bunks of the fore-cabin were covered in the same old-world map tapestry as the settee, while curtains of a satin stripe of maroon, forest green, aqua and gold complemented the gold and maroon wool rug. It was rich, sophisticated, and we were seduced. Every line of this magnificent vessel whispered to our souls and urged us to plunge forward into our dream.

She was a stuffed shirt, a bit of a snob, this grand lady that had stolen our hearts. She spent Sunday mornings vaunting herself at spiffy eateries in Newport Beach and wowing classic boat shows. Her name *Class Action* was emblazoned in enormous gold leaf lettering on her mahogany transom and cabin sides. She seemed structurally and aesthetically close to perfect but was woefully lacking in utility. She would have a bit to learn before she fitted us properly, but, well, we had a lot to learn ourselves. She had a firm keel, a great soul, and a willingness to bend to adventure. She also had two new engines and a sacrifice price. Early in January 1998 she became ours, and somewhat more gradually we came to understand that we had become hers.

For most of the first year of ownership we trod gently. We did not physically change her name, although it was changed in our hearts and in Coast Guard documentation. *Leone Felice* had been Bill's inspiration and a kind of retirement gift to himself; so the Italian equivalent of "Happy Lion" was entirely suitable. But this boat represented for us a new life together, and the name could not refer to only one animal. We settled on the name *i Gatti Felici*, "The Happy Cats." We needed a hailing port, which could be any city in the United States. We definitely did not want Bakersfield, the California city where we lived prior to retirement. We had been raised in St. Petersburg, Fla., but that name did not excite us either. It was too long and would be confused with Russia. So we settled on Naples, Fla., as a place we knew well and enjoyed and because of the Italian connection.

Gatti remained docked next to the yacht of Jerry, the craftsman who had rebuilt her. We valued his advice and help in making her more practical; he had built part of his heart into her, and we did not want to hurt his feelings with our changes. I was finishing teaching the school year; Bill was running a small consulting business as a mental buffer between leaving an executive position with an international oil company and retiring totally. Thus we were in Bakersfield during the week, and Jerry could keep an eye on his baby undisturbed.

Many changes were basic and necessary. While *Gatti* had a small refrigerator and bar sink, the ship's galley had been torn out, as had the shower in the head. In fact, the entire cabin, galley, and even the head had been carpeted with rich wool. The galley had been incorporated into the saloon and had no cooking facilities. More fundamentally, there was no windlass for the anchor, or any anchor for that matter. There were no electronics, no helm chair for the navigator. 1998 saw the purchase of a tender, *La Gattina* ("The Kitten"), an outboard motor, additional protective canvas, and installation of a water heater, microwave, small oven, and telephone. It also saw education on the endless upkeep of a wooden boat,

4

exploration of the local California coast, and a two-month sojourn in Italy to locate a port and slip.

The transfer and realization of dreams is a delicate business. Jerry bought a new wooden yacht project and busily began yet another multi-year renewal miracle. We spent many weekends basking almost totally immobilized on our beautiful teak decks. We had the boat, we had the goal, but we had not yet shifted our practical thinking from a work-oriented life in America to a leisure-oriented life in Italy. In many ways we were stultified, and the first changes we made probably demonstrate a lack of logical thinking. But we were approaching a full sea and were almost ready to take the current when it served.

Gatti by the mud bank at time of purchase.

The saloon looking forward to the cabin.

Where is the navigator's seat?

La Gattina joins the family.

CHAPTER II

PORT PLOTTING

'Open my heart and you will see
Graved inside of it, 'Italy'.'
Robert Browning, *De Gustibus*

Bill and I divided the months of June and July 1998 between an apartment in Rome and a little house in a tiny country village near Siena. We also engaged in a bit of port shopping. We had previously admired boats and explored delightful beaches, but we had never really looked at the actuality of having a boat in Italian waters. Was it truly feasible? Where did we want to establish a home port? Our friends in the States thought we were crazy. Were they right?

We began our sojourn as we always had in Rome, our favorite city. We had become very familiar with it over the years and had made interesting friends there. Some of these were people from whom we rented apartments or relatives of friends in the United States. Others were volunteers at a most amazing cat colony in the heart of ancient Rome; we had financially contributed to it over the years, and I actually worked in it myself this momentous summer. We were offered some interesting advice from these quarters as well as others. We were strongly encouraged to look at ports north of Rome, at least until we felt more at home. The consensus was that the possibility of theft was higher in the southern ports of the country and a boat left for months at a time would be particularly vulnerable. We were also repeatedly assured that our boat would be worth more on the market in Italy than in the States. Although we had no plans to sell her, this was still a comfort because we were facing shipping costs in the neighborhood of $15,000.

What surprised us most was to learn that the Italian peninsula and its islands offer relatively few good ports for a boat *Gatti*'s size. Imagine all that water and beauty combined with such geographic inhospitality! In our wanderings through Rome we serendipitously spotted in the back of a magazine kiosk a wonderful magazine called *Nauticard* that provided charts and data about every port in the country. The information was in Italian, but this posed no real problem for us. My reading ability far outdistanced my conversational skills. While we would eventually find similar information elsewhere, for a long time this was the only reference we had. Having collected what bits of local wisdom we could find and comprehend in Rome, we set off to do our own exploration.

We were not enthralled with the ports we could find in Ostia and Fiumicino, despite their closeness to Rome. The Tiber empties into the Tyrrhenian Sea between these two towns, and the area was very confusing to us. Narrow old roads ran along the sides of the river and a tall, imposing hedge concealed the boatworks or *cantieri* that lined the river banks. The time would come when we would be able to negotiate these areas and fill every nautical need, but even then, time and sleuthing would be necessary before we discovered which small openings in the forbidding hedge to duck into to find what we needed. Also the time would come when a dream port would materialize in the area, but that time had not yet come. There were also some pretty run-down neighborhoods in the area, and our Roman warnings about theft were fresh in our minds.

And so we headed north to our rental in Siena and began looking at ports to the north. We were not interested in the large port at Civitavecchia up the coast from Rome, which caters to huge cruise boats and other commercial traffic. Between Ostia and Civitavecchia we discovered the port of Riva di Traiano, which appeared to be brand new and beautiful. Its somewhat narrow entrance opened toward Civitavecchia, and the slips were folded in a circular protection of shore and breakwater. It appeared that eventually shops and cafes would surround the harbor: many were in the midst of construction. The port was perhaps a quarter full with power and sailboats of many nationalities securely moored. We were heartened to find that there were facilities in Italy that corresponded to our American conceptions of what a port should look like, but the Sunday we visited was scorching hot. It was 1 p.m. and everything was shut down. We continued on our way, thinking that this would be a good port to visit, but for now it lacked that essence of Italy we were looking for. It was too far away from towns, had no local color, and had a very transient feel. As we continued our drive, we discovered that there were many delightful little ports along this beautiful beach coast in the region of Lazio, but all were too small and were decidedly summer getaways.

The next ports we investigated were those in Tuscany. Some were too small, some appeared to be little more than canals, and some were too big and commercially oriented. Without question, the best of them all were the two ports at Mount Argentario – Porto Ercole and Santo Stefano. The coastline in Tuscany is pretty flat, and Argentario comes as a big surprise. Once an island, the mountain is now connected to the mainland and the city of Orbetello by a narrow, sandy causeway. The ports are tucked in at different sides of this mountain-island, and the Tuscan Archipelago lies in close proximity. The islands of Giglio and Elba are especially popular among boaters and visitors who arrive by ferry. Other smaller islands in the chain such as Monte Cristo are enticing areas for those lucky enough to have their own boats. Porto Ercole had a great deal of appeal for us because of its small-town feel and its picturesque medieval ruins. Santo Stefano is beautiful as well and in addition is home to one of the finest wooden boat restorers in the world. We were enchanted by these ports but maybe a little intimidated as well. They were different from what we had been used to in that they were harbors surrounded by towns rather than distinct port areas. While we vowed to come back and visit them on *i Gatti Felici*, we were not yet prepared to adapt to what we at the time perceived to be places so foreign to our experience. In addition, these ports also seemed somewhat isolated. Yes, one could find public transportation to the big train station in Orbetello, but it would have made us happier to have the station closer at hand. Although we planned to explore on *Gatti*, we also planned on using her as a convenient home-base from which we could travel easily to other parts of Europe.

At the end of our Tuscan sojourn, we decamped to one of our favorite Italian spots – the seaside town of Lérici just over the Tuscan border in the region of Liguria. A lack of certain amenities in San Lorenzo a Merse, the little village in which we had stayed near Siena, and the agony of hundreds of insect bites drove us to proceed directly to Lérici and forego investigating the ports between Grossetto and La Spezia. This was a shocking oversight to be sure, particularly in view of the fact that the bustling ports of Viareggio and Livorno are in this area, but we promised ourselves that we would rectify it sometime. The future seemed so strange at this point. We would really be living in Italy on a boat somewhere. But how would we decide where? How would all the complications of getting there resolve themselves? Such an abrupt change in direction in one's 50s certainly has its fears, but the exciting possibilities and broad horizons offered were too compelling to be ignored.

Beautiful, serene Lérici, rubbing shoulders with her neighbor San Terenzo, lies around the curved shores of the Gulf of Poets – the poets in question being Lord Byron and Percy Bysshe Shelley. It was one of their favorite places too. Byron was waiting here for Shelley's return by sailboat from a visit to Livorno when the news came that Shelley, a seaman, and a young boy had perished when their boat capsized. Shelley's home, a museum, and the naming of the gulf itself are testaments to the affection Italians felt for these men. The port of Lérici is so small as to be scarcely worthy of the name. It consists mainly of scores of small boats anchored to buoys offshore. A little tender boat is summoned by whistle for transport to and from these boats. There is a private dock where larger sailing craft tie up and a commercial dock where one can catch the ferry to Portovenere across the gulf, to the huge port of La Spezia that NATO and the Italian navy call home, or out into the Mediterranean to the towns of the Cinque Terre and north as far as picturesque Portofino.

One can be blissfully happy in Lérici! From the Hotel Shelley delle Palme's fifth floor breakfast room with its expanse of windows overlooking the gulf, or from the well-appointed swimming deck across the street right on the rocky shore, the whole area forms an idyllic panorama. To the left stands the great castle fortification intended to protect the northern boundary of the medieval city-state of Pisa with its massive walls rising from the sea. Across the gulf to the north gaze back serenely the fortifications of the Genovese city-state whose southern boundary lay here at Portovenere. A significant portion of the fortification does not appear to be intimidating at all today, made up as it is by seven-story pastel apartment buildings that face the port. But intimidating they could be when manned by angry defenders poised to dump hot oil on invaders who could find no alley or shelter between those tall walls. On the heights behind this line of defense sits a fort.

Perched in the gulf are the islands of Isola Palmaria and little Isola di Tino with its reassuring lighthouse guiding mariners from the Mediterranean into the gulf and the wharves of La Spezia. Topping a cliff to the sea side of Portovenere is the venerable church of San Pietro, movingly simple with its black and white stone. It is very old and weathered but not to the degree of the ancient Roman temple to Venus which sits on the same cliff and lends its name to the town. Looking to the right from the deck of the Hotel Shelley, about three miles within the entrance of the gulf stretches the great 12-cable breakwater that protects the bustling commercial and military harbor of La Spezia. A narrow channel at each end of the breakwater provides entrance to the big freighters and warships that visit or reside there. Sometimes a smudge of black smoke defiles the clear air as a freighter makes its way past the lighthouse and by the breakwater. O, yes, Lérici is a lovely port indeed, but not a permanent home for *i Gatti Felici.*

We next traversed the Ligurian coast from Riomaggiore in the Cinque Terre to Portofino. Time did not allow for covering more, but we knew we would be back often. Liguria is the province that embraces the great curve of the Italian Mediterranean from the towering white marble cliffs of Carrara all the way to the French border. We were well aware that captivating beauty awaited us all along the Riviera, but for this trip, we explored the Cinque Terre by foot, car, train and boat. The name refers to five little villages that perch on the cliffs high above the coast. The inhabitants concern themselves with fishing and tending grapevines that clutch the slopes at improbable angles and are tended from cable-car-like vehicles. The villages are connected by footpaths and terrifying trails etched into sheer cliffs, very popular with hikers in summer. None of the five offer anything like a port for a boat like *Gatti*, but we enjoyed exploring them nonetheless. We then moved northward to the pretty towns of Levanto and Sestri Levante, taking cool dips along the way and each time realizing that ports were few and small. Then we arrived at Lavagna.

The *porto turistico* at Lavagna is the largest yachting marina in Europe, with 1600 slips. This was a place that seemed to fill all our needs. There was a bustle of shipbuilding and repair. There were boats of all kinds from all over the world, and the excitement blended in with the Italian atmosphere we craved. Just across the rail tracks from the port area sat the medieval town of Lavagna, its narrow streets lined with little shops and cafes. It had the amenities of a modern port but also the proximity of an old Italian town. We fell in love with this place and hurried to the dockmaster's office. He seemed a bit confused when we asked about slip rental for a year. No, that was impossible; one could rent for only three months. He did concede, however, that after the first three months, there might be another three available. We then wandered about the port and came upon an office offering marine insurance, etc. A big, friendly dog greeted us at the door, followed by an equally friendly man who spoke about as much English as we spoke Italian. He assured us that he could provide a slip for a year as well as upkeep while we were out of the country. He gave us his card, and we left feeling jubilant that we had found a home. "Just fax me when you are ready. We will have all in order." What comforting words! We were quoted an annual price of about $4,000 for the slip, including water and electricity.

We returned to the hotel at Lérici happy cats indeed. Then, our two month stay in Italy being up, we drove back to Rome. Rome was hot. Rome was packed with tourists and those who prey on them. Bill's wallet was stolen on the bus the day before we returned to California and with it the name and number of our contact in Lavagna. We had not learned enough on this trip to go forward with moving *i Gatti Felici*, but we now knew there was a place for us in Italy such as we had dreamed of, and we could work in the direction of making that dream a living reality.

CHAPTER III

"H" DOCK

'Mud unto mud! – Death eddies near –
Not the appointed End, not here!
But somewhere, beyond Space and Time,
Is wetter water, slimier slime!'
Rupert Brooke, *Heaven*

While the Huntington Harbor Marina may not be the worst anchorage in a world that includes the Sargasso Sea, it truly lacked the amenities to be found in most civilized locations. *I Gatti Felici* had the misfortune to be moored at "H" dock, which was undoubtedly the strangest dock in a strange marina. "H" dock was actually newer than any of the others because it had burned down and been replaced in 1989. It will probably maintain the distinction of newest dock as long as the marina exists, for another conflagration is surely in its future. Our constant hope was to vacate it before that happened.

Not only did we have the great misfortune of being moored at this dock, but our slip lay lengthwise between the dock and a mud bank. At the best of times, we viewed slimy rocks and mud from our starboard portholes. Other times we were in real danger of grounding in the muck. The boats across the dock from us faced in, so a view from port revealed tall bows that looked for all the world as though they were about to broadside us. People lived on all these boats and each boat sported a dog. At various times during our year's stay here, all the people and all their dogs were at odds with one another. At no given time was everyone speaking to everyone. On one boat lived a somewhat rotund man who delighted in reclining naked on his upper deck. Pretty young women would arrive on weekends to administer massages under the glaring eye of the sun and the lowered eyes of the dock denizens. A few months later this boat was towed off under the armed escort of federal marshals.

Another boat nearby was a large cabin cruiser that had been resurrected by a strange couple who used it as an office and demonstration center. We gathered they did boat repair, remodeling and sales. Their great goal seemed to be to sell an old boat and then restore it. We never could quite figure out what was wrong with their own restored *Black Pearl*. About two-thirds back from her bow she made a distinct angular turn and then continued sternward from that point. It was rather like someone had done a sloppy job of gluing her back to her front. These people were friendly one day, combative the next, and nosey always. An eyeball could always be counted on at one porthole or another. When they weren't quarreling with dock-mates, they were quarreling below deck. We suspected that a fair amount of drinking was going on and, when two years later *Black Pearl* was driven upon the rocks outside Marina del Rey following a July 4 celebration, our suspicions were supported.

The marina boasted a species of ballroom that was rented out for parties, weddings and similar celebrations. Despite the obvious decrepitude of the structure and its contents, it enjoyed a relatively active booking. After dark the carpet stains were not so evident, and the assumption seemed to be that garlands of greenery or bunting of white netting would put the guests in a festive frame of mind. Valet parking also added a touch of glitz to the proceedings and a ton of frustration to those of us who rented slips. Theoretically we were provided with parking, but the limited spaces set up a situation that frequently became confrontational. "H" dock lay close to this structure, so many a night we fell into troubled sleep to the throbbing of third-class bands echoing from the mud bank.

Having once acquired a parking spot, the problem arose of toting our supplies to the boat and arriving with them and our limbs intact. The first entry gate to the marina was adjacent to this "club house." It was an iron swinging gate about 10 feet wide, secured to its post by an old sock in lieu of a latch. And a mighty tenacious old sock that was! During our stay there and for at least two years after we left, it showed no signs of wear whatever. After entering and resocking this gate, we had to traverse a quarter mile along the mud bank already mentioned. The first few feet, which ran along one side of the club house, were paved in concrete slabs of varying altitudes. Drops and rises of several inches between the slabs laid traps for unwitting toes. Beyond the sidewalk we plotted a careful path along the bank, attempting to avoid the deep furrows and crevices where the mud had slipped into the ocean. Adding to these difficulties, small, anemic palmettos, clinging to an uncertain life, were scattered about in no discernible pattern; we regularly embraced at least one of these sharp sentinels on the way because there was no lighting whatsoever between the parking lot and the boat.

Assuming that we negotiated all these horrors without mishap, the next trial was the gate at "H" dock. Whereas gate #1 had no latch, gate #2 was firmly and unalterably locked, and there were no keys. The only way to open it was to jerk directly upward with considerable vigor. Many times have I stood and sworn at this obstacle as I waited for assistance and many were the sprains and bruises sustained from throwing myself at it from various angles. This hell-gate having been passed through, if the tide were in, reaching the boat was now the relatively simple procedure of walking from bank to dock across a ramp. If the tide were out, a nearly vertical ramp had to be slid down to the floating dock level. If the weather were dry, one had a reasonable expectation of making it with parcels intact. When it was wet, Fate held the advantage.

Under this mobile ramp, living a life of privilege, resided a half dozen pigeons. As delightful as their home was, of greater pleasure to them was to perch, scratch or defecate upon our smooth teak decks, lustrous mahogany trim and burnished stainless fittings and rails. We waged a constant battle with these fowl, often awakening to their scratchy little goose-stepping on the foredeck above our bunks.

"H" dock was as far away from the "amenities" of the marina as was geographically possible. These amenities consisted of the showers and restrooms. To get there, one reversed the steps required to reach the boat. The ramp was mounted sideways and gate #2 shouldered open. The palmettos and furrows were avoided, and the old sock lifted off. The parking lot was passed and then two large condominium buildings. The restrooms were finally reached a full half mile from the slip. In this chamber of horrors the stall doors hung crazily from hinges secured by one screw and had no apparatus to lock into. The shower stall reeked of fungi and was hung with various mildew species. Every aspect was damp and dank and redolent of mysterious diseases.

We lived 150 miles from *Gatti* when she was moored at Huntington and more often than not arrived after dark. This fact transformed getting from car to boat from an annoyance to a major difficulty. However, many times we congratulated ourselves on having those many miles between ourselves and the weirdness that was "H" dock.

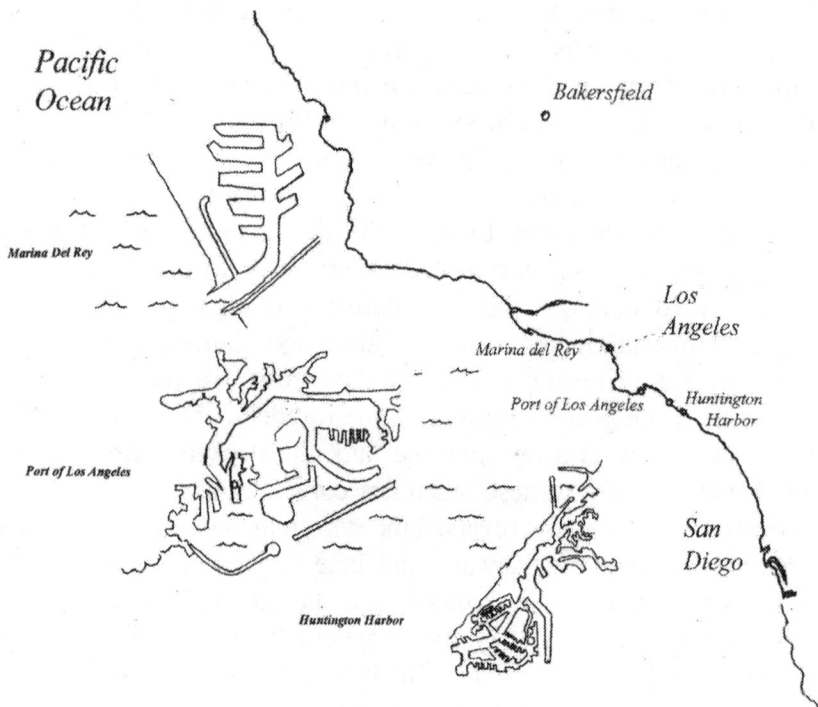

Pacific
Ocean

Bakersfield

Marina Del Rey

Los
Angeles

Marina del Rey

Port of Los Angeles

Huntington
Harbor

Port of Los Angeles

San
Diego

Huntington Harbor

Southern California Coast

CHAPTER IV

JERRY

'It was so old a ship – who knows, who knows?
And yet so beautiful, I watched in vain
To see the mast burst open with a rose,
And the whole deck put on its leaves again.'
James Elroy Flecker, *The Old Ships*

The question the reader may well ask is, "Given the other really nice locations in southern California, why did you stay at "H" dock?" The answer is a single word. "Jerry."

Jerry was the master, the godfather, of *Gatti*. He had purchased her as a derelict for a fraction of the rent due on her slip. He had transported her to a warehouse and for three years labored on her daily. Without regard to cost or time, he dismantled and lovingly recreated her. He transformed her into a showpiece not only externally, but internally as well. Every inch of wood, every screw, every liter of engine was the best that could be found.

Jerry parted with *Gatti* to purchase a vessel he had longed to own for years. It came on the market suddenly, and he had to move quickly. He now lived on this yacht with his wife and engaging Scottie dog, his bow pointed at us across "H" dock. He was unfailingly kind and courteous to us, generously sharing his wealth of naval knowledge and his time.

Jerry is a perfectionist, and when he owned her *Gatti* never had so much as a water mark on her bright work or stainless fittings and rails. Every morning she was wiped down and shined up; her mahogany was varnished three times a year and her decks twice. It had to have wounded his heart to see her less than perfect after she fell into our hands. But Jerry spent hours working with us, instructing us in the best ways to maintain her. Slowly we began to measure up to his mark.

We believe his gentleness and magnanimity were built into the boat as he restored her because she exudes an aura of stateliness and warmth that is distinctly Jerry.

CHAPTER V

ATTEMPTED ESCAPE FROM "H" DOCK

'The shattered water made a nasty din.
Great waves looked over others coming in,
And thought of doing something to the shore
That water never did to land before.
The clouds were low and hairy in the skies,
Like locks blown forward in the gleam of eyes.
You could not tell, and yet it looked as if
The shore was lucky in being backed by cliff,
And cliff in being backed by continent...'
Robert Frost, _Once by the Pacific_

Under a leaden sky and cold drizzle, _i Gatti Felici_ loosed her ties to "H" dock and slipped ghostlike through the channels of Huntington Harbor to the sea for the 30-mile voyage northward to Marina del Rey, where she was to have some davits fabricated. She passed by the munitions storage area in the restricted channel (yet another charm of this spot!) and ducked under the Pacific Coast Highway bridge. All was deserted, calm and silent. Wham! The first Pacific wave caught her off-guard, and she recoiled for a moment. Then Bill nosed her into the swelling waves and adjusted speed. _Gatti_ caught her breath, regained her composure, and persevered through eight miles of high seas and strong swells. Her bow awash in water, she drove forward powerfully and confidently.

Her skipper reveled in the weather while her navigator clung for dear life to the companionway. A unilateral decision was made that a second helm chair would be the next major purchase. Although we thought we had stowed items below well, this first real open water test revealed that we had not. Vases, books and cups dislodged and became flying missiles. The toaster oven door flew open, releasing a soaring flock of trays, pans and grill shelves. I went below and tried to secure the projectiles I plucked from the air, fighting to maintain a footing in this great cat that was leaping as violently as our domestic variety after prey. With amazement and gratitude I realized my stomach was not lurching. If it never got worse than this, I felt I could handle it.

Past the harbor entrance to Alamitos we sailed; past the entrance to Long Beach where the freighters hunkered behind the long breakwater that also offered us a mile or so of respite from the rolling swell. Then back into the open ocean past the point at Palos Verdes, where the waves boiled up against the sheer cliffs like an enormous bubble bath. On toward a point with a lighthouse and a huge rock that appeared to have been carelessly tossed into the sea by a Cyclops. And finally into the lee of Catalina Island, where the waves diminished and fell still.

Although the sky was steely, the rain had stopped and occasionally a weak sun tried to peep through. The angry gray and white sea had become a slick, wet-tar black. Onto this stage marine animals began to timidly appear and, growing more courageous as they saw no human life other than ours on the sea's broad expanse, staged a performance that left us enthralled. Out of the depths appeared a pod of bottlenose dolphins that followed playfully in our wake, performing jetes and pirouettes. As the dolphins lost interest and turned to other pursuits, a spout of foam heralded the presence of a migrating gray whale. Three times he spouted for us. The date was February 4, and we wondered if it was a newly pregnant female heading north early from her frolic in Baja's Sea of Cortez. Or could it be a late-arriving male teenager, tardy because his nosey explorations had detained him as he headed south?

We had just spotted our first jetliner catapulted into the heavens from Los Angeles International Airport when the next show began. Across our bow and headed inland was a sleek black seal undulating in leaps and dives through the waves, followed by another (or perhaps the same?) group of dolphins. We mused over this teaming. Were the dolphins chasing the seal? Were they playing? Were they after the same fish? Were they being pursued by the same enemy? They passed by quickly and were gone.

In this world so magical and removed from reality, *Gatti* had become a sentient creature herself and we the humans favored to glimpse it. We moved as one with the sea, and its rhythm throbbed through the ship and us. By degrees the magic began to fade. What the heck was that smell? Bad fish breath! We had come upon a number of large buoys, each supporting a dozen or so huge, indolent seals. A few bothered to stretch out their sleek necks to have a look at us; the rest continued to doze. A group of youngsters bounced together in the waves with their flippers sticking straight up like so many shark fins. Their big round eyes surveyed us from their little whiskered faces with interest but no fear.

By now the airplanes were shooting up with greater frequency as we approached the airport. One actually lumbered right at us at quite low altitude. And then we were at the breakwater of Marina del Rey. A broad, straight channel ran directly into the marina with its hundreds of piers and slips. What an exciting change this marina presented! Here thousands of boats were moored at proper facilities. We passed parks and the restaurants and shops of Fisherman's Village. Sea birds and seals were abundant. We turned starboard at the first inlet and found ourselves being waved into the work dock at the Yamaha Shipyard. We learned that in former times this had been a Chris-Craft shipyard and as such might have been a previous port of call for *Gatti*.

Doug Christiansen of Waterside Boat Works had made two stunning davits following some incomplete plans we had managed to track down from the Chris-Craft museum in Newport News. Jerry had never installed davits because he did not have the need for a tender and believed that their addition would detract from *Gatti's* classic lines. By following plans designed for the boat, we hoped to make her more functional without marring her beauty or authenticity. Doug had accomplished this beautifully using stainless steel in lieu of laminated wood.

Because of continuing rain, it took several days for the new davits to be installed. *Gatti* spent the time at the work dock basking in the compliments and admiration showered on her. It was the first time we had had her out in public, and we showed her off like proud new parents. When the job was completed, *Gatti* returned with reluctance to "H" dock to have her hull painted and to hoist up little *Gattina*, the disconsolate tender that had been left behind.

CHAPTER VI

ESCAPE FROM "H" DOCK

'Long have you timidly waded holding a plank by the shore,
Now I will you to be a bold swimmer
To jump off in the midst of the sea, rise again, nod to me,
Shout, and laughingly dash with your hair.'.
Walt Whitman, *Song of Myself*

March 1, 1999, was the day designated for *Gatti's* emancipation from "H" dock. The day had not begun propitiously on the home front. Family obligations had intruded on our lives and, as Bill had become more maniacally focused on boat work, I had become more resentful. I was still teaching, and that required that my students be uppermost in my mind. But Marina del Rey had shown us how much fun a decent marina could be, so we rented a slip there. We were eager to get out of Huntington for reasons beyond the general decrepitude of the place. It was time to put space between Jerry and his baby, plus Marina del Rey was a lot closer to Bakersfield, especially in the rush hour traffic of Friday evenings.

As we approached Los Angeles by car on moving day, it became abundantly evident that the fog over the city was not going to stir itself during the morning hours. That was all right; we had several things to do on *Gatti* before we would be ready to leave. We busied ourselves with rigging the new davits and scrubbing *La Gattina*. The fog meantime shrugged itself southward at mid-afternoon to be replaced by the increasing swells of an incoming storm.

At 3 p.m. we decided to make the run north. Jerry patted *Gatti's* freshly painted hull and whispered "Good-bye, Baby"; we pulled away from the dock, this time with *La Gattina* swinging merrily between her magnificent davits. Through the familiar harbor we sliced, past the munitions storage area where a huge military ship was presumably being outfitted with fire. Into the Pacific we poked our bow and discovered to our transitory delight that we were not violently buffeted as on our previous trip. But truth announced itself with one of the tall "rogue" waves the radio had been warning of. Bill was watching how *Gattina* was doing on her davits when I saw the monster wall of water tower above us. "Wave!" was all the sound that my strangled throat could gasp out. Immediately, Bill heard the word, saw the stark terror on my face and in my bulging eyes, and turned *Gatti's* bow toward the wave. Up, up, we rode and slid down the other side. And thus we continued up the coast to the point accented by the lighthouse. The sea was like some enormous dragon snoring with huge exhalations. Looking out over the tumultuous sea was like watching green coils quiveringly rise and fall. It seemed as if this was the whole world and there was no order anywhere in it. Nothing was predictable except the rolling waves that came and came. No time to regroup, no time for a deep breath, no time, no time except at length to cry out, "If only they would stop for a moment!" Up, down, and here came yet another wave to be mounted. And through it all, not one item fell from the shelves below. Even a table lamp that I had forgotten to stow stayed in place during this crazily smooth dance of up and down.

Past Alamitos we rose and dipped, ducked behind the breakwater at Long Beach and then back out. The enormous swells flung themselves upon the cliffs of Palos Verdes, threw up despairing, foamy arms, and slipped back down into the depths. Past the lighthouse with its far-flung boulder we bowed and curtsied. And now the sea, rather than smoothing out dark and slick as on our former trip, rumpled itself up like bolts of seersucker or crushed parchment. The huge swells subsided into heaves as though the fearsome dragon were awakening with great yawning and stretching.

And here, close to where we had earlier seen a whale, arose the great dark back of another. For about half a mile we watched two gray whales as they spouted and fluked. Again, we were the only vessel on this part of the sea and again we could feel ourselves embraced in a fantasyland, a wonderland that Nature was allowing us to be a fleeting part of. Before long, we reached the buoys where the halitosis seals had cavorted. Today they were well out of olfactory range, bouncing up and down upon the giant buoys like trained circus animals. The effect was comical but their incredible sense of balance roused our admiration.

The day had been gray and fog had been a real concern but now, as the sun sank, the western horizon cleared, and for a short time we followed the rays of liquid gold poured out before us on the ocean. Then, as the verdigris sky was polished to glowing copper, we turned toward the coast, where a great full moon beckoned us in to our new berth. Up the channel we continued to Marina del Rey, passing inviting restaurants behind whose windows romantic candles were being lit and the happy faces of relaxed couples were beaming in the warm glow. The docks at Fisherman's Village were crowded with the usual expectant corps of pelicans on the lookout for incoming fishing craft.

With the exception of taking on fuel, we had never docked *Gatti* any place other than in Huntington and the work dock at Marina del Rey. The work dock had been a simple mooring with lots of room to maneuver and, although the space in Huntington had been a difficult one, it hadn't presented the situation of boats lined up side by side at finger piers. A crosswind caught us on our first try, so we backed out and turned in again. Anticipating good entertainment, a harbor seal rolled over on his back so as to enjoy the amusing spectacle more comfortably. But we fooled him. This time we pulled in and tied up at the "H" dock of Marina del Rey.

CHAPTER VII

RETURN TO LAVAGNA

'O'er the glad waters of the dark-blue sea
Our thoughts as boundless, and our souls as free
Far as the breeze can bear, the billows foam,
Survey our empire, and behold our home!'
Lord Byron, *The Corsair*

From August of 1998 to March of 1999 we had busied ourselves with painting, varnishing, and moving *Gatti* to a place where more serious work could be undertaken. It was now time to get back to Italy and get some firm plans in place. Our Italian culture club's annual sojourn to Italy provided us an opportunity to do this at a very reasonable cost. And so it was that while our California friends toured Pisa, Siena, San Gimignano and Firenze, we caught a train to Lavagna to try to reconnect with the gentleman we had met there some seven months earlier. Those other Italian cities would soon be our playground; there was no need to make a rushed tour now.

Our train rumbled off from the bustling Firenze station under a gentle but cold drizzle. By the time we pulled into Pisa, the rain had pulled up into the clouds and the temperature had risen appreciably. From Pisa to La Spezia we sailed along in the fast and comfortable Eurostar train. At La Spezia's frenetic station we changed to the shabby local that wends its way up the coast and stops at small places such as Lavagna. Now the skies had cleared to the azure we remembered and a warm sun smiled welcomingly. Up through the Cinque Terre we lumbered, for the most part burrowing through tunnels blasted in the stone cliffs. At each quaint little village we popped out from our tunnel track like a rabbit taking stock of his surroundings.

And what incredible surroundings! Pop up at Riomaggiore for our first view of waves crashing against the cliffs. Pop up at Manarola, where the tiny fishing boats perch on their cliff walls awaiting the proper tides. Pop up at Corniglia, its vineyards clinging to sheer drops. Pop up at Vernazza, whose center is strategically hidden from sea approaches. Pop up at Monterosso, with its smooth flat beaches. Each quick glance caught at our hearts and imaginations. The view was not new to us, but who could ever grow accustomed to the awe? This was the first glimpse of our proposed home. Our earlier trip was one of exploration. This one was of settlement. Yes, we were really coming to this place. This was our chosen spot. How well would we grow to know it? How often would we ride this rabbit train along the magnificent Ligurian shore? See over there where we caught the boat to Lérici? Look! There is Levanto, where you swam and I collected serpentine rock! And thus the remembrances of summer flooded over us until we came to a bumpy, squeaking halt at the Lavagna station.

On our prior visit we had driven a car and paid little heed to train tracks. This round we were delighted to find ourselves stepping off the train right at the harbor. With almost eerie precision we walked directly to the office we had visited. The proprietor had posted a note on the door that he was out on the docks, so we whiled away the time until his return at an outdoor café on the wharf. We sipped an icy crisp local white wine and watched the boats dancing in their moorings. We tried to picture *Gatti* here, eager to carry us out into the Mediterranean. The breeze was soft, the air warm and clear, and to dream was easy.

We returned to the office at the exact moment as Dominic Asino and a friend. "Hello, Los Angeles!" he called out. In seven months the English of this found, lost and found again man had improved somewhat less than my Italian and in a polyglot of languages we exchanged information – how the wallet was stolen, how he had waited to hear from us, why one should ship to La Spezia rather than Genova, when a slip would be available. We resolved some basic issues. We would ship *Gatti* to arrive at the end of November. We would make solid confirmation with Dominic in September. This time he threw out numbers in the neighborhood of 12.500.000 lire a year for slip rental. This amounted to $6,500 per year rather than the original figure of $4,000. But by California standards this was not at all outrageous and, after all, we would be on the Italian Riviera. It appeared that we would be subletting someone's slip. We later came to understand that we were renting a slip that Dominic handled for the owner. We were told we would require a 16 meter slip and one of the best docks in this size range was – "H" dock! Of course Dominic had no way of comprehending our merriment at this information or our hilarity in snapping pictures of the great blue "H" emblazoned on the concrete of the dock.

We explored the docks at great length, taking special note of the boats moored there and the way they were moored. They were of all varieties and nationalities. The Italian boats had names, but few had home ports painted on their transoms. One large sailing vessel, *Leone,* was moored across from an open slip, and we fantasized that this would be ours. Of course, "slip" seems an odd word to use for a narrow, undelineated expanse of water with no finger piers. All the boats were moored stern-to with fenders hanging off their sides for protection. As the waves moved to and fro, so did the whole line of boats – all shrugging to one side and the other like so many sixth graders nudging one another in a row. Each boat had one or two mooring lines from the bow that were pulled taut by some unseen thing below the surface. The sterns were secured to the dock by two heavy lines connected to enormous springs that pulled and relaxed with the movement of the water. Each boat had a gangway of some type attached to the stern and pulled up so as not to strike the dock. These were made of wood or fiberglass and maneuvered by davits or hydraulic pumps. No single kind predominated, but they all appeared to be risky ways of climbing aboard a boat. We reflected with dismay on *Gatti's* high transom!

Although we did not spend a great deal of time in Lavagna on this visit, it appeared clear that we would find good facilities here. Workers were busy everywhere. The breakwater seemed strong and sheltering, the waters clear and blue. The tall mountains shouldered up to the harbor and the medieval city of Lavagna protectively. The atmosphere was quiet and the town had the flavor of Italy we were searching for.

A 24-hour train strike had been declared for Firenze that night, so we headed back with some trepidation as the witching hour approached. But we first pocketed three of Dominic's cards and distributed them among three different sections of ourselves and our luggage. Our lucky day closed as our train was the last to be admitted to the darkened train station in Firenze. Two days later we were safely back in the United States with all three cards still with us and an exciting deadline looming before us.

CHAPTER VIII

GETTING UNDERWAY

'And now I know that we must lift the sail
And catch the winds of destiny
Wherever they drive the boat.
To put meaning in one's life may end in madness,
But life without meaning is the torture
Of restlessness and vague desire –
It is a boat longing for the sea and yet afraid.'
Edgar Lee Masters, *"George Gray", Spoon River Anthology*

Boat life at Marina del Rey was dramatically different from that of Huntington Harbor. While we missed the neighborliness of Jerry and also missed witnessing the boat at "H" dock being escorted away by armed federal marshals, that was all that we missed. We especially did not miss the extra 40 miles of horrific Los Angeles traffic that snarled the freeways between the two marinas.

This new "H" dock was a working dock. Although some of our neighbors were permanent, most of the vessels were being prepped for sale, so there was always a great deal of purposeful activity around us. Three of the boats were fishing boats hired out for a day or two at a time by ardent anglers. Two large fishing party boats were moored a few docks from us. They would pass by in the morning loaded with pale, chatting novices fumbling with rods and generally ignoring the safety rules being blasted over the loudspeakers. In the evening they would pass us again on their way back in, loaded with very red (and some pretty green) passengers too exhausted to speak. Our restrooms and showers were close by and immaculate. There were even laundry facilities. The gates were fitted with functional locks and keys. A short walk away was Fisherman's Village with its jovial weekend crowds and bands and its quiet weekday dinners by the water. Across the narrow channel from our mooring was a large, green public park on a finger of land. Dog and cat walking, barbecues, music, Fourth of July fireworks, and various shows provided us a constantly changing kaleidoscope of life.

The big boat show held there in June 1999 really gave wings to our enterprise. Dozens of vendors of boating supplies plied their trade under white tents while dozens of new boats bobbed happily in the water. Hundreds of people, ourselves included, boarded boat after boat, longing, dreaming, garnering ideas for their own craft. We made two significant contacts that day. The first was the dealer for the elegant Riviera boats, imported from Australia. When he heard our plans, he suggested we visit his yard and purchase one of the cradles used in the ocean passage of one of his boats. He also gave us the name of a flat-bed truck operator who was so highly respected for his moving of large boats in and out of port that he had even been employed in transporting America Cup contenders. Our second contact was the dealer who was representing Aprea Mare, exquisitely crafted yachts manufactured in Sorrento, Italy. He lived in Italy six months of the year, knew Lavagna well, and whetted our enthusiasm. We had pretty well decided which electronics to purchase, but this show gave us a chance to share ideas and ask questions of some very knowledgeable people. We returned to *Gatti* enthusiastic to get on with business.

Our dock was being used by people being ferried across the channel to the show. They had to walk past *Gatti* on their way to and from the loading site. Our neighbors were amused by the numbers of people stopping to admire our 47-year-old boat. A brand new million dollar Cheoy Lee for sale across from us did not garner greater praise. We realized anew what a tremendous bargain *Gatti* had been, and the awesome cost of installing instrumentation was put in better perspective.

The following week Bill met with the highly touted truck driver, who took him to the Riviera yard and showed him cradles and how they could be modified to fit our boat. Greg's competence and experience were impressive. For $2,000 he would transport *Gatti* from Marina del Rey to his yard in Long Beach, fit a cradle to her, and take her thus ensconced to the freighter that would carry her to Italy. Confident that this part of our plan was in good hands, we took the costly plunge at the electronics store. We bought a high-quality VHF radio, auto pilot, radar unit, and combination GPS-sounder-plotter. Doug, whose superior imagination and craftsmanship had produced our davits, was commissioned to manufacture a stainless mast to accommodate the VHF and GPS antennae, the radar unit, lights, a hailer, and a telephone dome should we decide to invest in one.

Bill then busied himself in the time-consuming and intricate woodworking required to bring *Gatti* electronically into the 21st century without marring any of the beauty and fine craftsmanship bequeathed her by the mid-20th. A couple of times a week he would travel down to design supports and to measure the various instruments being installed. He would return to Bakersfield for the tedious cutting, routing and varnishing of superb woods. I worked on more mundane projects such as finishing up curtains, trying to get my inventiveness around a workable shower, and viewing our Bakersfield home from a marketing standpoint.

It was also at this juncture that Doug casually asked us one day if we had met the man on a sailboat in the harbor who lived in Italy. No, we had not, but we made it our immediate business to do so. We found Frank toiling under a straw hat on his 38-foot *Shearwater*. He interrupted his work to tell us he had had an apartment in Italy for nine years; he had traveled extensively; and he had plans to sail to Italy via the Pacific. He agreed to come by *Gatti* for a glass of wine that evening. What a dazzling world unfolded for us as we became acquainted with this remarkable man who would grow to be a good friend. Frank approved of our using crystal glasses, china dishes and silverware on board. He is about the only person in our experience who did not think us nuts on this issue. He had retired early from a thriving and remunerative medical practice in Los Angeles. When his children were grown, he sold his house, auctioned off his extensive wine cellar and proceeded to follow very personal and specific goals. He had rented an apartment in Bordighera, Italy, after exploring the coast very much as we had. Bordighera had called to him very much as Lavagna had to us. Bordighera is also in Liguria but very close to the French border. While Lavagna lies along the Riviera Levante (east of Genova), Bordighera lies on the Riviera Ponente (west of Genova). Frank had remodeled his apartment to his liking and had then set out on two major quests – to visit every country in the world and to equip his *Shearwater* with the most advanced technology possible. We found a kindred soul that night, and our hearts soared at having found someone who had actually set sail on a tide we yearned for.

Our sense of direction was gaining clarity at an amazing rate. We had fumbled around for so long and had suddenly found our way. Our attitude has always been to stay flexible and keep an ear open to Fate. And in the end, Fate has always led us in kindly directions. A visit to family in Florida in July led us to the decision to purchase a condominium on the Gulf of Mexico, and we made an offer on a unit. We returned to California inspired to complete our many unfinished remodeling projects and with a much more objective understanding of what lifestyle adjustments would have to be made if we were serious about pursuing this Italian dream. Even in view of the commitments we had already made, few of our friends took us seriously. After all, who really leaves a long-time home in California to live on a boat in Italy? Yes, we all talk of the grand adventures we would like to undertake, but few of us follow through. Even though we were determined to do this thing, it was hard for us to visualize actually living the dream. Thank goodness we were unaware of the difficulties that lay ahead or the pain we would experience in leaving our animals, gardens, and beautifully remodeled home.

We settled on a freight line and a shipping broker to handle all the paperwork. Because we were establishing ourselves as freelance writers and photographers, we were able to ship the boat under a carnet. The beauty of this plan was that she could stay in Italy for one year without being tied up in customs or subject to an import fee. We were not opposed to paying such a fee, but no one was able to give us even a ballpark prediction of what it might be. The drawback of the plan would become clear as our first year was drawing to a close. But that was a long way off and not part of our thinking. The actual shipping cost for *Gatti* was $13,000. To our delight we discovered that our freighter, *Cielo di San Francisco,* had a single cabin available on her Oct. 30 voyage to Genoa for $2100. We booked passage for *Gatti* and myself and spent the following week moving about in a daze. It had been decided. We were committed. Thanksgiving would be celebrated in Liguria.

CHAPTER IX

THE NAME CHANGE

'Even as the gift of life
You take the famous name you did not choose
And make it new.
You and the name exchange a power:
Its history is changed, becoming yours,
And yours by this: who calls this, calls you.'
Ann Ridler, *Choosing a Name*

Mariners are a superstitious lot, and every seaman knows that to change the name of a boat is to court disaster. Yet the name *Class Action* with which Jerry and his wife had christened the yacht was not one that we liked. After lengthy investigation of other possibilities and not a little hissing and claw-baring, we agreed to rename her *i Gatti Felici* – the happy cats. We had enough nautical savvy to comprehend the risk inherent in this decision and so we researched the topic. The yacht had not been named *Class Action* originally; it was simply her reconditioned name. This fact made us less apprehensive and we concluded that if we proceeded cautiously, we would be all right. We decided to follow a ritual outlined by the noted sailor John Vigor because it sounded like fun, and he actually allowed that a name change could be done safely if done properly. It never hurts to be on the safe side.

John Vigor is the author of a fine and useful book entitled *The Practical Mariner's Book of Knowledge*. Vigor's "little-known interdenominational de-naming ceremony" not only appealed to us but he additionally assures the reader that he has used it with great success and can recommend it to all "without hesitation." The de-naming ceremony is held after the old name has been totally expunged from the boat. Since *Gatti* did not have an old log book, in our case this applied to the name painted on the transom and the cabin and a baseball cap with the name embroidered on it. The

37

ceremony itself, we were instructed, should be short and involve supplication and libation. The supplication is addressed to Neptune, god of the sea; Aeolus, god of the winds; and any other deity one chooses. The libation consists of the best champagne that can be managed being poured over the bow. The supplicants are generously permitted to share the champagne. The gods are requested to forget the old name of the boat and they are reminded of that name. They are asked to protect the boat under her new name, to be revealed at the re-naming ceremony. Under no condition is the new name mentioned at this time. When the time is right, the ship is christened as though she were brand new. On that occasion the new name is announced, and more champagne is uncorked.

These niceties occasioned quite a lot of trouble for us. We had never called the boat anything but *i Gatti Felici*, but it took us a year to make the physical changes. We tried to be sensitive to the feelings of Jerry, who had breathed life into the vessel and named her as a good father ought. A few months after we purchased the boat, we told him we were changing the name but still did not act on it until the time came to repaint. Two beautiful mahogany panels, one on either side of the cabin, bore the name *Class Action* in gold. When these were removed a year after we bought the boat, we gave one to Jerry as a memento and Bill made a replacement. The remaining original was stripped down, but even after bleaching and sanding, the shadow of the name was still visible. We ran into the same problem when it came time to varnish the transom, but by dint of much sanding, bleaching and staining, we finally felt confident about staging the de-naming ceremony.

Many dates were set and altered. Two months in the spring offered blue moons but as each arrived, we had not yet stripped "*Class Action* – Newport Beach" from the broad, high mahogany transom. There was no reason to conduct the ceremony under a blue moon, or even just a full moon, that we knew about, but the unusual event of having two months with two full moons each in such a short span seemed propitious. But in the end, on Aug. 23, 1999, we were at last ready. It was a chilly, blustery night at Marina del Rey. A half-moon ducked in and out of wind-swept clouds and gathering fog. The dock was totally deserted except for Obie, the next-ship cat, who hospitably joined us on the foredeck. We generously frothed the bow with Veuve Cliquot and, filling our glasses, made our supplications. Addressing Neptune, Aeolus, Diana, and Jupiter, we begged that the name *Class Action* be forever expunged from their records and their goodwill be attached to the vessel under her new name. Obie added his plaintive meows in the direction of Isis for good measure.

The following day, Shannon Basso came on board to help us develop ideas for illustrating the new name. Shannon was another of those wonderful serendipitous meetings that seem to attach themselves to *Gatti* wherever she goes. Shannon just happened to be on the dock that day attending to other business and a neighbor pointed her in our direction. Shannon also happened to be clever, talented and wacky enough to give us exactly what we were looking for. The result was *i Gatti Felici* in script of Italian goldleaf outlined in emerald green. The last two "i's" were dotted with two gold and green cat eyes, the "c" sprouted whiskers, and two ears resembling seagulls in flight floated above. She had the two mahogany side panels painted in time for the renaming ceremony.

This event enjoyed the same procrastination as the previous one. After a series of delays, the renaming ceremony was set and the evening of Sept. 17, 1999, saw guests arriving at "H" dock. Jerry and his wife, friends we had made on the dock along with their friends boarded to the music of Andrea Bocelli's *Romanza*.

> *"Con te partirò*
> *Paesi che non ho mai*
> *Veduto e vissuto con te,*
> *Adesso si li vivrò.*
> *Con te partirò*
> *Su navi per mari*
> *Che, io lo so,*
> *No, no, non esitono più*
> *Con te li riviverò"*

("I will go with you to lands I have never seen or shared with you. Yes, now I shall experience them. I will go with you on ships across seas that I know exist no more. With you I will recreate them.")

Veuve Cliquot was again liberally foamed over both bow and glass rims and *i Gatti Felici* was presented to the universe with prayers for her safety and good adventures. The two side plates with her new name were affixed and an evening of joviality ensued. Jerry appeared pleased with the new name, and Obie stuck his bewhiskered face in at a saloon porthole to register his approval.

CHAPTER X

DEPARTURES

'Nothing great was ever achieved without enthusiasm.'
Ralph Waldo Emerson, *Experience*

Having stepped beyond dreams into the reality of actually shipping the boat, we found ourselves in a flurry of activity that was both physically exhausting and mind numbing. We had an actual departure date and so much to get ready.

Work began dockside on installing our selected electronics. Since *Gatti's* wiring was not up to this complexity, we decided to rewire the entire vessel to European current. This mammoth, time-consuming process was undertaken by Andrew, who arrived daily in his big gray hearse cum traveling workshop. Out went the microwave, toaster oven, coffee maker, heater, refrigerator and the beloved icemaker that we had installed after purchasing the boat. None of these appliances would work on the new voltage. Up came the wool carpets and hatch covers. Over all rained a shower of sawdust and wire snippets. Dirty tools were laid on upholstery and carpet. Oily footprints were tracked across pristine teak decks. Andrew's work area was immaculate and professional. His neat bundles of wire were a marvel to behold. Stately rows of organization marched behind the walls while chaos reigned without. Stepping around, behind and over Andrew was Mark, who was trying to install the electronics. Meanwhile, Doug was working overtime to implement in stainless steel the mast designed by Bill. It was loosely based on the wooden one made for the boat in 1952 but had added height and strength to accommodate modern electronics and antennae. Bill made the 100-plus mile run from Bakersfield to Marina del Rey a couple of times a week to ensure that all was going well and to intrude his constantly evolving ideas into the general confusion.

We managed to live part time on the boat during this mess. School was finally over for me, and I had officially retired. Now I was able to make the trip down during the week and concentrate on the boat rather than planning lessons and grading papers. I was also able to spend time watching Doug's extremely attractive welder. This young man, Paul, was the same age as our daughter. He had already been discovered by the entertainment moguls of Los Angeles and was making commercials when he wasn't working for Doug. Paul could go from a smudgy working stiff in jeans and T-shirt to a squeaky clean, suave Adonis in no time flat. His only difficulty seemed to be his fingernails, which did not recover as rapidly as his other body parts. There remained a certain ragged blackness to them that his agents went to some pains to obscure. His success was to grow as time went on, and it is as great a joy today to see him on television, in movies, and in photography books as it is to see him in deep concentration behind his welder's mask.

We also managed to complete the purchase of the condominium on the Florida Gulf beaches during this bizarre period of our lives. We had been raised in Florida, as mentioned earlier, and had some family there, including my mother, who was in an assisted living facility. We had decided that if we were going to spend half the year in Italy, it would be smarter to have a residence in the United States on the East Coast rather than the West. In addition, the stock market had been very strong and a condominium on the beach seemed like a good investment. Indeed, this turned out to be the case beyond our wildest expectations – the value of the property doubled in two years. It was furnished and ready to be rented out if that was what we decided to do. We made plans to fly to Florida on September 19, 1999 for the closing.

Sept. 18 found us on *Gatti* in a very happy state. The previous night we had celebrated the renaming, and this was the day of the Vessel Assist photo shoot. Vessel Assist is a sort of automobile club of the sea. Every year it positions a photo boat outside the breakwater of Marina del Rey as well as other locations and invites members to set up appointments for a complimentary photo taken underway. The timing makes the photos available for Christmas cards. Our Saturday appointment found the skies overcast and the Pacific a smooth, dark sheen. We spent the morning scrubbing *Gatti*'s exterior and making her presentable, at least to an unpracticed eye, from a distance. We were asked to circle the photo boat three times from various angles and at varying speeds, since she was such a classic craft and a possibility for the Vessel Assist newsletter. We did so with pleasure and a sense of accomplishment and returned to dock in high spirits. Yes, we were spending a lot of money, the work was messy, our nerves were shot, but what a unique, desirable, beautiful bark was ours. We tied up and Bill went off to the marine store to pick up yet another electronic gadget.

I busied myself on board cleaning up and stowing gear to the tune of the bilge pump and water spouting from our flank into the sea. I completed my tasks, but the bilge kept spewing out with more gusto than usual. I lifted the hatch cover and discovered with horror that water was flowing into the bilge at a good rate, actually creating a pretty strong current. The packing around the starboard rudder had worked loose. We knew that this area needed work but had hoped to address it when the boat was pulled. Well, it appeared the time to pull had arrived somewhat ahead of schedule. Bill returned from his errand; Doug was summoned from his own work on his old Chris-Craft; an exhausted diver who had just gratefully popped above the surface of the icy Pacific was prevailed upon to submerge yet again to repack. At the conclusion of this frantic activity, during which many people ran to *Gatti*'s succor, it was the considered opinion of all that she would be fine as long as she stayed put and her rudder didn't move. We would go to Florida for a week to close on our new property, and the following Monday *Gatti* would be pulled and her final preparations begun.

And that is what happened. We went to Florida and closed on the condominium. We threw a house-warming party and became reacquainted with high school friends we had not seen in some time. And we talked a lot to Doug on the telephone. He and Paul were hard at work on creating the remarkable mast. "It's enormous!" he cried plaintively across the continent. Bill agreed that the size could be reduced by one foot, but Doug was still concerned. However, the work went on. We decided not to rent the condo, but locked it up instead and flew back to California to see the marvel Doug had wrought.

When we returned, work proceeded at a rapid pace. *Gatti* ran over to the lift under her own power and was pulled, farewell Pacific waters sheeting off her hull. She was propped up in the Yamaha Boat Yard, where Andrew and the electronics man now had to climb a wobbly 20-foot ladder to reach the workplace. Doug's stainless steel mast had evolved into a large work of art that also had to be hoisted up and down for proper fit and proportion. Beyond being just a mast, it needed to hinge down in the event that we would canal in Europe as we hoped. There we would encounter quite low bridges. The painter got busy painting below the waterline, which Bill had not been able to do at dock.

We were still working on preparing the stern so Shannon could return to paint the new name on the transom. *Gatti*'s bottom was found to be enveloped in a strange plastic covering that had loosened in several places. With great trepidation we pulled off this skin. It was adhered tightly to the hull when Jerry had purchased the boat, so he had not removed it. The boat had been in a warehouse during its three-year renovation and the wood had shrunk. When it was returned to the water and the planks had swelled again, the covering had loosened. A communal prayer of thanksgiving went up to the heavens when we exposed under the covering a bottom in perfect condition, with planks that looked like new wood. However, we did have to replace the very expensive wormshoe, which was riddled with worms. This is a board of special wood which is attached along the bottom of the keel as a sacrificial wood to protect the hull from damage by marine life. It was the consensus at the boat yard that these worms were from the happy home of muck that had been our slip at Huntington. In addition to replacing the wormshoe, we also had to replace screws that had held the hull for almost 50 years. Since we had the opportunity (if not as much time as we would have liked), we refastened the hull with 2,000 bronze screws each topped with a little wooden plug.

In addition to making the mast, Doug and Paul also helped with this refastening, as well as repairing and replacing wood in the hull at the rudders that had become worn and leaky. Never did two men work so good-humoredly on so many different jobs. Since it was at this time that Paul's modeling career began to take off, he would work feverishly, throw aside his welder's mask and rush for the showers to be ready for an interview. His activity was a great source of humor for us all, Paul included. He is a young man whose work ethic is as outstanding as his physical attractiveness, and he does not take himself too seriously. After Paul would leave to model, work would continue, although it had lost a great deal of its flavor for some among us.

Doug working miracles in his shop

Paul delivers rudder et al.

Because of burn from too much zinc, we invested in an electronic system to monitor and correct the electrical flow around the hull. And so Tim was sent up the wobbly steps to snarl his wires among those of Andrew and Mark. Bill continued to ply his way back and forth between Bakersfield and Marina del Rey, designing and creating stands, boxes and covers for the new equipment so it would conform to the boat's classic cockpit and helm. Paint cans, brushes and tools bristled up through the sawdust in our garage as well as at the boat. Seldom has a more competent or more fun group of people worked so diligently, aggressively, or with more dedication against a quickly approaching deadline. Even poor Shannon showed up on a Saturday to paint *Gatti*'s name. She was amply rewarded, however: Paul worked that day as well.

The boat was to be loaded on a truck on Oct. 20 and taken to a yard in Wilmington to have her Riviera cradle fitted to her. Then she was to be taken to the Port of Los Angeles to be loaded onto *Cielo di San Francisco*, currently en route from Vancouver via Portland and Oakland. The night of Oct. 18, Bill and I pulled ourselves wearily up the long ladder and collapsed in our bunks. We slept high and dry in the shipyard because it was convenient; we could work into the night and be up early the next day to begin again. It was a bit awkward. We had no plumbing and had to make the treacherous climb to use the facilities.

At about 2 a.m. we awoke to a sound of shivering timbers and an odd swaying motion that felt nothing like the sea. "What is it?" we asked one another. But having lived in California for 20 years, we knew exactly what it was and yet were unable to comprehend the irony of it all. As I crouched on the floor between our bunks, petrified, Bill tried to reassure me that we were all right because the supports below us were chained together. Yet all the while he knew that the bottom had been painted that day, and the chains had not been reattached. He had thought to say something, but the probability of an earthquake had seemed so remote... For a full minute we swayed like helpless hatchlings in a nest listening to the creaking of *Gatti* and the other boats around her.

Gradually the swaying and the gratings slowed and ceased. "Now!" urged Bill, and he herded me to the ladder and helped my trembling legs cope with the wobbly rungs. We ran through the darkened yard filled with boats perched up on their tall, silly supports, around the long keels of sailboats, tripping over line and tools until we stopped breathless at the open area of the docks. Here most people still slept through what to them was gentle rocking, though the boats were nudging their jetties and complaining along with the groaning pilings. The earthquake, centered at Joshua Tree, was 7.5 on the Richter scale. Because the epicenter was in the middle of the desert, little damage was reported even though the shaking lasted far longer than usual.

Our desire to complete our tasks and escape the boatyard increased dramatically after this incident. But other events had also conspired to make the Yamaha Boatyard an unpleasant place. It had more than one earthquake shaking it up: new owners had taken over with new plans and visions. A terrible woman stalked about all day in spike heels and short, tight mini skirts, finding fault with everything around her. Every day a new edict was handed down, each more perverse and ridiculous than the previous. First to go were dogs in the yard. Poor old Teak, who had accompanied his owner Peter, our painter, to work every day since puppyhood, was exiled to his home in the city. Here he pined all day for his good friends at the yard. Next, animals living on boats were banned, including our good old buddy, Obie the cat. His owner, Rick, promptly weighed anchor and moved to another marina. A mother duck had hatched a brood and was raising it in our area to the great delight of all the residents. A little ramp had been especially constructed to help the ducklings get into and out of the water more easily. The ramp was now dismantled, and we were forbidden to feed the ducks. (Which is not to say that we did, indeed, stop.)

Following the expulsion of animals, boat steps and carts came under attack and ridiculous rules were levied against tenders. Even Paul's increasing fame and sought-after skills were useless weapons against this diabolical female. Wherever her heavily painted eye fell, evil ensued. The final outrage was that shops in the yard such as Doug's and the painter's could in future operate only from 8 a.m. to 5 p.m. on weekdays. Boat repair is in greatest demand on the weekends or after normal business hours. Had these rules been in effect when we pulled *Gatti*, we would never have met our deadline. As it was, these good artisans ignored the new rules and continued work on our boat after curfew. Fortunately for everyone, these owners soon sold out to new ones.

However, by the time Greg's big truck rolled into the yard to get *Gatti*, spirits were getting pretty frazzled; but Greg brought a focus and optimism with him that lifted our hearts. He brings such competence to his work as well as a reassuring can-do attitude, that even when you see your yacht centered in the air over a huge semi-truck, you don't feel totally unhinged. "This is no problem," he smiles, and you believe him. He inspected every inch of his supports and saw to it that *Gatti* rode comfortably. Then he set off down the Los Angeles freeway in time to beat rush hour. This was probably the most frightening stretch for the vessel on her journey to Italy. The rest of us watched her big gold name disappear down the road and shuffled our feet in the debris that lay around. We had done all that we could. Our work as a team had ended, and we were all sad, if relieved...

Gatti with Greg – swathed, lashed and ready to roll.

CHAPTER XI

GATTI ET AL. AT SEA

'Darkness settles on roofs and walls,
But the sea, the sea in the darkness calls;
The little waves with their soft, white hands,
Efface the footprints in the sands,
And the tide rises, the tide falls.'
Henry Wadsworth Longfellow,
The Tide Rises, the Tide Falls

Within a few days *Gatti* had been set in her cradle and affixed to a flat. We drove down to Greg's yard in Wilmington and found her perched high up on his truck, ready for her run to the loading dock at Long Beach. Her freighter was not yet in port, but that did not seem to concern anyone. Bill clambered high up on the cradle and boat to cover her with her ample canvas. When we bought the boat, Jerry had already had huge canvas covers made for her aft deck, windshield and transom. Bill had added to this over time, and *Gatti* and little *Gattina* were both now protected stem to stern with natty tan canvas slickers. We had weighed the pros and cons of shipping her covered. Had I not been accompanying her, we probably would not have risked losing the canvas at sea. As it turned out, it was a very good idea, since the crew cooperated with me in keeping it well lashed, and her varnished trim arrived in Italy in perfect form. This covering was the last service we could render *Gatti* in the United States and Bill carefully and lovingly secured her protective covers.

Off we went through the back streets of Wilmington, Greg driving his big semi with *Gatti*'s bow pointed courageously ahead high above him, a "pacer" pickup truck darting back and forth around the semi like a sheep herder, and our car bringing up the rear. We avoided taking out traffic signals, electric lines, and on-coming vehicles and arrived safely at the port gates. We said good-bye and watched as our baby slid through the high gates and disappeared

51

among the other trucks laden with cargo behind the stout chain-link fence. *Gatti* was now impounded in customs, and we returned home feeling a little lost.

The following days were haunted by the strangeness that accompanies such situations. You work single-mindedly on a project and, when there is no more to be done, a vacuity and adjustment period remains. For the first time, really, I thought about my impending voyage. Bill and I had never, in well over thirty years of marriage, been separated for such a long time, and we had never been separated without telephone access. I had never been at sea, out of sight of land. I would be traveling from the mild October weather of Southern California to the humid heat of the tropics to the cold late November weather of the North Atlantic and Europe. What was I to pack to wear? We were living from day to day, not knowing when the call would come to board. Valerie from World Freighter Cruises tried to keep me abreast of the freighter's movements, but I was not yet experienced in the complications that can make freighter schedules uncertain, and the day-to-day waiting was a bit unsettling.

I tried to keep my mind busy with assembling the things I thought I would need. I was looking forward to uninterrupted reading time, so I had a heavy collection of books. I had been trying for two years to knit a complicated fisherman's sweater for Bill with little success. I hoped to untangle the mess and make some headway with it and at the same time feel close to the love of my life. Because I had been studying Italian for three years, I had plenty of texts, books, and compact discs to work with. I purchased an elegant leather-bound journal in which to record my daily adventures and musings. Bill had given me an engraved wooden box filled with fine, personalized stationery. I would be able to post letters at our scheduled stops in Mazatlan, Mexico, Cartagena, Colombia, Valencia, Spain and Livorno, Italy. I also had what proved to be my most time-consuming item – a Magellan GSC 100. This was the first piece of navigational equipment I had ever dealt with, and it took the entire trip for me to be able to use it proficiently.

An explanation of the Magellan is in order here because, for some reason, this product never enjoyed wide popularity and newer technology has all but made it obsolete. Frank had introduced us to the Magellan; he had purchased one along with the other cutting-edge electronics he hoped to use on his voyage from Mexico to the Marqueses. While the Magellan performed all the functions of a good GPS, including the ability to set waypoints, determine speed and time of arrival, etc., it could also send and receive e-mail via satellite. Since no telephone lines were involved, it was the perfect tool for communicating at sea. The freighter would have a satellite phone, but it was expensive to use and the feedback made conversation unsatisfactory. It was wonderful to know it was there for emergencies, but my Magellan proved to be an excellent way to keep in daily contact with my family and made me feel much less isolated.

It was Oct. 26 when Valerie finally gave the word. *Cielo di San Francisco* was en route to Long Beach from Oakland, and I was informed to board at 10 a.m. the following day. Bill and I headed south early on the 27th. We stopped at a beverage warehouse and added several bottles of Blenheim ginger ale to my pile of stores, in hope that ginger really would stave off seasickness. We entered the shipyard but were not able to drive our own vehicle wharfside. Instead, we had to unload and reload everything into a security vehicle. Aside from drug searches in Cartagena, Colombia, this was the only security measure that was ever evident to me in any of our ports of call.

As our car pulled up to the freighter that was to be my home for the next 27 days, I was struck by her immense size. I was to learn that she was not very big as freighters go, but to my untutored eye she seemed enormously long and tall. Her white superstructure was located at her stern and rose seven levels, with the bridge atop that and the electronic equipment and flags still above that. At her stern flew a flag that was strange to me – St. Johns, Antigua, her flag of convenience. Spaced from the superstructure forward were three big yellow cranes. Her metal decks and rails were painted red and her hull black. Red lines painted from her hull to stern showed how low she was riding in the water. At this point many red lines were in evidence because she had already been unloaded and the reloading was just getting underway. We had been told that *Gatti* would doubtless be loaded last and we were hoping for some good photos of the grand event.

We lugged my things up a very straight, tall metal ladder to the deck. The first thing we saw on the cleared deck was *i Gatti Felici*. How beautiful she looked and what kind care had been shown her. Her flat rack had been firmly bolted to the deck and she looked snugly protected in her cradle. To her port towered a stack of containers, creating a wall between her and the sea. To her stern was the shielding superstructure. Her bow was just long enough, packaged as she was, to prevent a stack of containers from being loaded in front of her. The captain was later to grouse good-humoredly about this loss of income, while everyone agreed they had never seen a boat so well packed. *Gatti* had been patiently waiting dockside for four days now; we learned that she had made friends with many admiring longshoremen. It was possibly they who had ensured her secure and early loading in such a favored place. *Gatti* had been out of the water for 18 days and looked eager to be off and at least get some sea spray.

At this point the captain appeared, introduced himself and summoned a crew member to help us carry my bags up to my cabin. Up, up, up we climbed the steel steps in the superstructure, our steps and luggage making an echoing, clanging racket. On the seventh level we stopped, breathless and exhausted, shouldered open an impossibly heavy steel door, and looked down the long hallway we had stepped into. On the starboard side fore and aft were the spacious captain's quarters. Next to that, fore, was the purser's cabin, then a pilot's cabin, with the chief engineer's suite on the port side forward and a double passengers' suite aft. I had been told that a couple had booked accommodation, but this was not the case. I was to be the only passenger and the only woman aboard and would occupy the purser's cabin.

I looked around my new digs with satisfaction. There was a spacious bathroom with a shower. A large clothes closet; a couch with ample storage below; an inviting bunk heaped high with fluffy European pillows and a duvet of spotless white; a huge desk with locking drawers; and a refrigerator comprised the furnishings of the cabin. Behind the couch was a huge porthole that I could open manually. We ran over to it and there, far below us, was *Gatti*. With my port almost dead center and just below the bridge, I had a magnificent view of the ship and her precious cargo. I soon learned that *Cielo* was not even a year old yet and still under warranty, so my gleaming accommodations were indeed very special. I had lived at home until I married at age 19 and had never experienced the freedom of living alone. I love my family dearly and it was with a kind of guilty surprise that I realized I was looking forward to this experience with more enthusiasm than I would have imagined.

Bill helped me unpack and we locked *Gatti's* carnet in the desk. We explored the ship briefly with a crew member and then said a tearful goodbye. Bill had a lot to do at home and, it was not going to be easy. We had two dogs, four cats, three cockatiels, and a koi pond. The large house we had lovingly remodeled sat on a beautifully landscaped half acre of fruit trees, gardens, and a solar heated pool. We had hired house sitters often in the past with few complaints, but this time we were apprehensive. We had an uneasy feeling about the man involved, and some of the animals were very old. But I chalked up my concerns to the fact that I was edgy about being pretty much out of communication for a month and that we were on the threshold of creating a new life for ourselves. I imagine selfishness played a part as well since I so much wanted to do this thing. When I had said goodbye to the animals before we had left home, I had no idea that home would never be the same again. My beautiful yard would be altered, and I would never again see two of my pets. Bill had difficult days indeed before him but, of course, we knew none of these things at the time, and our separation was difficult enough to face.

After Bill left, I began poking around like an inquisitive puppy. Large cranes on the wharf were stacking containers on and below our decks. So much cargo was on the deck and on the dock that it was almost impossible to distinguish between the two. The cranes moved up and down a track, squawking, honking and clanging, directed by a man who appeared improbably small in a little cage high up in the mechanism. Large trucks drove alongside and either received or surrendered containers. Despite the undeniably accurate placement of goods, it seemed obvious to me that a passenger should not venture out while such activities were in progress. So I mostly contented myself with looking out of my porthole and trying to make sense of a system totally alien to me.

Over the course of the day, I acquainted myself with the basic layout of the ship and spent brief moments at meals with some crewmen, but it was clear that loading days curtailed social niceties. At dinner time, the tiny men abandoned their perches high aloft the cranes, the longshoremen disappeared, and I assumed we would be casting off soon. The big, dirty barge that had been tied to our port side refueling us all day had been pushed down the channel, and I was certainly ready to go. Then at 6:30 p.m. I heard the rumble of trucks, the cranes started up again, and the loading resumed. Brilliant lights illuminated the entire work area: the one on the crane nearest my porthole turned my cabin into broad daylight. My nerves began to fray. It had been a long, emotional day. My brain had absorbed so much information and confused perceptions that it seemed I could hold no more. In addition, the work was getting more personal as far as I was concerned. Whereas earlier the containers had been stacked six deep in our cavernous holds, they were now being stacked on deck directly below my line of sight. Here they came, climbing the side of the superstructure at an alarming rate, and swinging by my face to be set down intimidatingly close to *Gatti*. At the moment it seemed very probable they would climb above my porthole and obliterate my view.

But mercifully at 11 p.m. the cranes went squawking querulously down their tracks, extinguished their lights and, throwing their arms toward the heavens, fell silent. Bright lights still flooded my cabin as men clambered over what appeared to be very wobbly stacks of cargo, tightening down turnbuckles, but the blessed quiet was enough to drop me into an exhausted sleep. At 2:30 a.m. I was awakened by a toot-toot, and we began to pivot from our dock and edge down the channel. Under the Vincent Thomas Bridge; past a clock with "Port of Los Angeles" glowing a spooky blue-violet; past naval vessels, closed restaurants and slumbering yachts. Then the channel opened like an airport runway, flanked by red lights to port and green to starboard. Past the lighthouse with its embracing arms of green light and warning/comforting calls; past the familiar breakwater where *Gatti* had sought temporary refuge from the rolling seas, we pushed our way through the night. A pilot boat raced to our side, picked up our pilot, gave a couple toots, and pulling away from our side, made a swooping turn back to shore. We pointed our bow toward the offshore oil rigs dancing like fairy lights on the dark sea. *Gatti* and I were on our way to Italy.

The next morning over breakfast with Captain Lessing and the chief engineer I began to understand the routine. There were two dining rooms – one for officers and one for crew. I was to eat with the officers at the table reserved for the German captain, the Austrian chief engineer, and the Filipino first mate. Three other officers, two of them Romanian, kept very much to themselves as they dined together at a second table in the same room. The 19 members of the Filipino crew ate in the second dining room, separated from us by the galley. The cook was also Filipino as was the "Master's man," Ray, a young fellow on his first voyage, who spoke no English. For that matter, no one spoke English very well, and yet all activity on board as well as that between the ship and port was conducted in English. I never did get beyond being mystified about how the system operated so well. Ray served three meals each day at specified hours. Food in the officers' mess had a decidedly Bavarian bent. Food for the crew was much different and, speaking purely from an olfactory point of view for I never entered the crew's mess, of a distinctly fish and rice flavor.

We left Los Angeles behind in the wee hours of the morning and arrived in Mazatlan, Mexico, in the wee hours of the morning on my third day at sea. How much I learned in that short time and how acclimated I became to this new way of life! My attitude and abilities had been quickly assessed and I was given full run of the ship. This meant most wonderfully that the bridge and the bow were in my domain, and I immediately recognized their value. When we were docked, the bridge was locked for security; when we were in the process of loading or the canal linemen were on board, I was denied access to the bow. Otherwise, I could go where I wished and when I wished. The first day a deck chair was set up on the bridge for me, but I soon preferred to do my sunning forward and spend my bridge time inside with the fascinating, complex and initially indecipherable navigational instruments. There was always a watch set on the bridge and, especially in the mornings, several people would be there as the captain updated his log and various officers reported to him. As we became better friends and my interests became obvious, I was given lessons and homework in seamanship.

The 360 degree panorama of open sea was a wonder for me to behold, both from the height of the bridge and the plunging bow. The bow was as far away as one could get from the vibration of the ship and the activities of the crew. Aside from morning wash downs and other routines, most of the day no one had reason to be out there. I would cart out my Magellan, books, an ice chest, and suntan oil and be in heaven for hours. Here were wound the mammoth ropes, the size of my waist, and I could climb or sit on great metal spool-type posts. The steel ribs running horizontally inside the hull made perfect climbing platforms. In addition, there were steel ladders up the sides.

Gatti buckled up on *Cielo*.

The mesmerizing magic of the sea certainly cut into my reading time. I spent hours and hours atop the ladder at the very prow from which little could be seen aside from the blue of the sea melding with the blue of the sky. The air was pure and clean, the swish of the waves as we parted them soothing to the soul. I pretended to be Christopher Columbus scanning the horizon for a smudge of land, not knowing what to expect ahead. One day an albatross spent some time swooping and ducking about me. On others I saw spouting whales and playful dolphins. On one occasion a great sea turtle swam by. Flying fish would suddenly break the surface and skim above the waves. By the time we arrived at our first stop, a new persona was already forming in me. I was now brave enough to run up and down the stairs outside the superstructure and to negotiate the lonely trip to the bow. I had recognized my total ignorance of things nautical and knew where my immediate intellectual pursuits would lie. I was renewing a childhood fascination with astronomy and beginning to feel a part of the cosmos. Most of all, I understood that I loved the sea and never wanted to be off it very long for the rest of my life.

Our stop in Mazatlan was my first complete experience of arrival and departure, loading and unloading. We arrived before dawn and a distinct change in the ship's vibration wakened me. I looked out to see a brilliantly lit peninsula guarded by enormous rocks. With great stealth and precision we navigated around them and, as the sun was trying its best to color the smudgy horizon, we swung north and passed through a breakwater with so narrow an opening, that I held my breath. Inside the breakwater two tugs were standing by, ready to pounce. As we entered the narrow channel, they moved in and ran along our flanks like a couple of collies. Between us and the buoys they ran, poking us in place as needed. When we were well into the channel, they pivoted us around completely and, putting their heads down, shoved us up to the quay, their powerful engines creating smooth, round maelstroms in the sea.

The activity was considerably different from what I was to experience in other ports. Container ports are a relatively new phenomenon and have somewhat different requirements from traditional wharves. The biggest demand is for space. Most of the world's commerce is conducted via containers, so there are millions of them globally. Ports designed for containers are generally constructed away from towns, where there is more area and land prices are lower. The port at Mazatlan was small by any standard. In fact, only smaller freighters such as we were could service it. Here there were no tracks and noisy shore cranes. Instead, three men climbed high up into our three yellow cranes, we revved up our generators, and they got to work. Even though it was a Saturday, the men worked hard all day and deep into the night. I watched the off-loading with horror from my porthole. The operator of the crane closest to my cabin was almost at eye-level. The dock workers would run up on the containers, attach four cable lines to two of them, and the crane operator would swing them over to the wharf. These were small containers, the ones you can see loaded two to a semi-truck, as opposed to the more commonly seen long single one. They were hauled up, knocking together in the air with the men below guiding and balancing them. I observed the end of the off-loading with relief and was pleased to see that the loading would consist of only long containers. These were not so bad; only one at a time was lifted, but the workers still ran below pushing on the suspended cargo. It appeared that life was considered cheap in Mazatlan.

The following day was the last day of October and the end of Daylight Saving Time. At 6:30 in the morning we were ready to leave Mexico. The two tugs stood off our side like two friendly puppies, and one actually had a dog on board barking excitedly. Two huge lines were attached to our port side stern by the barking tug, our engine rumbled to life, and we were tugged away from shore. Then the lines were removed, and we were nudged gently with the snub-nosed bow of the tug. We now headed for the breakwater under our own power and were underway with no further help. The two tugs waited and watched from behind the breakwater for a few minutes, then turned back to their Sunday pursuits.

All about us were tiny fishing boats glinting through the water like minnows. Most were occupied by two men with a heaped net between them. As we threaded our careful way among them, the pilot ran down from the high bridge, ran down toward the bow and descended a terrifyingly long rope ladder. His boat ran up alongside us and hovered until the pilot was able to leap aboard. A wave of his hand indicated that he was all right, and then the boat was gone. I looked sadly back at Mazatlan, barely visible through the filth belched out by a huge power plant. The magnificent Sierra Madre were all but obscured by the thick gray effluvium. We added our own burst of roiling black smoke, which trailed off into a sulphurous yellow. This was a different view of the beautiful Mazatlan I had enjoyed vacationing at in youth.

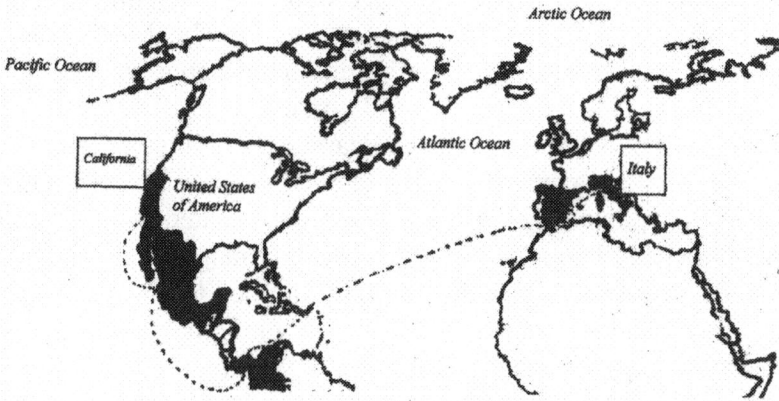

The Voyage

Ports of call: California, Mexico, Panama, Colombia, Spain, Italy.

The next four and a half days we spent en route to Panama. All Saints Day and All Souls Day passed with no break in routine that I could see. Our second night back at sea we encountered our first good swell, and I felt the first lurch of my stomach. While its contents stayed in place, the contents of my cabin did not. Writing materials flew about the place; a dreadful noise issued from the refrigerator. I stupidly opened it only to be attacked by a cascade of icy Coke cans. Bill was delighted to be informed of this experience via the Magellan. He assumed we had passed the place where his literary hero, Horatio Hornblower, had sunk the *Navidad* in novelist C.S. Forester's series. I checked our chart on the bridge and, sure enough, early that morning we had passed the Gulf of Tehuantepec. It is near here that the Sierras end and the winds from the Gulf of Campeche sweep over a narrow neck of land. The captain warned me that we would encounter this phenomenon in the Mediterranean, where a similar geographic configuration accounts for the fierce storms that sweep across the Gulf of Leon in France.

South of Mexico we sailed past Nicaragua, El Salvador, and Costa Rica. The stars and planets at night seemed so large and close that it was easy to spot constellations. The moon floated like an amber canoe on the sea. The sunsets were incredibly magnificent and lasted for a very long time. After the sun had dropped below the horizon, the entire sea and sky glowed in shades of pink, magenta, and red. I had become accustomed to seeing my world as essentially 360 unrestricted degrees, but I had always thought of sunsets as being visible only on the western horizon. This total wash of color over my entire field of vision was breathtaking; every night was different and grand, and each evening I was held on deck in its thrall.

The time seemed to be a relaxed one for everyone, and the crew had the leisure and interest to help me overcome my plentiful deficiencies. They ran off conversion tables for me, filled the pool with warm tropical salt water, and provided me with waypoints to enter into my Magellan. Every morning I checked my coordinates and speed with those of *Cielo* and happily found myself in agreement. As we approached Panama, the captain provided me with information and brochures on the Canal so I could better understand what was going on when we got there. The crew was excited about the Canal and the stop at Cartagena on the other side. But not as much enthusiasm was expressed for the ocean crossing afterward. The nearer we got to the Canal, the more freighter traffic and sea trash we encountered. Finally, on Thursday we dropped anchor amidst about two dozen other merchant vessels in Panama Bay. Our engine shut down, and we began to rock gently, as a boat ought.

We had had a couple rain storms during the trip down, but now it began to rain more often. The rain had been a bit of a godsend for an uninvited passenger on board. When we left Mazatlan, a tall white heron had sailed with us, perched on the top of a big orange container near *Gatti's* bow. The captain had predicted that he would probably die of hunger or thirst. I had tried taking food out to him, but he would have none of my fare. He looked miserable and forlorn. A few times he had flown out over the water, his long legs trailing behind him, in search of fish, but I never saw him dive into the water. The rain, which had collected in puddles on some containers that had tarpaulin covers rather than steel tops, was able to quench his thirst. I wondered about his family. I wondered about the stowaways who try to survive hidden away in containers. But this bird was lucky. Just before we chugged into the bay, he had thrown himself into the wind and flapped off to his new home. At least he could speak the language.

CHAPTER XII

TWO CONTINENTS, TWO
OCEANS, TWO BOATS

"Nothing of him that doth fade,
But doth suffer a sea-change
Into something rich and strange."
William Shakespeare, *The Tempest*

The morning of my ninth day at sea, I awakened at 2 a.m. to find a changed scene beyond my porthole. Our neighboring freighter had disappeared, we had weighed anchor and were heading off in the darkness toward an island. As had always been the case to this point, I had missed the boarding of the pilot, but there he was up on the bridge with the captain, the third mate and a helmsman. The night was velvety dark, with brilliant stars that faded as we approached the Canal. The lights of Panama City's towering skyscrapers defined the coast. We passed under the string of lights outlining the Bridge of the Americas, which carries the Pan American Highway. As tall as it appeared from a distance, our bridge was not far below it. The Panama Canal Commission Building was lit up like a castle and certainly looked as big as one. The wheelhouse was pitch-black; only the various electronic screens glowed in various colors. On the water, the buoy lights shone very brightly.

All was calm, hushed and controlled in the wheelhouse. "Hard port!" says the pilot quietly. Hard port!" says the mate loudly. "Hard port, sir!" says the helmsman. Then, "Midships!" says the pilot. "Midships!"; "Midships, sir!" "10 to starboard!"; "10 to starboard!"; "10 to starboard, sir!" This was my first experience on the bridge at night with a pilot aboard. How odd it was to see the captain standing by, lending assistance to the pilot and not in control of the navigation. I also gained a better appreciation of the importance of darkness on the bridge. The wheelhouse was only one flight of well-lighted steel stairs outside my cabin door. At the top of the stairs was an unbelievably heavy door. All the doors to the wheelhouse were heavy; the whole area could be locked down and fortified. Before this inner door would open, the stair lights would go off and be replaced by a red night-vision light. There was always a nautical chart with a desk light shining on it so our progress could be charted, but at night a thick black curtain was drawn around this table to prevent a single ray's escape. Bright light can destroy night vision for up to half an hour – not a desirable condition at sea any time, let alone when one approaches the Panama Canal.

Tugs appeared out of the dark and nudged us into the first Miraflores Lock. Fore and aft we were connected to cables attached to locomotives that clanged like San Francisco cable cars. Six linemen marched onto our poop deck and handled all the rope work. I looked down on them from the bridge and marveled. Their precise rhythm made them appear almost robotic as their 12 heavy-gloved hands pulled on the thick lines and tied them off. Their six hardhats as viewed from above made them resemble the Fisher-Price toy men of my children's babyhood. When they boarded or disembarked, they walked in step in a straight line. The cable cars clattered along their tracks under powerful lights and then positioned themselves to maintain the correct tension on the cables to keep us perfectly centered in the lock.

The lock accommodates freighters up to 13 containers wide. At 12 containers wide, we were shaving things pretty close. The heavy floodgates clanged closed behind us and, as water poured in in torrents, we were lifted up, up 40 feet. The same procedure was re-enacted in the second lock. Released onto our new level, we chugged along Miraflores Lake to the Pedro Miguel Locks. This is actually one two-way traffic lock. By the time we moved out of it onto a still higher level, the sun was beginning to rise. I had been living with the sun rising upon the left out of the sea. This morning we had made an obvious turn, pointed in a much more promising Italian direction. For the next three hours we navigated the Gaillard Cut, and I pretended I was on the *African Queen*. The pilot chatted with me overlooking *Gatti* for a while and then retired to the pilot's cabin next to mine for a well-deserved nap.

On both sides lay jungle and mountains and little islands. Palms, breadfruit, mangoes, silk trees, vines and grasses all vied for a root or tendril hold. Raptor birds perched on treetops; swallows flitted in and out of the teeming growth. The din of bird singing, squawking, shrieking and chirping was deafening. And I had always thought my two cockatiels were loud! The weather lent itself well to my African imaginings as warm rains began. After each shower a mist would rise over the trees and down the rain would come again. This waterway was actually fairly wide, and the captain was able to pass two slower moving freighters with great satisfaction. He was unabashedly proud of his shiny new craft and her 21 knots and flaunted her whenever possible.

We passed large vessels headed west as well, among them two cruise ships that resembled two big white martin houses afloat with hundreds of round port openings. During the showers, we could see hundreds of noses pressed against the observation windows. When the rains took a break, hoards of people crammed onto a comparatively small aft deck. As for myself, I clasped my hands behind my back and strolled the breadth of my bridge in solitary splendor, looking down pityingly at those huddled masses, with a certain self-satisfaction at my beautiful yacht poised on the deck far below me. I was marching to a different drummer all right, and I loved the beat.

The Panama Canal is not run on a first-come, first-served basis. Schedules are made and hefty tolls are collected. If a vessel misses its appointment, it loses its fee. So even though we had passed those other slower ships, we had to wait our turn at the last lock for them to catch up to us and be taken through. This Gatun Lock consists of three chambers, and passage requires a good chunk of time. Many times throughout this long, long day, I had seen huge signs proclaiming Panama's readiness to transport the world into the new millennium. In a matter of a few weeks the United States would be turning the Canal over to Panama, and the excitement was evident everywhere. As we entered this final big lock to be lowered gradually into the Atlantic, I looked at the last of these signs and in my heart wished the country success. The Canal is very old, the technology so involved, and the link so vital.

Outside the lock, a dozen or so ships lay at anchor awaiting their turn to head to the Pacific. The waters of the great eastern ocean were rolling with vigor and rain was lashing down as I made my way to my bunk after so many exciting hours on the bridge. How wonderful it was to be at sea again! It was only 7 p.m., but I fell into a deep sleep and awakened the next morning to find us tied up in Cartagena. I had been at sea 10 days and the scheduling − or lack of it − had become a part of me. The activities of day or night depended on where we were. Thus far, we had approached and left harbors in the dark. Meals were served at scheduled times, but we were passing a time zone with every 15 degrees of longitude and actual time pretty much lost its significance. Each time zone crossed would bring the chief engineer on the intercom. "Advance time one hour," his deep voice would announce in heavily accented English. By the time we were well into the Atlantic crossing, time had become the sun and dinner. It was probably a good thing I had no telephone.

In the end, we spent four full days in Cartagena and I came to know the port well from a variety of perspectives. We had a broken cable on our number one crane and this seemed an ideal place to have it repaired. *Cielo* was under warranty until the end of December, and it was already Nov. 6. Besides, Cartagena's location makes it a hub for global transportation of goods to and from South America, and we were scheduled to meet one of *Cielo*'s sister ships there. We were unloading goods from Vancouver and the United States' West Coast, plus some kind of nuts from Mexico – all designated for shipment south. We would be loading up with Central and South American goods for the European market. The wharf area itself made me think of Jim Hawkins of *Treasure Island* on his arrival in Bristol. It was modern and old-fashioned at the same time. Ships from around the globe tied up, were unloaded and reloaded, and sent on their way with amazing speed. The cargo was not all stashed in containers either. There were large quantities of timber and bales of cotton. These latter were lifted by a huge chain with many hooks of tremendous size dangling from the end. Men deep down in the cargo holds crammed the hooks into the cotton and the enormous mass of dirty white fluff was swung into the air.

Our first full day in Cartagena was a Saturday, and I was urged to go into town. I was a little concerned about being a single American female in Colombia but was assured my fears were unfounded, and so they proved to be. The crew waved me off, and I felt as though I had 20 big brothers to keep on eye on my comings and goings. The Atlantic coast of Colombia seemed more like a Caribbean island than a troubled South American country. I descended the long ladder from the deck to discover an extensive port area chock full of cavernous storage sheds and acres of containers piled high. I eventually located a bus that carried me, along with dock workers, to the gate. It soon became apparent that my recent intensive studies of Italian and exposure to German dinner conversation had done much to undermine my limited grasp of Spanish. However, I managed to hail a cab and get into town.

The area I visited that day was within old fort walls. The narrow streets were overhung with elegant little balconies in startling states of disrepair. Mayan-type hammocks on the balconies hinted that nights here were probably as stifling hot as the day was. It was early morning in November and already it was difficult to breathe and a real effort to walk with any enthusiasm. The crew had warned me that I would be inundated by emerald salesmen, but aside from the cab driver, who offered me something that looked like an ancient wad of chlorophyll chewing gum stuck on a card, no one bothered me.

With the help of several very kind people I was able to complete my errands in town. I found a bookstore and negotiated the purchase of a book about the city. I found a cool, dark hole in a wall lined with ancient telephone booths filled with people unburdening themselves in a wave of loquacity. An operator at an old, scarred wooden desk took my number, motioned me into one of the equally scarred wooden booths, and put a call through to Bill. I had talked with him only once since our separation, on a very expensive and unsatisfactory SAT phone aboard ship. Now I had a wonderful, newsy chat. I could tell that all was not going smoothly, but he covered well.

I then made my way to a quite odd post office, at which I mailed letters to my children. The captain had assured me that I could use U.S. currency, so I had no pesitos. This had caused a minor problem at the bookstore and phone place, but entrepreneurs seem to overcome these problems with more ease than do government employees. The woman behind the postal counter bound my letters in official stamps, seals and cellophane tape. I had tried to tell her that I had U.S. dollars before she began, but I guess she thought I was saying the letters were going to the U.S. In any event, I now proffered her my dollars. Impasse! It appeared that she could not undo what she had done nor could she take my currency. She settled back with stolid complacency and watched me. I felt like the unfortunate damsels in fairy tales who are ordered to spin straw into gold. At length a young man came up with a calculator. After a price was determined and I assured them I did not need change, the transaction was completed. I decided that from then on I would take advantage of the captain's offer to post my mail when we were in port. My adventures in town had exhausted me and I caught a cab back to my ship.

Work was progressing rapidly and not at all to my liking. The wharf cranes were tending to the containers fore but the aft was being loaded by our crane. This was the first time we had been docked with our port side to the quay and *Gatti* and I felt the strain. It was one thing to have containers heaped around her, but to have them swung over her, grappling hooks almost scratching her canvas, was quite another. When work stopped for the evening, I breathed a sigh of relief and collapsed. Practically everyone else on board went out on the town. It was their first time off ship in a long while and wouldn't happen again until they got to Italy. This time it was I who sent them off like a fond mother, and they promised to bring back pesitos.

The following day, Sunday, proved to be one of the fullest of the entire voyage. At breakfast I met two German technicians who had been flown in to repair our crane. Two ships had left during the night, and our sister ship *Cielo di Canada* had come in. The captain arrived at the table with an envelope addressed to him. Inside was a formal invitation written in French. As nearly as any of us could make out, a very important function was going to take place at the wharf that night. A transatlantic regatta from Le Havre to Cartagena had been completed and awards were to be given out. In the lower right hand corner were the words "traje: color bianco." Do we need a white pass? Do we have to wear white? Is it white tie? Do we bring white wine? We were mystified, but I agreed to accompany the captain that evening. At the same time he told me he was going sightseeing to Fort San Felipe that afternoon and invited me to go along. The second mate had procured some pesitos for me, so I agreed to give Cartagena another shot.

The afternoon was great fun; we hired a cab and driver to show us around. It appeared that the captain and I were the only two people on Earth not to have seen the movie *Romancing the Stone,* and we took a hard hit in the estimation of our driver. But then I asked to see Gabriel García Marquez's house and that somewhat repaired our damaged image. We drove up a winding mountain road to an old monastery from which we had a magnificent view of the area. We could see *Cielo* far off in a port that appeared minuscule from this height. Off to one side, within its eight kilometer wall, sat old Cartagena; to the other side lay the "new," a massive stretch of sorry poverty. We then visited Fort San Felipe and a most fascinating naval museum where a little withered old man with a cane led us about, his lively personality and wit recreating local history from 1533 to the present. As evening approached, we returned to our ship to prepare for the next outing.

Just in case we were to wear white, we dressed in the lightest colors we could find. The closest we could come was khaki. We made our way off the ship and about the port as carefully as we could so our smart duds would not be smudged by the omnipresent oil and dirt of such locations. We walked along the quay where cranes were busy loading and skipjacks darted among trucks, containers, and workers. We were almost mowed down by one of these backing out of the way of a motorcade. Then we were nearly flattened by the motorcade itself. It consisted of vehicles bearing the president of Colombia, Dr. Andres Pastrana Arango, and a couple dozen of the world's most gorgeous women all decked out in dazzling white gowns.

We entered the area of celebration from the back door, so to speak, and took our seats on folding chairs draped with white covers. Several hundred of these chairs were lined up on risers facing a ship moored along the quay. What a magnificent ship she was! She was the *Gloria*, Colombia's naval training tall ship. Her towering wooden masts seemed to support the sky. Her brass gleamed, and a spiffy naval band on board was tuning up. Elegant women with smooth, bronzed skin, heavy gold jewelry, and brilliant white outfits entered through what must have been the main gate on the arms of dashing gentlemen also eye-achingly in white. Waiters in purest white circulated among the seats, serving cocktails from white-napkined trays. Excited Spanish and French flowed from those in white and eddied around the German-Italian-English speakers hunkered down in khaki. I mused over whether a duck landing among a flock of swans shared the feelings I had. The evening was a resounding success in spite of our sartorial handicap.

The festivities included the stirring national anthems of Colombia and France; awards to the winners of the Ruga de Café Regatta; a haunting bugle call of *Taps* in honor of a contender lost at sea off the Azores; an address by the Colombian president; and the presentation of the Miss Colombia contestants. All of this was conducted first in Spanish and then in French, so it took twice as long. The deck of the *Gloria* served as a stage, and background sound was provided by the

71

clangs, honks, and rumbles of a loading operation at a freighter moored nearby. At the close of the formalities, wonderful entertainment was presented including the arrival of Juan Valdez with his coffee-laden donkey, folklorico groups, bands, and a finale of extravagant fireworks. The beautiful alabaster crowd then dined on dainty hors d'oeuvres while the captain and I threaded our way back among the mechanics of the port like two wharf rats. Back on his own deck with his attentive crew at his beck and call, the captain took a deep breath and appeared to physically expand. I scurried to my cabin to make a note to never, ever travel again without a white outfit.

Monday found us still at dock with no hope of leaving before Tuesday afternoon at best. Our cranes were functioning, but the loading was behind schedule. *Cielo di Canada* had required some work as well but since she had a Canal appointment and no wish to forfeit her $60,000 passage fee, she had fled westward during the night. Because we were delayed, we swapped some cargo with yet another sister ship we had not expected to meet up with. *Gatti* and I certainly had had fun at this port, but we were eager to get underway. We wanted to get back to sea, and we wanted to get to Italy. The rest of the crew must have had similar stirrings because everyone was grumpy all day. Like any good captain with a nose for unrest and mutiny, ours devised a diversion for the afternoon.

Chief among our many safety devices aboard was a self-contained lifeboat. It was a neon orange capsule that hung at our stern and was equipped with food and water to sustain our entire crew for a couple days. During my initial safety tour early in the voyage, I had been allowed to peek inside at its rows of seats with their sturdy seatbelts. The boat was brand new like everything else on board, so it was decided that this would be a good time for the crew to try out its state-of-the-art lifesaving features. To my extreme displeasure, "the passenger" was forbidden to take part in this exercise. This and not being allowed to climb down to see the bow thruster were the only activities the captain ever denied me, so I had to assume he had good reasons for the exclusion. To soothe my disappointment, I was put in charge of the camera. The crew filed obediently into the little capsule tilted off the stern at a 30-degree angle and buckled up. The door was closed and latched. Whoosh! The little craft shot off our stern like the wind, half-submerged, and then bobbed up. Two hatches and the back door opened and heads popped out. It looked like a miniature version of the *Monitor*. The tiny boat motored around to starboard, and the crew climbed up the long, swinging ladder used by the pilots. With three crew remaining on board her, the little orange ark then motored back to our stern, was attached by hooks, and eventually drawn back up into position. There was much swinging about during this stage; the three eventually exited, streaming perspiration and looking green around the gills. It was certainly a valuable experience for us all – even those of us who only stood and photographed – and served to get us all in better spirits. The captain fairly sprinted up to his quarters to send off his digital photos to the ship's owners.

I awakened early on Tuesday and watched the sun rise on what was finally to be our last day in port. I watched as the east changed from pink, to apricot, to gold. To the west, storm clouds were piling up in shades of purple. A single pink cloud hung against the gray above the monastery on top of the hill far above us. Only two ships lay quietly at dock, and the quays were covered with large puddles left from an overnight shower. Everything was motionless except the silent birds. Some plants and debris floated on the glassy water. Two gulls spotted some food and in moments 18 more had appeared, but even their garrulous cries were muffled in the quiet dawn. A rooster crowed in the distance. I heard a soft rattle in our rigging and looked up to see a crewman running up our flags. Neither of us spoke; we drank in the peaceful freshness. At the harbor mouth sat the orange inflatable that patrolled the harbor, engine off. It was a magical time as the liquid sun floated an exploratory path across the placid water and, finding all well, peeked with greater audacity over the horizon. The glass of the skyscrapers to the west suddenly gleamed. The harbor boat's engine coughed to life and the little dinghy turned back reluctantly to land. The first truck of the day honked imperiously. Day had come to Cartagena.

Around breakfast time ships began to enter the port – a big cruise ship, a sea construction vessel, and a huge white Del Monte boat. A hotel bus appeared and began shuttling cruise passengers into town. Those poor souls were deprived of the joys of port buses and cab negotiations. In deference to these tourists as well as the health of Colombia's economy, some shops and a communication center were set up in the port not far from our berth. I spent the entire afternoon at this facility running errands for crewmen who could not leave the ship. Having photos developed was their big interest. I bought Havana rums for Bill and the captain. It seemed strange being able to do this after decades of U.S. embargo against Cuban products. But I was not on my way to the United States. Thus the thought of customs had actually crossed my mind as I returned to *Cielo* toward evening, but I was hardly prepared for what awaited me there.

When loading had begun that morning, a half dozen uniformed men had arrived. They began randomly checking containers as they were loaded. Since they were requiring that every tenth one or so be opened and examined, we were being slowed down considerably and no one on board was harboring happy feelings toward these men. Now as I returned to my ship, I was subjected to a search as well. Everything in my backpack and purse was taken out and scrutinized. The utmost courtesy was shown me and my person was not touched, but the procedure was very annoying. How inconceivable that before very long such procedures – and worse – would become routine in my own homeland! I was permitted to board and the slow loading continued. When it was completed, divers were sent down below to see if we had drugs attached to our water intakes. No drugs were found, but some kind of shells were. Down went yet more divers to pry open the shells!

It was 11:15 p.m. when we finally pulled away from dock and headed down the long, narrow channel. At the mouth of the Boca Chica we passed the coastal fort, ablaze in light. Our pilot swung down his ladder to his waiting boat and was borne off at high speed into the Colombian night. We adjusted our engine and headed for sea.

Pushing freight eastward.

CHAPTER XIII

EASTWARD, HO!

'Roll on, thou deep and dark blue Ocean – roll!
Ten thousand fleets sweep over thee in vain.'
Lord Byron, *Childe Harold's Pilgrimage*

As we headed for Mona Pass and the open Atlantic, I reflected that I had been at sea for two weeks. I had learned a lot in a short time. On my fifteenth day we passed Puerto Rico and did not see land again until day 23. The crossing was obviously the part of the trip the crew liked least, but several Filipino crew members were going home for Christmas after *Cielo* made the return trip to Vancouver and the big hope was that we would just make good time. While the Pacific leg of the trip was certainly a sea cruise, somehow it had not seemed like such a big deal to *Gatti* and me. After all, we had played in that ocean before, and the ship was pretty much following the coast line. But now, as we headed northeast across the broad Atlantic, life took on a more serious aspect. Just beyond the Mona Pass we had a big barbecue with chicken, steaks, sausage, pork chops, and plenty of German beer. The entire crew, barring the poor third mate on watch, partied under colored lights, singing far into the night. All the songs were American and accompanied by an acoustic guitar. "Take me home, country roads…West Virginia, mountain mamma, take me home…" carried over the dark seas in heavily accented bass tones. In a way the songs were funny, but there was nothing humorous about the nostalgia for home and the personal loneliness that welled up from those throats. We had hung a tarpaulin to break the already freshening winds, and that evening was our last social time.

From that point on everyone was busy dealing with weather that was far from pleasant. A late-season hurricane had formed just behind us in the Mona Pass, but our problems came from a storm in the North Sea. For days we bucked and plunged in six meter waves. I lost any fears I had harbored about the security of the containers.

Despite sheeting rain and tremendous walls of water washing over the decks, all the cargo stayed firmly in place. *Cielo* and *Gatti* actually reveled in the weather. It is true that water at times puddled on her canvas and during the highest winds her coverings began to tear loose, but the crew was quick to heed the passenger's instructions and kept *Gatti* as dry and secure as possible. By the time we left the waters of the Atlantic, she looked like she had spent a night in Lilliput, so lashed down and around her were her canvas cloaks.

I spent the voyage learning many noteworthy things. There is a good reason for the bars on the walls near the toilet. One can eat, albeit with difficulty, while clutching the table with one hand so as not to skid all over the mess. A soft bunk is a good place to stay when loose items are flying about in a steel cabin. The most important thing I learned was, of course, that I had a lot to learn. As the days wore on and the weather made it impossible to follow my earlier pleasant pursuits, I spent most of my time in the wheelhouse. I poured over my copied conversion tables, and I learned about great circles and waypoints. I had daily lessons in knots, gauging wind speed, wave height, and cloud reading. I learned to understand nautical charts and the use of dividers.

And while all this was taking place, Bill was tidying up affairs at home; flying to London to set up venues for handling banking, insurance and legal matters; and taking a train to Genova to prepare for our arrival. I was a part of so much excitement and yet, at the same time, was being held captive by the angry sea, which seemed determined to slow us down and hold us in a kind of limbo. We had already lost so much time in Cartagena and now had to lower the RPMs of our engine to cope with the high seas that struck us broadside and sent shudders through the vessel. But the time came when we got closer to the protection of land and the winds shifted. All of us began making predictions as to what time we would reach the Strait of Gibralter.

On day 23, Nov. 18, we began to see other ships. My Magellan began receiving and transmitting messages with more reliability. The seas were calm and the weather turned cold. There was a half moon and the clouds were dissipating, making it likely that we would see stars for the first time in several nights. At 7 p.m. mine joined the other pairs of eager eyes on the bridge scanning eastward through the darkness. I could relate to Paul Revere straining forward on his mount to catch the first rays from the Old North Church. Suddenly, out of the void gleamed Africa – a lighthouse at the tip of Morocco. Then to our port flashed out the 2/1 signal of the light at Trafalgar. We checked in by radio with the control at Tarifa and once again we were navigating interesting waters in the dark; but no one cared.

The Strait was like a two-lane highway with ships great and small navigating in both directions. We had our radio on and learned the names, cargoes, destinations and ports of departure of vessels entering the area. The brilliant lights of a fort in Africa on our starboard side vied with the magnificent Rock jutting up on our port. It was peculiar to look at the shorelines and think of these land masses as continents rather than countries. The captain put me to work finding lighthouses and lighted buoys on the chart and then identifying them by their flash sequences as we passed them. There were so many that I was able to master this new lesson. At 11 p.m. we left the Strait at last and the waters of the Mediterranean Sea bathed our hull. Below us lay the waters that were to be our new home, placid and inviting under the dangling stars and beaming moon.

The following morning the sun rose over a smooth, soft sea. In sharp contrast to the desolate, endless miles of ocean, we were now surrounded by vessels of all kinds – freighters and sailing craft alike. White sails dazzled before backdrops of bright blue sky and tall mauve mountains that appeared to march right up to the coastline. Along the coast of Spain we sailed while I picked out gleaming alabaster cities and expansive beaches with the mate's binoculars. Manned by lone fishermen, small fishing craft of ancient vintage, paint peeling and rust-stained, rode at anchor just outside the shipping lane. Despite the beauty of the weather, the captain reported that a strong gale was tearing at Genova after striking Savona so hard that containers had actually been flung around the port. It was a source of amusement on the bridge to picture Bill, newly arrived in Genova, wondering why on earth he was bringing a boat to such a place. It was generally agreed that while we were not happy about our delays, at least the storm would clear out before we approached Italy.

At sunset we sent out a radio call for the Valencia pilot. He did not come racing out as our former pilots had, and we actually made a large circle in the sea as we waited impatiently. Finally he arrived and guided us in through a breakwater flanked by green lights to our starboard and red to port. The frisky tugs were waiting for us and nudged us up to dock. An employee of the shipping line was waiting to come aboard, laden with mail. I had forgotten about mail, but no one else had. The ship's central office looked like feeding time at the zoo. Paper ripped as some men dove right in. Others of us scurried away, our unopened treasure clutched close, to devour in our own private corners. Like animals with bones, we gnawed at our treats, stretching out the pleasure for many hours.

Loading began immediately, but the captain was still glum. We were supposed to be in Genova today, and we would now be doing well to get there by the 23rd. He had a flight to Hamburg on the 24th. Our chief engineer also had plans to return to Austria for the holidays, but his mail included orders designed to ruin anyone's day. He was told to report immediately to Bilbao and board a freighter bound for Buenos Aires. A new German engineer replaced him.

The freighter port at Valencia was brand new and relatively small and quiet. Since it is located a fair distance from town and no one had Spanish currency for a bus ride in, I amused myself by watching activities in the nearby yacht basin from my bridge perch. Several little prams were taking advantage of the sun just outside the basin, either racing or getting lessons from a larger sailboat in their midst. When the sun finally surrendered to threatening clouds, the tiny sailboats paraded back into their basin behind the larger craft like so many obedient little ducklings. That pleasure port was crammed with beautiful power and sailing vessels; *Gatti* and I imagined what it was going to be like to be moored in a similar port in only a few days.

Gatti was finding more immediate friends as well. Several big boats, all shrink wrapped, were being loaded onto *Cielo* with a great lack of ceremony. They had neither flatbeds nor positions of importance. In fact, they were piled above containers and not properly on deck at all. The frenetic loading continued until close to midnight. Then we pulled in our bright yellow cranes and gave ourselves over to the two little tugs. Our engine roared to life and the familiar vibrations, squeaks and rattles, and comfortable rocking lulled me to sleep. Next stop, Italy!

The air was growing a lot colder, even though the sun still was shining. Ahead of us though, the sky was gray. This was my fourth Sunday aboard – my fourth special dinner of steak and ice cream. It would be my last. I felt the tension beginning to build. What would life be on land? I had grown to love the sea and could not imagine being held by the restraints of dry land. But I knew Bill was waiting for me and happy preparations had already been made. Via my Magellan I learned that we were to be berthed in Posto G-56 (no "H" dock after all). By tomorrow we would have a cell phone and bank account. I packed my things, figured out tips, and paid my freighter bill: two faxes, one telephone call, some small change in postage, a case of Diet Coke and some mineral water.

I fell asleep that Sunday night to the familiar and comforting vibrations of our engine but wakened to a strange feeling the following morning. Our engine was shut down, but from my porthole I could see we were still at sea just outside the harbor of Livorno. As it turned out, we had arrived at Livorno at 4 a.m. and, since no one would answer our call, had dropped anchor. The crew was greatly annoyed, but it seemed reasonable to me that a port should slow down on Sunday. I was already thinking like an Italian and was gratified that for the first time I was really going to enter a port in daylight. At 8 a.m. we were informed that there was no room for us yet. Anti-Italian sentiment was now running even higher on board. I was told that the port had been threatened with boycott by the freighter line for such laid-back attitudes, and this was its last chance.

It seemed to me that Livorno had blown its last chance big-time. But this was not my problem. I had breakfast and went above to take a look at the coast. The air was icy and the mountains towering behind the port were snow-covered. We received word that the pilot would board us at 10 a.m. Since this was my first chance to see a pilot actually arrive, I went to the bow, where the anchors were being hauled in. A clomping racket assaulted my ears as the huge chain links wound over one another on their giant winding spools, pulled up from the deep by equally vocal windlasses. Steam rose from the dripping metal. A most amazing assortment of mud and squirming mucky creatures fell off as the mammoth metal links dragged across the deck and were circled over and over one another. Mooring lines were laid out ready for action; there was not one clear spot on all that spacious bow. In short, this was no longer the quiet, private refuge I had grown so fond of.

At the appointed hour, the high-speed pilot boat raced out to our starboard side and held itself in position until the pilot could find a foothold on our dangling ladder. He hit the deck running and never stopped until he was in the wheelhouse. I arrived there, winded, several minutes later, and he was already directing us to the harbor mouth breathing normally and in perfect control. He was the first pilot aside from the Panama pilot ever to note my existence and when the captain introduced me, he showed courtly pleasure. Ah, Italy!

Over the next hour we made our cautious way into what was to me our most fascinating port of call. It reminded me a bit of Venice, with channels leading off channels and bustling activity everywhere. We passed towering grain elevators; dry docks; acres of new cars awaiting shipment or delivery; oil tanks; ferries to Elba, Corsica, and Sardegna; cruise ships laid up for the winter; and a fleet of black tug boats scuttling about tirelessly. The noise of hammering, beeping, shouting, tooting, whistling, and sloshing filled the air as we were nosed up the channel, turned completely around and tied securely to the wharf. The tugs and pilot left, the wheelhouse was locked down, and the off-loading began; I remained on the bridge to take everything in. This was my first day in Italy with *Gatti* and my last day aboard what had become my beloved Alma Mater. I did not want to go ashore until I could do so with Bill.

The view was spectacular. To our stern were two Moby Line ferries moored side by side, white with big blue whales painted on them. What a common sight this line would one day be to me, but at the time the name just made me smile. To our bow was moored another cargo vessel similar to *Cielo*. To starboard I could see over the mole to the open water. There, ships were lined up to enter very much like airplanes being directed by a control tower. On the docks themselves, the activity was fevered and quite different from what I had observed so far. The docks appeared to be very old and poorly maintained. Huge puddles of dirty water lay everywhere. While the trucks approached the loading area in generally the same fashion as in other places, there was a kind of recklessness here. Loads were not balanced too securely. The turns to and from the area were tight and the trucks more or less dodged one another around them with furious honking. Adding to that mayhem was the fact that several official cars and motor scooters were parked between the crane tracks. There was a general haphazardness I hadn't seen elsewhere.

I had scarcely returned to my cabin when I heard a soft knock on the door. I opened it to find Bill standing there. He had lost a great deal of weight while coping with his own trials and looked trim and fit. Of course, he would have looked like an angel in any condition. How strange it was to see him in that setting that had been my world alone for so long. He had taken the train to Livorno from Genova to get *Gatti*'s carnet in hope that the port personnel could release her more expeditiously from customs if they got a head start. I removed the documents from the drawer in which I had locked them a lifetime ago. Bill had an hour before his long return train trip, so we checked on *Gatti* and I showed him around the bridge and my other favorite spots. Before dusk we parted, expecting to see one another by noon the following day. He had rented a suite at a hotel in Voltri, the container port just to the north of Genova, for our much anticipated reunion.

That time assessment had not been predicated on Italian schedules and technical problems. Although the loading proceeded late into the night, it was not completed until about noon the next day. In addition, our bow thruster was not functioning properly. With *Cielo*'s warranty rapidly running out, the captain had called in technicians from the Norwegian manufacturer. They finished up about the same time as the loading, and then we had another hour's wait while holds were checked for stowaways. Apparently emigrants attempt to get to Canada by hiding out in containers, and Vancouver would be *Cielo*'s first stop in North America on her return voyage. I could not even begin to imagine the horror of such a voyage. The wonder is not that desperate people routinely die horrible deaths in such ventures, but rather that anyone survives.

The sun was low on the horizon when the tugs shepherded us back through the channel to the Mediterranean. The captain was in a foul humor. The port had insisted that we employ two tugs for the job when he felt that one was sufficient. Pejorative language was applied to the Italians. It seems we also had to pay a steeper bribe than usual to officials – nine cases of cigarettes and a good deal of whiskey. The concern was that we now had a limited supply for the personnel at Voltri. Furthermore, the captain was due to return to Germany the next day and the outlook for doing so was not good. His replacement was coming to Genova from Germany, but the huge snow storm that had made the mountain peaks so beautiful to me had caused airports across Europe to close. The new captain was now on a train trying to make his way through the Alps. If he did not arrive in time, our good captain would have to turn his back on a cozy Christmas and Millennium celebration with his wife and children and head *Cielo* back across the Atlantic. He spent the entire trip up the Italian coast dealing with administrative details in his cabin in a very bad mood.

I spent the trip in the wheelhouse taking in every detail of my new land. As usual, it was dark when we passed the places I most wanted to see, but the night was clear, crisp and invigorating, and the lights on shore shone with remarkable clarity. We passed the Serchio and Arno rivers where they empty into the sea west of Pisa. I recognized the entrance to the Gulf of Poets at La Spezia and picked out the villages of the Cinque Terre high above us. Further up the coast I spotted the lighthouse on the Portofino promontory. Soon the lights delineating Genova and her extensive suburbs grew denser and denser. The sea was dark, with only a few flecks of light from vessels and navigational aids. The large and busy "old" port of Genova was bright with lights and the coastline stood out clearly. The brilliant blanket of urban lights pushed inland to the mountains, then became a sparse sprinkling as houses climbed the mountains. At last only a twinkle or two could be caught. We passed by all the port lights, never altering our speed, and seemed to be heading away from Genova when we made a turn to starboard and entered the dark, quiet port of Voltri. All activity had ceased for the day and we were the only ship at the wharf. An officious Italian customs inspector boarded, and he and the captain sequestered themselves for quite some time. The customs official declared that everything had been shut down for the night and everyone was to remain on board until business the next day.

"I have a passenger on board whose husband is waiting for her here," pleaded the kind captain.

"She can go. Everyone else stays," was the response.

And so it was that late on the 27th day of the voyage, I fled the ship, leaving both good friends and *Gatti* behind.

Pilot finally caught in the act.

CHAPTER XIV

DAYS OF THANKSGIVING

'Our life is closed, our life begins,
The long, long anchorage we leave.
The ship is clear at last, she leaps!
She swiftly courses from the shore.
Joy, shipmate, joy.'
Walt Whitman, *Joy, Shipmate, Joy*

The day following my disembarkation was an active one indeed. We had many details to finish up before *Gatti* would be released from customs. We were informed that her incarceration at the port of Genova Voltri could be anywhere from two or three days to God-only-knew how long. We caught the regional train in Voltri and headed south to Lavagna along the east side of the Italian Riviera. While Bill had been awaiting my arrival, he had made this 30 kilometer trip several times, but for me it was all new and exciting. The train first stopped at the two major stations in Genova – Principe and Brignole – and then headed down tracks affixed to what must be some of the most desirable real estate in the world. We were on the mountainsides hugging the coast, alternating views of the Ligurian Sea with quick stops in picturesque towns that seemed to run vertically down to the great rocks at the coastline – towns whose names trembled enticingly on the tongue and then fell from the lips like music. Sori, Recco, Rapallo, Santa Margherita, Portofino, Zoagli, Chiavari, and finally Lavagna.

Everywhere richly colored flowers were blooming, cascading down hillsides and balconies and climbing rocks and trellises. Oranges and lemons stood out brilliantly against shiny dark green foliage. We stepped off the train, and in two minutes we were in Dominic's office, where we were expected. Off we went into town and made a first stop at the bank, where we opened an account. We were presented with a checkbook a good twelve inches long. At that time, the exchange rate was 1500 old lire to $1. By the time the astronomically long numbers were spelled out on a check, their length and complexity were impressive.

From there we went to an electronics store and purchased a cell phone complete with an indecipherable instruction book. Every Italian worth his salt has a cell phone, and it never crossed Dominic's mind that we could possibly survive without one. Then it was back to the port, where we were shown the slip or *posto barca* we had rented for a year and that would actually prove to be our Italian home for over two years. We were six slips in from the fairway on "G" dock and, given our "H" dock history, this seemed like a positive development.

Dominic explained that *lavagna* is the Italian word for "blackboard." Local quarries in the mountains that overshadowed us produce some of the highest quality slate in the world and local businesses provide the majority of blackboards globally. The actual word for "slate" is *ardesia,* and Dominic pointed out several shops that sold articles made from the smooth black stone. We look back on the first two days with Dominic with some wonder. He was organized and informative. These were the only two days in our long association with him that this was so.

After completing our business in Lavagna, we boarded the train for our return trip to Voltri. Past the magnificent seascapes, past the exquisite towns, through the dirty, bustling stations of Genova, we made our way back to the hotel near the container port. The suite Bill had rented was equipped with a grand whirlpool tub. He had filled the room with candles, flowers, and chocolates. A cold bottle of wine with a proper starched napkin about its neck sat in a silver cooler beaded with frosty droplets. I had arrived so late the night before that I had not had time or energy to enjoy these gifts of my husband of 36 years, now turned Italian lover. *Cielo* had offered only showers, and I had not enjoyed a tub bath in a month. I had never enjoyed a bath in a tub like this in my life. Bill and I were sybaritically enjoying same after our eventful day when there was a knock at the door. A fax had been delivered stating that our *Gatti* could be claimed the very next day. We put in a frantic call to Dominic, who agreed to meet us at the port of Voltri the following morning.

As it happened, the following day was Thanksgiving Day; never before has a morning unfolded with such promise. Despite its being the end of November, the air was warm and caressing, the sky was blue with a rare clarity, the sea was tranquil, and the world seemed clear, pure and perfect. Not surprisingly, we arrived at the port gate before Dominic or any of the officials involved, but we were permitted entry. There floated *Cielo* moored to the quay but all loaded and ready to begin her long trek back to Cartagena. On the wharf only a few feet from her starboard side sat *Gatti* like a little sister. She was still trussed up and mounted on her flatbed and sat high above us.

I called up to the bosun and his crew who were by now hanging over *Cielo*'s side and greeting me enthusiastically. The new captain had made it through the alpine blizzards and arrived just in time for Captain Lessing to make his flight home to his family and the holidays. My seafaring friends especially wanted to draw my attention to the Ferretti yacht they had loaded. This large, expensive and beautiful Italian boat was perched on the top tier of a stack of containers. Looking fearfully over a bow that would be pounded by sea and wind, she sat unprotected and vulnerable. No extraordinary services would be rendered her in her long passage. A tug came tooting up to *Cielo,* who revved her enormous engine in happy response and the heavy dock lines were thrown off. The new captain and a new female German passenger stood on the bridge that had been my station for so long. The rest of the crew was unchanged. *Gatti* and I watched with mixed emotions as the crew waved, the second mate danced on the foredeck and our good friend *Cielo di San Francisco* turned her stern to us and pointed her bow toward the Americas.

So it is with changing tides. Life is laid bare and re-covered. What is weak or dead is nudged up on the shore and abandoned. What lives scrambles back into the current. This was no time to be maudlin. We were ready to launch into that current; already men had brought ladders and were clambering on *Gatti*, removing her bonds and canvas. Dominic and his partner, Angelo, had arrived and the paperwork was being sorted out. The fact that the yacht was entering under carnet made this process relatively easy and we were led to believe that it had greatly cut down on time spent in customs. We could stay in Italy legally for one year and whatever difficulties might arise would come when they would come.

Cielo with her little sister to starboard.

At length *Gatti* was stripped of her protective coverings and lashings and ready for action. The huge crane came squeaking down its track like a disgruntled hen and positioned itself over the cradle. The boat just barely fit between the mammoth steel legs. Heavy belts were carefully positioned around the hull. Nothing was rushed or overlooked. Several adjustments were made in the strap placements before she was freed from her cradle and lifted high, high above us. Then she was moved forward until she hung 50 feet above the aquamarine waters of the Ligurian Sea. A collective breath was held as she was lowered down, down until her keel parted the surface and her hull settled comfortably into her new environs. Among cheers, *ciaos* and smiles, Dominic, Bill and I leaped aboard and started her engines, so long silent. Purring like the happy cat she is, *Gatti* turned her bow toward the breakwater and followed *Cielo* into the open sea.

As we came around the breakwater, a wave caught us broadside and we were baptized in an exhilarating and surprisingly salty splat in the face. The day was unparalleled joy. In the warmth of the Italian sun we were speeding over a smooth sea along a fairytale coast. Ancient and medieval towns, monasteries, castles, imposing stone villas with exquisitely landscaped saltwater swimming pools, beaches, tall church steeples atop the highest peaks, stark cliffs and cascades of brilliant flowers went fleeting by like a movie. The little towns we had passed through on the train could be seen tumbling down to the coast and even the train itself, like a tiny Lionel model, could be seen making its way around and through the mountains. The water was as limpid as a spring. Dominic rejoiced in the speed and quiet of the 700 horses fueled by gasoline rather than the diesel fuel to which he was accustomed. *Gatti* rejoiced in the sea. Bill and I rejoiced in a dream come true that still seemed so much a dream.

A good thing it was, too, that Dominic sped along the 30 odd miles to our berth at Lavagna. *Gatti* was taking on water and in big gulps too. Having been out of the water 59 days now, her wooden planks had dried out and now required time to swell. She was also operating with only one centrally located bilge pump. Jerry had not installed the large pump that boats need at their sterns to expel bilge water pushed back when the vessel is under power. We had known that two more pumps were needed but had decided to have them installed once we were settled in Italy. It was also a good idea to speed along since the fact that the *Guardia Costiera* (the Italian Coast Guard equivalent) was on midday break was advantageous to us. We could not locate our U.S. flag under all the piled canvas and were running illegally under Dominic's registration number. In addition, our beautiful new mast lay supine in its hinged position on our foredeck, so our antennae were not functional, and we were not flying our Italian flag of courtesy.

Angelo, who had driven back from Voltri with our luggage, was waiting at our slip as we tore triumphantly around the breakwater at the Porto Turistico di Lavagna. How strange it seemed to back toward the cement jetty, squiggling in between two big sailboats protected only by their fenders. How could we ever squeeze into such a narrow space? But as we backed, our neighbors moved genially aside. Our stern was made fast with two lines and a third was picked up out of the water at our stern with a boat hook and walked forward to secure the bow. This procedure remained a mystery for some time but that was fine. We had no plans to go anywhere any time soon. For the moment we had a boat to bail, unpack and make livable. We had a new town to explore and a whole new way of life to work out. All these thoughts passed through our minds, and we looked at each other and grinned. It was a day for non-stop grinning and irrepressible smiles. The happy cats were on the crest of a wave and everything appeared perfect as far as eye could see.

Gatti tastes a new sea.

I taste a new sea.

Mast still down, headed out.

CHAPTER XV

SETTLING IN

'Still as a slave before his lord,
The ocean hath no blast;
His great bright eye most silently
Up to the moon is cast –

If he may know which way to go;
For she guides him smooth or grim.
See, brother, see! How graciously
She looketh down on him.'
  Samuel Taylor Coleridge,
  The Rime of the Ancient Mariner

It was an unseasonably warm afternoon when *Gatti* tied up at her new berth. She was six slips from the end of the jetty, flanked by two sailboats a little longer than she. *Rachele* rocked softly to port and *Bo Drum* to starboard. No one was on either boat and, for that matter, we had the entire jetty, which was home to some 80 big boats, to ourselves. One of our first concerns involved getting on and off the boat. Since we did not have a gangway or *passerella,* we had to leap from the transom to the jetty.

We had barely started practicing this interesting maneuver when the *passeggiata* began. This is the daily stroll Italians traditionally take in the late afternoon. At the Port of Lavagna it consisted for the most part of elderly townspeople wandering down the docks and stopping to observe boats as the mood dictated. In the early days this staring was a little unsettling to us, but we soon learned to go about our business with unconcern. The first notice we took of this first *passeggiata* was when we heard a voice on dock. There stood a rotund, elderly gentleman with his hands crossed over his chest.

"*Bellissima! Bellissima!*" he was saying aloud and yet to himself. We thanked him for the compliment and later learned that he was a boat designer and builder of some renown. A beautiful example of his skill floated further down our jetty. *Moscatello Bello Bello* was a marvel of fiberglass and wood craftsmanship. This delightful gentleman was only a precursor of many strollers who paused to look at the new kid on the block, to comment among themselves, and to chuckle at our name and hailing port. In retrospect we are not sure whether there were more people than usual out that evening because we were a novelty or whether over time we just got used to relaxed Italians walking and chatting before the dinner hour. Or perhaps it was simply that it was an exquisite late November day.

We had sent an exuberant message to Frank via the Magellan announcing our arrival and received a response in short order. "Congratulations! You broke out!" We hadn't really looked at it quite that way before, but the concept pleased us greatly. Many people make big plans, spin fabulous dreams, and eye outgoing tides with longing; but not so many have the fortitude to actually jump in and sail away. We had, and we suddenly felt very proud of ourselves.

We spent time trying to get a handle on the method of mooring that is called *cima* a *terra* in Italian. Between two concrete, fixed jetties or *pontili* a huge chain is laid parallel on the seabed. At each berth, or *posto barca,* a second strong perpendicular chain is laid partway to the berth with a mooring line attached at its end. To this mooring line is attached a smaller rope line that runs to the jetty and is secured. A little float tied to this last line (commonly referred to as the slime line) holds it at the water's surface for easier retrieval. The idea is to back your vessel into your berth while this line lies on the bottom so as not to cut the line or foul your propellers. If you are lucky, someone on the jetty will take your boathook from you, snag your line where it is secured to the pier, and return the boathook to you with the line dripping off it. All this time, of course, the helmsman is holding the vessel close enough to the dock for all this handling to occur across the water without cramming his stern into the concrete jetty. If fortune does not smile, you run off your wobbly *passerella* with boathook in hand, leap over the intervening water to the jetty, snag the line and then jump back on, assuming the helmsman has not moved forward too far.

Once the feet are on deck and the line in hand (yes, literally in hand, slippery, filthy, shell-encrusted and worse!), you abandon the boathook and "walk" your line up to the bow, dripping green slime on your white sides and teak decks as you go. At the bow, you kneel and begin to haul up your mooring line until the chain is tight and you are able to tie off your bow line at the distance from the jetty that you wish. I have seen quite small women do this efficiently, but I, alas, am not among them. The lines and chain are very heavy and securing them to the bow is hard. We were to learn that Bill would not be a suave Italian captain aloof in his helm seat while his crew performed this task. We would devise a plan whereby I secured the aft lines first and he would then go forward. It is a plan that is most likely to achieve success when a boat is moored on either side of you.

We discovered early on that few people were living *"a bordo"* because winter is not the best time to enjoy life on the Ligurian Sea. Our delightful run down from Voltri had apparently been a particularly beneficent gift from the gods. As is true of so many of life's blessings, we are often ignorant of their worth at the time. We had not paid much attention to weather patterns because, frankly, we had a lot to do and learn before we could even think about venturing from our dock. For example, learning how to leave it and get back in were, of course, of primary importance. The crew on the freighter had spoken of cyclonic storms such as the gale that had struck Italy as we were approaching from Spain. The dock folk spoke of the *Libeccio, Tramontano, Scirocco, Levante, Ponente* and *Mistral* as though they were close family relations. We understood precious little Italian and no weather patterns at all, so we put our minds to other things. It had always been warm and beautiful when we had been in Lavagna before and, hey, how bad could a wind from Africa be anyway? Our eyes were opened very soon and very wide.

The day after our arrival we began experiencing some peculiar weather. At any rate it was plenty peculiar to us. To begin with, it began to get cold, windy and rainy. We had had the boat rewired in California for Italian current, but we had not had access to Italian outlets. Enter our first visitor, Amerigo – excellent electrician, mad septuagenarian motorcyclist, and fervent Americaphile. He took care of our immediate, critical needs and we gave him a USA baseball cap in addition to his charge. We could now plug in appliances. Bill and I hoofed it around town and bought a refrigerator, convection toaster oven, iron, and heater. Thus when affairs meteorological took a truly nasty turn, we were moderately prepared.

This appliance shopping would have been a simple undertaking had we had a car and an understanding of where to find what we needed. We learned right away that our yacht service would be of no help in such endeavors. As it was, our efforts were sort of hit and miss. Lavagna did not have any appliance stores, although we did locate our refrigerator in a hardware store there. It was delivered to us literally on the back of a poor man who made his way down the long *pontile,* avoiding as best he could the mass of lines that lay everywhere. The other items we found by making the long walk to the much larger city of Chiavari, which lies on the other side of the Entella River. Chiavari is a good-sized town with sidewalks covered by medieval porticos that we much appreciated, since it rained seemingly incessantly.

The second mate on *Cielo* had introduced me to an instrument on board that appeared to be just what *Gatti* needed. As soon as we had sailed past Gibralter, the Navtex had become a daily functioning companion. It printed out on heat-sensitive paper all kinds of interesting information, and in English to boot. It warned of errant buoys, malfunctioning lighthouses, overdue mariners, submarine exercises and offered detailed weather forecasts and warnings. This information was so good that the crew often clipped items and attached them to the log. We had decided we would definitely purchase one of these wonders, but for the time being we depended on what bits of information we could glean. We had our VHF radio reports and forecasts from the Genoa newspaper, but we began to gauge our expectations more by the precautionary measures being taken by our neighbors. The day might be sunny and mild with amorous couples strolling arm in arm down the jetty, but if Luigi were tightening his lines, surely something was in the wind, and we followed suit.

Some of the boats were locally owned and the owners came by every so often to check on them. Many vessels were owned by residents of France or wealthy inland cities like Milan, and these were cared for by port personnel or by yacht services. Most importantly, at this point in our Ligurian sojourn the port workers were very conscientious and reliable. They would ride their bicycles the length of each jetty a couple times each day, checking on lines, the height of gangways, loose halyards and the like. The jetties were an obstacle course at the best of times. The Italians apparently have no comprehension of "flemishing" – arranging excess line in a tight, flat coil on the pier. Lines were strewn everywhere, power cords and water hoses were allowed to loop down into the water or entangle themselves with whatever else might be lying about the pier. One undesirable aspect of the *cima a terra* mooring scheme is that when you pull away from the dock, there is no good way to organize the lines you leave behind. The solution is simply to throw your aft lines onto the pier from deck and hope no one kills himself on them in your absence. The bowline is simply dropped in the water where it sinks for later retrieval. The port personnel were quite agile cyclers and avoided all the entrapments that lay about with the sanguine attitude born of never having known any other way of docking.

Our biggest meteorological disturbance began the Monday of Christmas week and coincided with the vicious storm of the century that felled thousands of historic trees in Versailles and wreaked havoc across the European continent. The damage in terms of human life, environmental harm and economic loss was horrendous. Yet, while this storm was particularly ferocious, its pattern was not too different from what we had experienced since our arrival and would find to be consistent throughout our stay in the Ligurian Sea.

The Friday and Saturday preceding Christmas weekend brought us soft, warmish rains. Sunday presented a brief clearing, the sun brilliant in a cerulean sky. But a strangely disquieting lapping had begun to lick around our hull. Later a low moaning began in the air around us, and the winds picked up. At first the gusts were far apart. Clouds began to blow in, trying to obliterate the sun but never quite succeeding; bright rays kept escaping around the ragged edges. By Monday we were in the teeth of a gale that warned us how quickly the sea can change.

When I was first bemused by the stern-tied boats poking one another like sixth graders in a line, I did not visualize what the comparison might be were a disturbance to erupt in the classroom. What an apropos simile! In the buffeting of the winds now howling about us, the boats began to react violently and unpleasantly. Masts angled down the long line of vessels moored to the jetty, looking all in one direction. Then they righted themselves, only to sink down and peer in the other. One boat would kick at her neighbor, only to receive a surreptitious punch in the ribs. Gangways plunged up and down from the halyards of tall masts or careened crazily from port to starboard. *Gatti* and her portside neighbor *Rachele* rubbed shoulders so briskly that Bill braved the elements to go out and buy two additional big round fenders. This trip was rendered more stimulating by the fact that we did not yet have a gangway.

At one point *Gatti* rose so high as to be almost looking down *Rachele*'s hatch. Most improper behavior, to be sure. *Rachele* retaliated by swinging her teak gangway over *Gatti's* aft deck. The port was in a truly undisciplined state. Flags at one moment flew taut to the east. Then a few moments later, with sharp snaps, they were streaming westward. The bouncing and jostling created a cacophony of squeaking, scratching, scrapey rubbing. Fenders compressed between vessels squealed and squawked. Canvas flapped and shrouds hammered. Rigging slapped and a roar ran through the classroom, modulating between dull and horrific. The wind screamed across the open sea and created haunting howls as it swept between masts and lines. Spray was thrown up hissing above the seawall and an occasional wave would cascade over the top with the thunder of a waterfall. The sail of a vessel three *posti* to our port flung itself loose with the report of a rifle. It flapped and plunged angrily until port personnel arrived to vanquish it.

Gatti had not only not gotten her gangway yet; she did not yet have the powerful springs on her stern lines that were providing a large measure of control to our neighbors. We had pulled ourselves out on our bowline a fair way from dock, but were in real danger of whamming our transom against it. We also had only one bow line instead of the two that many boats had. This did not contribute much to our peace of mind in such an unprecedented situation. But *Gatti*'s neighbors proved to be as loyal as most sixth graders basically are to one another and held her in place without too much complaint. There was nothing for us to do but stay holed up in our cabin. Instead of traditional Christmas decorations from home, we had bought beautiful foil-wrapped Christmas candies and strung them about festively. Our new little heater kept us cozy and snug. And so we were oddly comfortable and content as our home plunged and rolled and the candies danced and bobbed cheerfully around us.

The violence of this storm sent the clouds scuttling, and the following day the sun rose in an air almost painfully clear and pure. The tall mountain peaks around Genova wore sparkling white mantles and, while the harbor was frosty, the sun's beams were warm and encouraging. Like little groundhogs, we poked our noses out of the companionway and, finding the weather surprisingly fine, ventured to the deck. We made the hazardous passage from deck to dock and proceeded directly to Dominic's office. We wanted a second bowline, springs and a gangway – and we wanted them now.

Both Dominic and Angelo were already well aware that boarding was a great problem for me. Even on the calm day we had arrived, it was difficult. When the seas kicked up, transit became problematic. One night we had resorted to climbing on our good neighbor *Bo Drum* and thence over the side rails to *Gatti*. Another night the water had been so rough and high that it had taken four people to get me aboard. Young, lithe Angelo had found this a particularly comic situation. With his toes flexed on the pier, he arched his back over the foaming gap of water, his hands on our stern rail. "I will be your bridge," he laughed. While irrepressible Angelo was the first to break into grins over a situation, he was also the first to come up with solutions; that stormy night had truly demonstrated that we needed help. Angelo agreed to go to the factory and order a *passerella,* while Dominic assumed the job of acquiring springs and heavy-duty lines.

It was now Tuesday of Christmas week, and we caught the train to Genova to pick up a rental car. The towns along the route were gradually becoming real to us and no longer just magical names and picture postcards. Each was unique but also in many ways the same, each with its little train station and houses marching straight up the mountains on one side and rolling down to the rocky sea on the other. Many of the buildings dated to medieval times, frequently decorated with *trompe l'oeil* exteriors that made them appear to be marvels of art and architecture. The homes marched along the railroad tracks, their windows filled with flapping laundry and flowers spilling out over the balconies. Yes, we were becoming familiar with the towns, but the familiarity never dulled their enchantment.

Driving back down the coast road that night, the differences were more apparent than the likenesses. Each town was alight with its own unique Christmas decorations hung above the narrow streets. These were not random blinking lights. These were parades of brilliantly lit butterflies, colorful flowers of recognizable species, bells, and doves. Rapallo sported a kind of interplanetary display. Christmas shoppers bustled in and out of gleaming little shops, stopping to talk and gesticulate in the cold air. Behind us the tall peaks were silhouetted as a close-to-full moon rose above those before us. As we rounded one curve, we would see it full behind a church steeple; coming around another she would appear to be laughingly balanced on a sharp peak; then again the single bright eye would peer at us around a mountain summit. By the time we snuggled into our bunks, she was beaming directly down our hatch.

On Wednesday we took advantage of having a car to drive up the steep, curving, narrow roads into the sparsely populated hinterland. The mountains soar dramatically from the sea as high as 1200 meters, and the views are breathtaking. We found icicles but no snow. The chestnuts, oaks, and olives shivered in the cold stillness. The mountains that flank the sea are typically covered with groves of olive trees. These lend a lovely silver-green shimmer to the slopes and, at this time of year, also a touch of orange. Strung under the trees were acres of orange netting attached so that the precious olives would be caught like so many clumsy acrobats and prevented from rolling down the mountains.

We noticed smoke rising from among the trees and learned that this was not just a seasonal phenomenon. Trimmings from the trees are burned to prevent disease, and it appeared that trimming took place all year. The immediate burning of the wood must indeed be a necessary health measure; surely the very thrifty Ligurians would otherwise add it to their piles of winter firewood. Whether the smoke quickly dissipated in the blue summer skies or was pressed down the mountainsides by ponderous winter fog, one could always be sure of seeing fires burning somewhere in the hills. It almost seemed as though smoke signals could be sent from farm to farm, hilltop to hilltop and, for all we knew, perhaps they were. On this particular trip, most of the olives had already been harvested and scurried off to the presses in the tiny three-wheeled *Apes* that buzz about like the bees they are named after, but the nets remained for a few weeks more. It has to be a horrendous chore to lay them out, roll them back up and, worst of all, clear them of leaves and branches.

We discovered quaint churches and our first monument to the partisans who hid in these heights during World War II. Cut into stone was the moving story of a group of poverty-stricken locals killed while preparing *farinata* for Allied soldiers. This was our first monument but was not to be our last. Throughout the rugged terrain and thick forests of the inland mountains, we would come across stone remembrances of brave and desperate men. It became a source of great frustration to me that my Italian wasn't better and my Genovese dialect non-existent. Most of the people living in these areas are very old and many of the *rustici* or old stone farmhouses are falling into tragic ruins. As one elderly lady sadly told us, "The young move away and do not come back. They don't even return to die." But the old folks are still there and are dying there and their stories are perishing with them, with no one to record the heroism that was acted out in those rugged places. I wonder how many of my own countrymen owed their lives to these crafty and resourceful mountain dwellers.

We returned to port from these explorations to find *Gatti* sporting two big springs on mammoth stern lines. A true ancient mariner had spliced the rope around shackles, and his labor was a real work of art. While these lines, whose girth was equal to that of my wrist, later proved to be much heavier than required and even occasioned the replacement of bittes on the boat, we were delighted. A second bow chain had been rigged as well, and *Gatti* was beginning to feel like a real Italian. She surged forward, and her springs pulled and relaxed like shock absorbers. Just as good was the comforting sound they made. They murmured and clicked in a barely audible voice. All the boats the whole length of the jetty on both sides moved back and forth at various speeds and forces and the springs chattered softly together as though the boats were sharing notes with one another and the sea.

That night marked the rare and magical convergence of the winter solstice and the full moon. The inky sky was calm, cloudless and breathless in anticipation. The moon rose majestically, so slowly, so enormous, so close. No other illumination was required on this night that seemed of mythical proportions. The moon beams reflected from the worshipful calm of the Ligurian Sea and metamorphosed the metal fittings of ships into miniature lamps. The boats rocked quietly in place between their bowlines and murmuring springed aft lines. All was hushed and almost reverential. So much of our new life was strange and wonderful, and we almost could have believed that this historic moon could be a nightly occurrence.

The next day, Thursday, we drove to Milano to gather our first holiday arrivals – our daughter and son-in-law from New York. We found Piedmonte and Lombardia very cold indeed. Snow clung to the bare branches of trees and the stubble of corn and sunflowers in the wide, flat fields. Fog shrouded the area, enhancing the feeling of darkness and depression. But it would have taken a lot more than mid-winter weather to dampen our spirits. Joyfully we all reunited and returned to the sea. We loaded our arms with suitcases and presents and headed from the car to the boat.

As we rounded on "G" dock, a laughing Angelo and Dominic appeared out of the dark, their faces wreathed in smiles like mischievous elves. "Go see your boat!" they urged excitedly. In their boyish delight they could scarcely endure introductions to our family. Laden as we were, we rushed down the *pontile*. There, attached to our davits and projecting behind our boat, was a beautiful latticed teak *passerella* with just the hint of a gentle arch. Two stainless steel balustrades linked with a guide rope gave security above while two little wheels beneath rolled back and forth on the dock as the boat moved. A steel pin on the gangway dropped into a receptacle that had been inserted at the top of the stern. Lines from the davits provided lateral stability and the ability to raise or lower the gangway. *Gatti* was now a true European and we strode over our new bridge with a renewed confidence in our dreams.

It was very cold and very still in Lavagna that night. *Gatti* lay motionless between her new lines, her new *passerella* at rest on the dock. Sometime during the night a telltale lapping began to slap our bow. The moon became overcast. By morning it was cloudy and an odd moaning was building.....

Gatti learns Italian ways near an impaired control tower.

Ports of Lavagna and Chiavari looking towards Monte di Portofino.

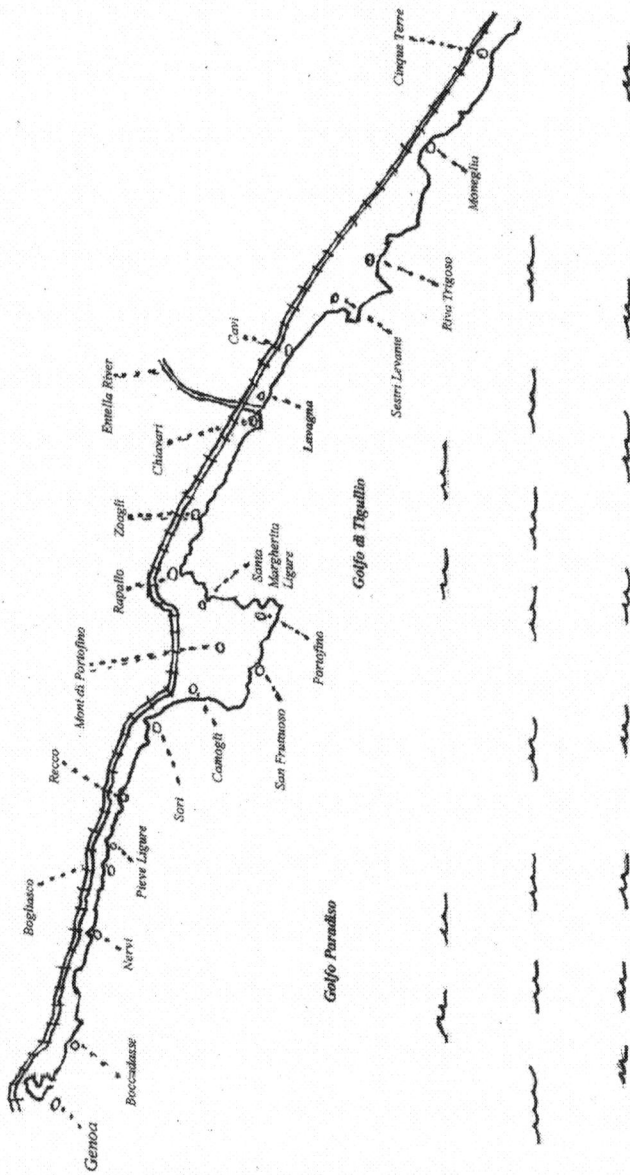

Coastal towns of the Riviera Levante

CHAPTER XVI

STORM AND SONG

'The air broke into a mist with bells'
Robert Browning, *The Patriot*

Every other Christmas Eve we had spent in Italy we had attended midnight Mass. For some reason we did not do so this year. Perhaps it was the happiness of having our daughter with us and the expectation of our son's arrival in two days. Perhaps it was the fact that Catholic churches in Lavagna and Chiavari did not seem as welcoming to non-Catholics as those in Rome. Perhaps it was the exhaustion of the preceding weeks. But probably it was the bells at noon on December 24 that made all other traditional celebration pale in comparison.

There are rare moments in our lives when we are blessed with a kind of epiphany of the senses, an expansion that floods beyond the confines of the body. It has nothing to do with intellectual thought, but is more properly a profound quickening of the spirit, during which the bodily senses pour out beyond the strictures of bone and skin and the soul becomes for an instant a part of the great life force. A part of the wonder is that it occurs so rarely that it is rendered precious indeed. It was the bells on the Gulf of Tigullio at noon on this day of Christmas Eve that touched my soul in such a way. Words cannot do justice to the chorus of the bells – bells tumbling over themselves with joy. Seemingly every mountain top in Liguria is surmounted by a church. From the Portofino promontory to the north of us to Sestri Levante, poking out into the sea to our south, the whole bay reverberated with music.

Some of the bells were playing carols, some chimed the hour, others called the faithful to church. Since each church was in a different location, at a different elevation, with different bells, the ringing echoed and re-echoed, confused and exuberant. Some silver, some gold, some bass toned, every metal throat threw to heaven its own unique version of joy. At times the tones would come together in mellow harmony, at others the notes would be discordant. It reminded me of the beauty of little children singing all together with glad faces, sure they are making lovely music. What they are actually producing is scarcely in that category, but it is celestial in its own right. I stood alone on the aft deck bathed in the ebullience which seemed to cascade down the mountainsides, to sweep from one end of the gulf to the other and back, and even to waft in from the open sea. It was an orgasm of the ears, a filling of the heart. At length the outpouring began to lessen and gradually drift away as the tolling of the hour was ended or the carol completed. One by one bells would slow, lower their voices and be silenced. One now could hear the church in Chiavari across the river alone doling out the hours in golden, dulcet tones. As the last quavering sounds faded away, I could hear the soft squeaking of springs, the subdued murmur of rigging, and the gentle plash of water moving under the jetty. Maybe this was not a sensual epiphany, but it was the sound of a real, live dream.

The family spread out, gathering in the last of the breads, cheeses, wines, *focaccia*, *farinata*, and traditional *panettone* cakes. Our major celebration would not be held that night but when our family would be entire. At dusk we visited the little open-air port chapel. This quiet corner of the port was covered by a roof of striped canvas beneath which was a small altar flanked by candles and terra cotta pots of flowering plants. With much love a nativity scene had been laid out on an adjacent slope of soil dotted with flower clumps and small bushes. The ceramic animals took their ease under plant stems. The shepherds rested beside little pools sunk in the earth. Small white pebbles by day and tiny lights by night delineated the vagrant path that led at last to the makeshift barn where Mary and Joseph were positioned expectantly before a still-empty manger. The simplicity, attention to detail, and devotion put into this scene created a most moving *presepe*.

On Christmas morning a visit to the *presepe* revealed that a baby now rested under the gaze of Mary and Joseph. Traditionally, in Italy the youngest child of the family is accorded the honor of placing Jesus in the manger at midnight on Christmas Eve. At the Port of Lavagna, I don't know. Because we still had the car, we spent the rest of Christmas Day driving along the coast to the south. Excellent *autostrade* connect the coastal towns, but we elected to be more adventuresome. Some of our route lay deep under the mountains in tunnels that had once held railway tracks. These tunnels are long, straight, narrow – and one way. The road surface is smooth and fast and the whole effect eerily recalls a James Bond movie. Traffic lights located outside the tunnels provide directional guidance.

Our destination was Monterosso, the most northerly of the Cinque Terre. When we were not in the depths of tunnels, we were inching our way around precipitous mountain curves increasingly obscured by incoming clouds pushed against the mountain face. At length we picked our way down through the vertical olive groves and vineyards to downtown. The shops were closed, of course, but many people were walking along the waterfront observing the sea. These were not the mobs of summer, but the stalwart oldtimers who brave the winter here. All were looking at the sea with a touch of apprehension. Astonishingly huge waves were beginning to pile along the shore. This was the fringe of the storm that was making a disaster of this Christmas Day across Europe.

The day following Christmas, St. Stephen's Day, we repeated the depressing drive to the airport at Malpensa and returned with our son and his girlfriend. Lavagna was literally kicking up a storm when we arrived home. Enormous waves were striking the high breakwater wall, throwing spray high above it which then frothed down into the harbor. The occasional wave that actually washed over threatened a tall crane that had been doing some work on the harbor side of the wall. All of Lavagna was out to view the spectacle, strolling along the long promenade at the beach and past the boats rollicking at dock. This night we experienced the benefits of our new system of lines. While the boats were still moving sideways as before, much more of *Gatti*'s movement was focused fore and aft. In fact, being aboard her was much like being astride a horse (and occasionally pitched off!). She would seem to gallop forward at full speed only to be taken up abruptly by her bow lines and powerful stern springs. Back she would jerk, toss her head to the wind, shuffle from side to side, and leap forward again. There was a bit of gastric unease that evening, but the bright candies (by now becoming severely reduced in number) still bobbed about merrily, the wine flowed freely, and Ciarán, our son-in-law, manfully managed to lead us in song accompanied by the guitar.

Although this particular storm did not pass quickly, it didn't bother us for long. All six of us took the train to Rome for a four-day visit to welcome in the new year, century and millennium. We shopped, ate, enriched our souls in galleries and churches, and joined the 400,000 other revelers who at midnight created a seismic event in Piazza del Popolo. This is a place where one can feel like an integral part of history. It is a place where for millenia people have been coming together to celebrate events large and small. Tired, but happy, we boarded the train for home on Jan. 2, 2000, with about a million other people. We stood all the long way, crowded, jostled, but triumphant.

Two by two we saw our family off to the United States. We stayed on until Jan. 18. The weather remained much the same, alternately sunny and stormy. We covered *Gatti* snugly in her canvas and prepared to leave her for the first time in a new land. We thought she would be well looked after, but it was a wrench to leave her all the same. Dominic drove us over to the Chiavari train station and helped carry our luggage in. With hearty kisses to both cheeks he assured us that April would be beautiful.

The port chapel.

CHAPTER XVII

BREAKING OUT

'When lilacs last in the dooryard bloom'd,
And the great star early droop'd in the western sky of night,
I mourn'd and yet shall mourn with every returning spring.'
Walt Whitman, *When Lilacs Last in the Dooryard Bloom'd*

For the most part Bill had enjoyed his 31-year career at the international oil company he had joined after college. He had moved up the corporate ladder and had interesting assignments working for people who valued his abilities. But we never were part of the corporate family. We are very private people, who separated our social activities from our employment associations. In both Houston and Bakersfield we lived on fairly large pieces of property and put our leisure energies into gardening, remodeling, pets, and raising our two children. Bill's last two years at the company had not been good ones, however. His position was secure, he was highly respected and the pay was good, but the American economy was not. He was frequently put in the uncomfortable and truly distressing position of terminating good employees and friends. We decided that this was not a life we were enjoying or could even tolerate. It was pointless to continue to work under conditions that were bound to result in physical and emotional harm when it was not necessary to do so. Therefore, as soon as he had acquired the requisite number of retirement points, Bill announced his decision to leave the company.

Because we were in the enviable position of planning our own destiny, within human parameters, retirement was relatively painless for Bill. We attended a retirement seminar in Seattle and had a lovely mini-vacation in the process. Bill's last years with the corporation had involved political activity at the state level, and he had formed some strong friendships in this arena. Within a few days of his retirement, he was ensconced in a small office with a local political friend some years his senior. They worked as a part-time consulting firm and had a very good time. They accepted only clients with good causes and kept their minds and contacts sharp and active. The office never made any money to speak of, but it did not lose any either. It provided a place outside the home where Bill could do his own thing and also use his skills. Here he was also able to indulge his interest in the stock market. The office provided a bridge between the corporate world and retirement. The stock activity later provided the same bridge between having an office and having an active business interest at home.

Retirement was not at all hard for me. I taught high school Latin and English for six years before we began a family. After the children were born, I stayed home to rear them. I returned to teaching part-time at a private school where the pay was low but the sense of fulfillment great. My teaching income was never of any great significance so its loss had very little impact on our lives. I had no benefits or vested economic interests. While I enjoyed teaching and was blessed with the gift of effectively sharing knowledge with young people, I have always enjoyed many other things as well for which I had little time when I was working. I taught for two years after Bill retired just to retain some continuity in this passage of life, but we were also doing a great deal of boat preparation during this time as well.

The retirement seminar had been very specific. We were advised not to move out of our communities but rather retain friends, doctors and general social familiarity. We did not pay any attention whatsoever to this advice. The city of Bakersfield had deteriorated over our 20 year stay there, particularly in our neighborhood. Our children were employed elsewhere, and our only other family lived in Florida. California was a long way from Italy, and we saw little to persuade us to stay. As we threw ourselves into working on *Gatti* and spent a great deal of our time at Marina del Rey, we distanced ourselves even further from our Bakersfield connections. We knew that sooner or later we would be leaving California, but we buried ourselves in the work of the moment and pushed the implications of the move to the back of our minds. The purchase of the condominium in Florida while we were working on the boat at Marina del Rey was the only concession made so far to our eventual move. The condo was furnished and ready for rental and, although we never did rent it out, that was our general plan. But we had not emotionally faced up to leaving our beautiful home. Our hearts could not yet go there.

In metaphorical terms, an unexpected current threw us headlong and bruised onto our altered course. We returned to Bakersfield in mid-January still bursting with the excitement of our happy times in Italy. The future sparkled with promise. We had made the break, against all odds and predictions. We had our home in Italy, and now the dream would begin to unfold as envisioned. Ha! The fickle currents of life were running in unpleasant directions. Our lifestyle in Bakersfield had always presented us with travel problems. The house itself was lovely, and 20 years of remodeling had made it truly our own and reflective of our love of Italy. It was set on a terraced half acre of very private, beautiful land with 18 mature, bearing fruit trees of many varieties, grape vines, a kitchen garden, formal rose gardens, and a large solar-warmed pool. All required constant attendance, which we enthusiastically supplied. We also had birds, cats, dogs and the occasional rabbit.

In the past our work schedules had pretty well dictated summer travel, and it had not been too hard to find house-sitters willing to accept payment to share the pleasures of what almost amounted to a resort. All had done perfectly adequate jobs. But this particular trip posed more problems than before. For one thing, it was winter, and the pool and yard were not big draws.

Also, some of our former sitters were away at school. The time approached for me to board the freighter, and we had not yet found anyone to undertake the job from mid-November to mid-January. At the witching hour, some acquaintances from our Italian club suggested that their son might be interested. He was, and I boarded the freighter convincing myself that all would be well. The tiny gnawing doubt in my heart was pushed into a corner, but in the two weeks between my departure and Bill's, Bill developed severe reservations about this man. But our plans were set; our son promised to come down from Sacramento to check on things, and we left. We were unaware at the time how utterly we had left our way of life behind.

We returned to California through Los Angeles, and even though we were tired after the 12-hour flight, we stopped in to see Doug and Paul at their shop and Jerry on his boat at Huntington Beach. After all, they had been partners in this whole enterprise, and we were loaded down with photos and beautiful books to share. It was late at night when we turned into our driveway in Bakersfield, and so the full impact of the disaster was not apparent until the following day. The facts we learned that night were heavy enough. The house was filthy beyond description. The man had remarried and actually moved into our home with his pregnant bride and his son by a previous marriage. One of the three birds was dead, and the dog looked terrible. We had barely fallen exhausted into bed when the telephone rang. A woman began screaming at us, asking who we were and demanding to know where her son was. As the sun rose the following morning, the disaster to our property came into focus. The beautiful hybrid tea roses had been whacked back with a chain saw. Every tree had been "pruned" to within an inch of life and the poor severed boughs were still piled around the trunks. We took the dog to our vet as soon as he opened his office. The doctor, with great oaths, moved him into surgery immediately, where a kidney, damaged by abuse, had to be removed. We wept and wept and felt as though the tears would never stop as our hearts dissolved in grief.

And thus it was Circumstance that made a crucial decision for us, hard and cruel as it was at the time. Our son took his recuperating dog to Sacramento. The bird that had been killed was the female mate of a pair of cockatiels who had loved and hatched many eggs over an eight-year period. The male wailed in his grief and added to our own sense of loss and self-recrimination. We found a home for him with a family that had a female. The remaining bird was the young daughter of this doting pair, and she went off happily to live with a delightful little boy. We put the house on the market and made two cross- country road trips to Florida with what furnishings would fit into the condo.

In short, by the time we returned to the boat in April, we had sold the house, torn ourselves from the soil and our animals, and moved into a condominium a continent away. We were on the sixth floor, encased above and below by concrete. No animals were permitted, and a guard was aware of our every ingress and egress. This is assuredly not the recommended way to retire, but we kept stalwart hearts. It was a new millennium; we had a new residence in Florida which, despite its culture shock, was very beautiful and valuable; we had our boat in Italy; our daughter was due to graduate in May with a degree in law. The year, in balance, looked as though it would be a wonderful one despite the cruel upheaval we had just experienced.

CHAPTER XVIII

OPENING AND CLOSING DOORS

'There lies the port; the vessel puffs her sail:
There gloom the dark broad seas.'
Lord Tennyson, *Ulysses*

On April 3 for the first time we locked a door behind us without having to find house sitters. My sister was caring for the three pathetic African violets with which I had tried to console myself. No other living thing was dependent upon us. We drove a rented car to Miami and caught an Alitalia flight to Genova via Milano. The flight was still over eight hours long, but so much better than the 12 hours from California. It was raining and cold in Milano. Our flight to Genova brought us south as far as Lavagna, where we made a wide, sweeping turn back up the coast. Just at that point the sun broke through, and we saw our new locale stretched out below us. There was the Entella River flowing from the mountains into the Ligurian Sea. To the north was the fairly large city of Chiavari with its surprisingly small port. To the south lay much smaller Lavagna with its surprisingly large port. Somewhere directly below our boat waited our arrival.

The burst of sunlight that permitted our glimpse of this scene was brief indeed. Genova was as cold and wet as Milano had been. We took the airport bus to the Brignole train station and got thoroughly soaked hauling our luggage across the street from bus to train. We travel very lightly as far as our personal needs are concerned, but this time we had a lot of stuff for *Gatti,* including pots and pans and that highly touted Navtex instrument. We even had a neighing hobby horse for Dominic's little daughter. We had the choice of taking a relatively good fast train that would disgorge us in Chiavari or a much slower regional train that stopped in Lavagna. We opted for the latter because we would not have to transfer everything for a cab ride to the port. So we stopped at every station along the way and became reacquainted with all the little coastal towns. There were no merrily dancing holiday lights. Each one looked a little dreary hunkered down under the lowering clouds.

Soon we stopped at the big station at Chiavari and began to transfer our luggage to a post closer to the train door for a fast exit at the next stop. This accomplished, I huddled with the baggage in the tiny station house while Bill trudged to the port to get a dock cart. We loaded up and made our bumpy way along the seawall, half the length of the port, and finally the long way down "G" dock. We lowered our *passerella* and trotted on deck. Bill took out *Gatti*'s big old-fashioned key and turned it in the lock. For the first time we had returned to our Italian home. Dominic had offered no help to make our travel easier, but he had pulled back the canvas and aired out the boat. Breathlessly we passed through the companionway. She was clean, warm, cozy, home. Smiling back at us were the photos of our children. Stacked neatly in the bookcase were our favorites. We rushed to the drawers below our bunks and to our closets and, yes, sure enough, there were our own clothes. In the galley were our own food, our wedding silver, our china dishware. This was not the rented apartment to which we had become accustomed during our previous stays. We could not contain our glee. This was truly ours, and it comforted our hearts. A part of us resided in Italy and welcomed us home from the maelstrom we had just escaped.

The next few days were full of kisses to both cheeks, *ciaos* and happy reunions. Our previous stay had endeared us to local shopkeepers and restaurateurs, who have very scant business during the winter months. One tiny restaurant in particular had perfected my favorite pizza and also turned out the best *farinata* around. This is a Ligurian staple made of *ceci* (garbanzo bean or chickpea) flour and olive oil, which is then poured out in a thin layer onto an enormous round copper pan and baked in a wood-fired oven. The resultant product is crispy, warm and utterly delicious. The shopkeepers were happy to welcome us back, and we were contented to bask before the big open wood-fired ovens and stuff ourselves with the foods we had been craving. All of this was very, very good. But the good weather Dominic had promised was nowhere evident.

Having been raised in a tourist town, we are aware of the official line …"this weather is so unusual…it never rains in April… we've never had a cold snap like this before…" But in this instance even the natives did not understand the peculiar weather patterns that we experienced. It had been raining pretty steadily for three weeks prior to our arrival and there had been some unseasonably high winds. Mud slides had loosened the foundations and roots of some of the stone houses and olive groves that cling to the mountainsides. A sailboat entering the port had been swept up on the shore, and Dominic had posted chilling photos of the poor craft beached on her side. The crane which had been working in such jeopardy on the breakwater at Christmas actually had been washed off with its workmen. No one had been hurt in these incidents, but the weather definitely had not been following expectations. We had no sooner settled in than a storm like the ones we had in December whipped in. This time the workmen on the breakwater prudently puffed off in their crane and a good thing it was too. In the winter we had seen tremendous waves breaking against the breakwater, sending up plumes of spray. This time, monstrous waves rolled right over the tops of the protecting rocks. Great white horses thundered past the port entrance.

For two weeks we did not remove *Gatti*'s canvas. It was too wet to store and it was so dreary outside anyway that the draping didn't matter. Actually, the weather was pretty immaterial to us for some time; we were physically and emotionally spent. The first day back we slept 22 hours straight. What bliss it can be to pull up your gangway and rock in your bunk to the sound of rain pattering on the deck above and waves slapping at your sides. It is like leaving the hard world behind and finding refuge in the safe womb of Mother Nature.

We had brought with us the fabulous Navtex instrument that had fascinated me on *Cielo*. It had to be special ordered from a marine supplier in California as there were no Navtex stations operational in the United States at that time. It is an attractive box of relatively small dimensions, so we installed it in the head and engaged Amerigo to connect the antenna. With great anticipation we turned it on. Nothing! Italy had no functioning stations yet either. The closest working station appeared to be Toulon and as much as we fiddled and begged, no peep came from it. It was several weeks later that we heard a strange whirring sound coming from the head in the middle of the night. We raced in with great excitement to find the paper tape being printed out.

"019*U*C Apr 01
TTT AVURNAV TOULON 145/*1
PROVENCE
On 12 APR ***Q from 1800Z *0 2100*+*-* 9*34-5*9,'?* -
:5 8,
43-?),030 *6*:7*   **R*LLELS*FNRW**WN
*A*WA...ME*I**ANS   *C**OAEPBE   *A
P*YA*TOE******
CANCEL*T*IS *22100*+*.-5***.:**= "

No, this message meant nothing to us either, and we disgustedly put the Navtex to the back of our minds even though we left it on and periodically received further bits of gibberish that did nothing at all to inform us. Occasionally we made out words along the lines of "submarines," "war surplus" and such.

The week before Easter brought a new feel to the air, as if a life force were swelling. The crane had moved back, this time accompanied by a parade of cement trucks that made daily treks to and from the seawall, where huge cement creatures were being formed. They were made in the shape of jacks such as are used in the game but of mammoth proportions. As they were formed, they were positioned leg to leg, three deep, down the length of the breakwater. We came up with several surmises as to what their use might be but were flummoxed when eventually they were loaded on barges and dumped into the sea about a mile from port. We learned in time that they were rip rap serving as a protective layer over a new sewer line. Other cranes appeared on the beach and at the river mouth. The latter seemed to be laying a sand bar across the mouth of the Entella River. The others were part of a beach cleanup and preparation that included major sand grooming and placement of pipes that would hold the supports of cabanas.

The town had the feel of a field of daffodils in the spring. The air may be gray and chilly, but vivid green spikes are beginning to push through the soil and there is the tingling of the tremendous thrust and life force at work. And, like awakening one morning to see hundreds of beaming, bright yellow faces, so we awoke on Good Friday to crowds of happy people. The dock was nearly impassable for the baby carriages and miniature bicycles. Towels hung drying over transoms, and packed boats rocked to laughter and activity. Sails were run up and motors coughed to life for the first time in months.

A steady stream of boats entered and left the port, with shapely, bikini-clad beauties poised at their bows. People were laying in food left and right – everything from supermarket staples to the traditional dove-shaped *Colomba* cakes that filled the pastry shop windows. Shops opened along the port overnight as though by magic. A new gelato shop flung open its doors with a mind-boggling array of delicious options. A newsstand filled with brightly colored glossy magazines materialized where only yesterday there had been a bare wall. Hotels that had been locked and barred now posted no vacancy signs. Our favorite little restaurant, where often we had been the only patrons on a cold, raw night, now had its rows of long wooden tables and benches filled with diners crushed hip to hip. The open wood-fired oven spewed out pizzas, *farinata*, grilled meats and sea creatures as fast as the exhausted owners could load and unload it. The weather was still having its ups and downs, but the ups were certainly getting the better of the game.

Easter weekend was the time for the first leg of a tall ship regatta. The regatta was to form in Cadiz, Spain, sail to Boston and Halifax, and then re-cross the Atlantic to complete the voyage at Amsterdam. Half the ships gathered together in Southampton for the run to Cadiz. The other half assembled in Genova. How exciting it was to see the antique port crammed with the tall masts of historic vessels! Many of the ships were open to the public the two days preceding Easter, so we took the train up to tour the *Amerigo Vespucci* and some others. The weather was perfect and no one was taking it for granted. Part of the tall ship celebration involved a linen-laid table that stretched all the way around the old port. Two thousand people seated at this table were served traditional local fare while thousands of others milled about visiting ships, shops and chandleries, trying to avoid collisions with hundreds of formally attired waiters. We walked the decks of the *Vespucci* with awe. If only *Gatti* could be maintained to the standard of perfection of that proud lady! Having several hundred good-looking sailors around obviously has more than one benefit.

The tall ships were scheduled to depart for Cadiz on Easter morning. Before turning westward, however, they sailed down to Camogli to bid a formal adieu to Italy. We hopped the local train once again and stepped out on the station platform at Camogli to the boom of a cannon. We rushed over to the old brick wall that overlooks the harbor and gasped with delight. There, so far below us, offshore of this charming little medieval harbor, lay the tall ships under sail. They looked like great white seabirds in flight surrounded by clouds of seagulls, so numerous were the sail and power boats that fluttered excitedly around them. From an ancient tower at the edge of the port, small puffs of smoke billowed out from time to time, followed by a cannon's rumble. We fairly flew down the steep steps and through the narrow alleys that took us through town to the beach.

The sun was warm and the beach was crowded with beautiful young women so intent on acquiring tans that they neither raised their heads to watch the ships nor twitched a muscle as cannon shots rang out above them. A little children's park had been erected and happy cries mingled with the laughter that was everywhere. We rushed past and found seats on the sun-warmed rocks that compose the breakwater. A loudspeaker had been set up, over which we could hear a government official communicate with each ship in its turn. Each captain, in his own native language, thanked the community and wished a happy Easter to all. The official responded in like tongue, wishing Godspeed and fair wind. Then a respectful cannon volley rumbled from the old fort that guards the harbor entrance. This protocol continued for some time into the afternoon, as we perched out on our rocks absorbing the sun and surroundings. At last a final volley heralded the departure of the regatta. Fire boats appeared, spraying great arcs of water, as the huge birds spread wider wings and headed to sea. At a distance they almost looked like giant pine trees planted in the waves. Many of the larger accompanying boats sailed out of sight with the regatta. The smaller ones turned regretfully back to shore. We mirrored these latter and climbed back on the train to Lavagna.

Back on our deck, we enjoyed the vivacious atmosphere bewitching the town. Boats began arriving back in port after the exciting day on the Ligurian Sea. Bow to stern they came southward, past our breakwater. We could see the mast tops float by, then turn in through the narrow entrance into the harbor. They passed by us as they proceeded up the fairway to back snugly into their slips. A late afternoon stroll down the beach promenade revealed that bathing beauties were not unique to Camogli or ship bows. We had also magically created our own children's park and the little carousel was squawking cheerfully. A small stream had been somehow manufactured, which flowed down the beach to the waves through hundreds of lounges and colorful umbrellas. Teenagers were attempting to surf at the mouth of the Entella, and we concluded that the sand bar had been created with that activity in mind.

The day had been very close to perfection. What marred it was a reminder from our own homeland that the world can be a harsh and ugly place. As we sat on the breakwater in Camogli on this gorgeous Easter day, people walked by with Sunday newspapers tucked under their arms. The choice of newspaper reflected the political leaning or civic pride of the carrier, but the identical color photo covered the better part of each front page. There was a grotesque man in a black mask holding a machine gun against a terrified child backed into a closet. Little Elian Gonzalez cast a shadow across that day and, although they were unassociated with him, the image presaged deeper shadows to fall over our happiness.

Bill with Doug's mast.

CHAPTER XIX

THE VALLEY OF THE SHADOW
AND THE SUN

'In *Endymion*, I leapt headlong into the sea, and thereby
have become better acquainted with the soundings, the
quicksands, and the rocks, than if I had stayed upon the
green shores and piped a silly pipe, and took tea and
comfortable advice.'

John Keats, *To James Hassey*

We had a full week of enjoying this return to our boat. We resolved
bilge and associated electrical problems. We bought a hot plate and
practiced crossing back and forth on our *passerella*. It was not
always an option to have the little wheels on the jetty and, when they
were not there, the gangway would swing from side to side from the
lines attached to the davits and tilt down from the pin in the stern
under the weight of transiting bodies. Tides would raise and lower it.
In this latter instance, passing boats or whipping winds could send it
smashing into the pier. This happened more than once. We had to
develop a routine to remember to pull it up when we were not using
it. When we first got the gangway, we needed to have the end sitting
on the pier so we could traverse it. We even clung to the little hand
rail. We rapidly progressed to the point that we could hop a foot or so
from the pier to the gangway without much thought. At length we
became so accomplished that we could leap onto it loaded with
grocery bags. Even though the early steps were tenuous and timid,
over time we have become as proficient as anyone else in the port.
Actually, we are probably a lot more proficient because our
passerella had been especially manufactured for an American vessel
designed to be boarded from the side rather than the stern. While
Italian yachtsmen can stride confidently over their *passerelle* that jut
out solidly from sterns at the touch of a remote control button, they

look as foolish as we did at first as they cling to our swaying, wobbling invention.

During this period we also spent time trying to learn knots, and Bill worked out a congenial relationship with Dominic and Angelo. They charged a monthly fee for caring for *Gatti* in our absence and a lower fee when we were in residence. This was annoying, since they did nothing for the boat when we were there and precious little when we were not. Other yacht services were providing their clients with boat washing and other amenities. We were receiving none of these, based on the excuse that our boat was our home and Italians place great store on the sanctity of privacy. The great benefit we did receive was that Bill had a key to the office at the port and a desk for his computer. He could go over after hours, when the time was good in America for e-mailing and stock transactions and analysis. The market was still highly profitable and Bill's energy was well-spent. Use of the office justified the monthly charge because we did not have a telephone connection at the dock. Dominic was also useful in recommending workmen such as Amerigo and ordering things such as a windlass. Generally speaking, we were happy with the deal we had struck.

In early May we closed *Gatti* up and flew to New York. We hastily bought suitable clothing and as proud parents watched our daughter file down the aisle at Madison Square Garden to receive her Doctorate in Jurisprudence from the New York University School of Law. Our plan had been to fly back to Italy from New York, but family medical problems had developed in Florida, and we took the train there to see if we could be of assistance. That stay stretched to a month as we dealt not only with family problems but with the growing recognition that condominium life was a serious oversight by Dante when he was constructing his circles of Hell.

If we had been returning to our home in Bakersfield, the jolt would not have been as harsh. There everything would have been unfolding in an accustomed order that filled my heart with peace. The roses and iris would be in bloom. The plum, almond and early season apricot trees would have shed their delicate blossoms back in March and now be well on their way to fruiting. The grapes would be plumping up, the tiny orbs of citrus would be free of their fragrant white petals and the pomegranate would be ablaze with scarlet trumpet-shaped flowers.

As it was, we checked through the guard house and punched the elevator button to the sixth floor. The first day or two everything was fine. We felt like millionaires as we trotted from room to room rediscovering things we had done without – a washer and dryer, a walk-in closet packed with clothes and shoes, a bathtub, a toilet that did not have to be pumped to flush. From one side of the condo we looked down on the water of Blind Pass and the Intracoastal Waterway beyond; from the other we could see across the white sand beaches to the Gulf of Mexico. At night from our bed we watched the white light up the coast at John's Pass flash the Morse code letter "A" – one long, one short – to signify safe water. On the premises were a sparkling warm pool that we did not have to maintain and two cars that would take us wherever we wished, whenever we wished.

But despite all these nice things, within a week I was in tears. There was no cycle of life here. I felt acutely my being cut off from the soil and the compression of the concrete above and below me on my soul. The lines of Gerard Manley Hopkins' poem *God's Grandeur* ran through my heart – "the soil is bare now, nor can foot feel, being shod." Beyond my feeling of physical alienation was the discovery that many people sharing this tropical paradise were beyond unpleasant.

During this month three positive things did happen. The family illness that had prompted the trip was not life threatening. I was able to visit my mother twice at her care facility. She had suffered from Alzheimer's disease for many years, and it was clear to me on this trip that the end of her ordeal was near. I was able to hug her and tell her that she would soon be freed from the hell that had held her so long. I could feel her relax and see her smile and almost believe that she knew who I was. The third event was our discovery of the Coast Guard Auxiliary.

For some time we had been concerned about our naval competence on both a personal and legal level. Since *Gatti* is a U.S. documented vessel, we were not required to have European Union licenses to operate her, but we were awed by the level of competence required to obtain one. Bill was a great boat handler, but his understanding of navigational law was sketchy and my understanding of anything nautical at all was close to nil. We knew at least as much as the average American boater, but, unfortunately, that is not very much. In retrospect we see how very naïve we were, but at least we recognized our deficiencies.

When we bought the boat, she had not one spark of electronic equipment on her. She had been restored with an eye to period authenticity rather than function. When we had her rewired by Andy in Marina del Rey, we spent a great deal of time selecting high quality instrumentation that would fit into areas hidden behind the lovely mahogany drawers and doors on the boat's deck. We left the United States confident that we had equipment that would provide the best security one can expect at sea. But who could know that our handsome radar screen would display only neon blobs of green that squirmed around like radioactive amoebae? The miraculous sounder/plotter/GPS which was able to split into three screens displaying spectra of lovely colors, made even less sense. Even the VHF radio was a gremlin. Intellectually, I knew how to use it. I kept it turned to the calling channel, listened in on channels and followed the daily weather reports in Italian and English, but the thought of pressing that button and calling out paralyzed me with fright. Fortunately, we are not youngsters who know it all. We are seniors who recognize how much of the world we do not know, but we do know where to go to learn.

Our Coast Guard Auxiliary was a heaven-sent blessing. Most of the members were older than we and possessed decades of military and maritime experience, which they were eager to share. They welcomed us with open arms and enthusiasm. They helped us double up on some basic boating classes so we would be eligible to become members and take the advanced courses. We labored over our lessons and tests, and by year's end we were charting radar targets on maneuvering boards, laying out dead reckoning courses and learning to adjust for current and wind. We were not experts, but passing the Coast Guard Advanced Navigation course is not child's play.

Of course, all this education took time, and it was now only June and we were just getting started. Even at that, we returned to the boat feeling that we were getting our world back in order and making good progress in educating ourselves. The Florida illness had complicated our travel plans and, as it was now prime tourist season, we could not find tickets to Italy at anything close to a reasonable cost. In the end we flew to Zurich and took the train to Genova. This was a beautiful, peaceful journey, and we arrived back on *Gatti* happy but tired. As usual, we holed up and slept for hours.

When we awakened, there was an e-mail on the Magellan from my sister. Our mother had died. My sister would handle the arrangements in Florida; Bill and I would fly to Pennsylvania and arrange the funeral. The three of us constituted my mother's immediate family. We had a couple days to organize things on *Gatti* and found an airline that provided seats at bereavement fares. On our layover between JFK and Pittsburgh, we called my sister to assure her that we were in the country and on top of things. Strangely, no one answered the telephone, and it was not until midnight in a Pittsburgh motel that we learned she had suffered a sudden, unexplained collapse and was not expected to survive the night. Altering our plans, we rushed the funeral and flew once again to Florida. We found the situation there still grim but improving. We stayed in Florida as long as we could be of use and then returned to Italy. The airline actually gave credence to this remarkably horrible story and were generous in discounting the fare and providing us with seating.

We arrived back on *Gatti* again, this time utterly spent and grateful for the serenity we always gain from her. Our 56th and 58th birthdays had passed two days earlier. Our children, of course, had remembered us, but they were far away. Charles was in California and Nicole and her husband were taking a summer hiatus to study Spanish in Barcelona. My sister had been in no condition to recognize the day, and the loss of my mother assumed a new poignancy. In our absence, which had been more extended than we planned, Dominic had seen fit to unplug the electric power to the boat. This had resulted in our finding a refrigerator full of rotted, molded food and close to $2,000 of my arthritis medicine destroyed. What made this more upsetting was that the drug was considered experimental in Italy at the time and could not be shipped into the country.

But we did not have time or inclination to dwell on misfortune. Between Bill's e-mailing from Dominic's office and my trusty satellite-powered Magellan, we were able to keep in close touch with our loved ones and my sister's steady recovery. One of the reasons we had returned to Italy as soon as we had was that we were expecting our first guests. Andy, our California electrician, was flying to Boston to rendezvous with his lady friend, a doctor there. From Boston they were coming to Lavagna to spend time with us before continuing their European vacation. We truly did not feel up to entertaining after the blows the year had dealt us so far, but Andy and Chris proved to be just the tonic we needed. They were young, fun, eager and totally invigorating.

Between our unplanned comings and goings, the bad weather and our timidity, we had taken *Gatti* out of port only twice. Angelo had run over to Sestri Levante with us for fuel once, and we had sailed to Rapallo and Portofino. Another time we had gone to Sestri ourselves and anchored there to clean *Gatti*'s bottom. Sestri Levante forms the lower peninsula that, with the promontory of Portofino, shapes the Gulf of Tigullio, also known as the Bay of Marconi, in honor of the man who did a great deal of his scientific work here. The peninsula used to be an island, which eventually became connected to the mainland. This accounts for the fact that it appears to be a tall mountain attached to the mainland by a low causeway. The actual port at Sestri is in the Bay of Silence on the side facing away from Lavagna. It is a beautiful spot but too small for a boat of *Gatti*'s size. But the gentle curve on the gulf side provides excellent anchorage for swimming and bottom cleaning. When we were in California we had hired a diver to clean the bottom monthly to stay ahead of the dreadful flabby creatures that attached themselves and grew with incredible speed. Surprisingly, in Lavagna there was hardly any growth at all. Because European vessels are not required to have black water holding tanks, it is a bad idea to dive in a big port, but Sestri is not an enclosed port and the water is beautiful and clear. On a calm day it was a pleasant chore to wipe away the thin, fragile film that had grown on the hull.

Now that we had two able-bodied friends on board, we became more adventuresome. Summer had brought a great bustle of activity to our dock. Vessels that had spent the long, cold months closed up, now had railings and masts festooned with drying towels and bathing suits. Happy families and friends reunited over wine and festive dinners on aft decks. Bicycles, shoes, and toys made the dock even more difficult to negotiate as they tangled with hoses and lines. A steady flow of boats moved in and out of the harbor, so we switched on our engines and gleefully joined the parade. We did not cover a lot of area, but the area around us was wonderful and sought out by some of the most fashionable yachts in the world.

We began by roaring over to Portofino and anchoring outside the popular harbor. When Angelo had gone over with us earlier, he had pointed out a lovely little cove that did not have a mooring charge. All that was required was to arrive sometime around noon and claim a spot. And what a terrific spot we found! Not far from the harbor entrance we dropped our anchor for the first time from our new windlass. As it clanked and whirred, we watched our new anchor descend through the limpid waters, the chain feeding smoothly along the cogs of this marvelous machine. From being a prima donna without so much as an anchor, *Gatti* now had a windlass, 75 meters of chain, lots of additional line and two anchors. She was rapidly becoming a very functional vessel. We carried our second anchor aft in *La Gattina* and lodged it in the rocks on shore. Thus secured, from this vantage point we observed the transits of mega-yachts and their passengers, the fun-seeking throngs on the ferries that all summer long hop from one idyllic port to another, and the totally contented people in their little boats anchored all around us. We prepared our dinner on board because Andy was interested in how well our inverters worked and how much energy was drawn from our batteries. He declared himself pleased, we congratulated him on his electrical expertise, and we dined like emperors on our private barge.

Dinner completed, the dishes were washed in the sea since we had not yet faced the chore of replacing the 50-year-old fresh water tank aboard. Then we all piled into little *Gattina* and tied up for the first time in the divine little port. We had visited many times in all seasons from land side, but seeing the town from the water was splendid. We walked around the quay, where people aboard the yachts were dressing formally for dinner on decks waiting with linen covered tables, lighted candles, and towering floral displays. Starched crews were waiting for the guests to arrive, every now and again giving a surreptitious rub to a smudge on a glossy brass rail. We enjoyed cappuccino by the slapping water's edge and watched fashionable ladies in spike heels try to negotiate the cobble-stone streets to the exclusive little shops. Then we climbed back into our tiny tender and putted out to *Gatti*.

Behind us was a chattering world of pretense. As we curved around the harbor entrance, we saw *Gatti* take shape in the darkness as she waited for us in her quiet elegance. Her classic lines were striking as she lay rocking gently before a backdrop of venerable old villas that climbed the cliff of rocks and flowers. As the last packed ferries of the day passed us on their way out of port, the passengers may have thought of us as being privileged and, if they did, they were right. We lay on deck trying to form constellations from the brilliant points so large and clear against the velvet black of the heavens. Peace was beginning to spread once again in our hearts and we felt very humble and, at the same time, very special.

Morning was announced by the first bright-yellow bus honking its way around the agonizingly tight curves of the promontory; the excited shouts of children in little boats already gathering for a day of summer swimming and fun; the sputtering of fishing boats going out or already returning with their catches to be sold to the stylish restaurants. There is no train station in Portofino. Train passengers headed here must disembark at Santa Margherita Ligure and either hike the pleasant trail provided or catch the buses which scurry back and forth all day. When we had lolled about long enough to suit our fancy, we went exploring. This activity presents *Gatti* at her best. Her powerful gas engines are smooth and muffled. Her sleek design makes her a joy to speed in. Gasoline is expensive in Europe and we do not lightly indulge in speed, but this time we did and savored it fully. We explored our coast to the north, making our way around the promontory to the ancient little port at Camogli, where we had watched the departure of the tall ships. We stuck our bow in to see the medieval church at San Fruttuoso; it can be reached only by sea or a hike of many hours over the mountainous peninsula. Wiry mountain goats leaped from rock to rock as we ran offshore. We checked out the grand yachts of the rich and famous and their imitators that were lying off the scenic beach at Paragi and circled the tall cruise ships whose passengers are so insulated from the sea.

One of the greatest highs of the trip was our return to port. Having additional hands on board gave me a welcome shot of confidence. Bill expertly aimed our stern between *Bo Drum* and *Rachele,* who slid sideways without reproach to let us in. I lowered our *passerella*, ran off, jumped to the dock, and threw a line to Andy, who secured us. I did it smoothly, unthinkingly, and very well. In my "retirement" I overcame horrors haunting me since my earliest gym classes. Our stern now secure, and our neighbors nudging back in close to hear *Gatti*'s tales of adventure, Bill shut down the engines and walking our slimy and dripping bow line up with a boat hook, secured our *cima a terra.*

Our daughter's summer in Spain was coming to a close, so we left the boat for Andy and Chris to enjoy in privacy for a few days before they continued on to Venice. We took the night train to Barcelona and returned a week later with our daughter by ferry. It was now August, and what a change had befallen the port. As though an evacuation warning had been sounded, the port had emptied of towels, shoes, bicycles, people and boats. The Port of Lavagna looked like an empty parking lot. The great month of vacation had begun, but who could ever have guessed such a dramatic start? Our neighbors had left for a month in Sardinia, Corsica, the Pontine Islands or one of the hundreds of other attractive spots around the Mediterranean, Adriatic, Ionian and Aegean Seas in this wonderful month of liberty. We had other visitors and cruises and another night at Portofino. Then Bill and I packed up and returned to Florida. Nicole and Ciarán stayed on longer and then closed up *Gatti* for the winter. We had been visited by friends and family and for a time life had been very good. We had experienced glimpses of those rare occurrences where all is truly perfect and not a single aspect could be improved.

In a way we were actually eager to return to Florida. Aside from seeing my sister, I had medicine, which I had not had since Dominic's presumptuous unplugging, waiting for me, and we were eager to continue our Coast Guard courses. A very disturbing question had arisen in regard to navigation. I had been reading an Italian book which displayed the usual diagram of the buoyage systems in ports. Everything followed the normal configuration except that the red and green lights were reversed from what we knew to be correct. Dominic and everyone we asked agreed that the book was correct, and they looked at us warily. What was this phrase "red-right-return" that we kept spouting? Why would you want a red light on your starboard side? Green is the color for starboard. Green to green; that's the way to return to port. That certainly sounded more reasonable to us, but our confusion and concern could not be resolved by anyone we asked.

We needed information! I had learned a little bit about electronics during this trip, but mostly I had learned how little I knew. I still had not had to gut up to that horrid little radio that disturbed my sleep. Also, Bill and I had discovered that we needed to work out problems posed by our physical disabilities. His hearing was not good, and we needed to work out a better communication system, especially during anchoring. My rheumatoid arthritis was in check, but handling lines and other duties that required strong hands presented challenges to me. We needed to learn about meteorology and winds. And we knew many of these needs could be met in Florida.

The challenges were many, but what baby would ever try to stand or speak if he could see the difficulties in the future? What lover would follow his heart if he had even a glimpse of the pain that love can inflict? It is the search and discovery in life that give it zest. It is the recognition of fear and overcoming it that gives us courage. It is the awareness of our ignorance that gives rise to the desire to learn and expand our thinking. It is in continued learning, bravery and achievement that we find pride in ourselves, purpose for being, and joy in the voyage of life.

CHAPTER XX

COMPLICATIONS, ADVANCES
AND COMPATRIOTS

"If the law supposes that," said Mr. Bumble…
"the law is a ass – a idiot."
Charles Dickens, *Oliver Twist*

From August 2000 until January 2001 we worked at resolving problems. We went to condominium meetings and made some good friends and a number of virulent enemies. We sorely missed our animals and investigated changing the "no pet" policy. My, my, what a tempestuous tide that was! Bill got a hearing aid and resolved to do his part to improve our communication problems at sea. We were sworn in as Coast Guard auxiliarists and attended our meetings and classes in starched nautical uniforms. We labored over currents, winds and vectors. I learned about true North, magnetic North, variation and deviation and trembled to think that I had ever dared put to sea in my former ignorance. When I had stood at the bow of the freighter pretending to be Christopher Columbus, I had thought of him as being pretty much in the dark insofar as knowing where he was going was concerned. I figured he had been taking a really big gamble. I now blushed at such a thought. He knew so much more than my poor brain could ever process and his "gamble" was backed by a strong knowledge of physical phenomena that I had never heard of before.

Best of all, we learned about Regions A and B. It is beyond my ability to grasp why, but the world has two buoyage systems. One would think that our oceans and seas, which flow into one another, could be spared the petty nationalism of humans. But, no. The systems are basically the same except for one highly significant difference. When returning to port in Region A, which involves the Eastern Atlantic coast, the Indian Ocean, most of the West Pacific coast and a couple Caribbean islands, one enters the harbor with green on his starboard side and red to port. Just the opposite holds true for Region B. This accounts for the "red - right - return" mnemonic device those of us sailing in the Americas must learn. We have been told this system originated during the American Revolution, when patriots reversed the colors of the harbor lights to confuse and destroy British vessels.

The big problem we did not resolve was our legal status. Most of the boats brought in to Italy by freighter are new imports, and the dealer pays an import tax on these. Other boats that come from the Americas usually either sail in from a transatlantic crossing or come by water transport from Florida or a couple other East Coast sites. In the latter case, boats are sailed into a transport vessel and cradled. The water is then drained out, somewhat like a dry dock, and the ocean passage is made. Off the coast of France, the transport is flooded and the boats sail out to their ports of choice. The protocol is to check in with the port captain, have papers stamped, and follow the laws of the host country. In the past, the regulations were very clear. A tourist could stay in a host country for three or six months, depending on the country, without a visa, after which he would be required to leave, if only for one day. Simply stated, we could have stayed in Italy for 180 days, visited France for the weekend, and returned to Italy for another 180 days. In practice, the Italians had this law on the books only because the United States limits an Italian's stay in a similar manner. As long as you were "on holiday" and living independently, the economy was happy for the income.

When the European Union was formed, the laws grew more confused for everyone. Because all Europe was now functioning as a unit, it became necessary to leave the EU every 180 days. The closest non-EU port at that time was in Malta – a long and very expensive distance away. The other way around this mess for a boat with *Gatti*'s agenda was to "lay up" the vessel six months of the year. The rules governing this procedure were also in a state of flux, but the general idea was that when you left the boat to return to America, you locked her up and entrusted the keys and papers to the port captain. On your return, he was to stamp the papers as though you had just entered the port. In reality, no one wanted to be bothered to stamp anything, so the rules were more theoretical than observed.

Gatti presented special complications. There was no water transport to take her from the West Coast. To truck her to Florida was expensive and not recommended for an old lady of wood construction. No one could place a value on her for customs in Italy and, if there were problems, she might wind up stuck in customs for some period. With her work at the shipyard and her long transport, it was important that she get back in the water without delay. There was discussion about security at the container port storage and the real possibility of theft, especially of our electronic equipment. These were the reasons the shipping broker had urged us to get a carnet.

The carnet is a document issued by the Department of Commerce that is, simply put, a passport for goods. If an American business person were attending a trade show in Europe, he could bring in samples under carnet, which would protect him from import tax. The carnet has a life of one year. Within that time period the goods need to be taken out of the country or the tax paid. Physically it is a beautiful, big, official-looking document of several pages. The first page is signed by customs on entry to a port and the last page is signed by customs on exit. The carnet is designed for goods such as computers and cameras, not boats. In fact, to the best of our knowledge, *Gatti* is the only boat ever issued one. We applied for one, listing our business as freelance writers and photographers, an accurate description, as we had already published several travel articles and planned to expand this activity. The carnet worked like a charm. It established a value for an old boat and got her into the water the day after she was unloaded in Genova.

It was now November of 2000 and *Gatti* had been in Italian waters one year. For six months we had been tirelessly trying to meet the conditions of the carnet. No one had ever heard of such a document, and no one was willing to sign off on it. We had followed the letter of the law in laying her up and leaving our papers with Dominic to be carried to the port captain. This is something we discovered Dominic had never done and never did do during our entire stay in Liguria. We kept getting contradictory messages from him. At one point everything would be fine. No one cared that we were there. We flew our national colors, and the *Guardia di Finanza*, *Guardia Costiera*, *carabinieri*, and every other government official responsible for law enforcement at the port were well aware of our presence. Then there would be a panic. I would read an article in the newspaper about vessels being impounded which were flying U.S. flags illegally. These boats were involved in smuggling and tax evasion which, of course, we were not; but there was still some suspicion being directed at boats flying U.S. flags. Another time

Dominic called us in Florida, breathlessly announcing that the boat could not be laid up in the water and he was preparing to pull it for six months. Yet another time he suggested we – or he – should fly to Malta and pay $1,000 for a stamp showing we had been there by boat.

In November Bill made a solo trip to Italy in yet another attempt to get matters in order. From the beginning, we had been using a fine lawyer and insurance agency in Genova and we knew from them that we had been following legal practice in laying up the boat. We were not interested in the Malta idea; we realized we were guests in the country and were doing our best to understand and abide by the law. To say we had been to a place we had not been, and to pay a bribe to a government official to confirm the lie, did not seem like a good thing for us to do. Bill's arrival in Italy coincided with the United States presidential election, which held the world in limbo, and a devastating storm that sank dozens of multi-million dollar yachts in the trendy port at Rapallo. Despite the chaos, he did succeed in visiting an official in Chiavari with Angelo and giving the latter power of attorney to act on our behalf. He left a check to be used to pay whatever taxes might be levied. We just wanted to be legal. He returned home and we celebrated the holidays with a big open house on Christmas Eve, assuming that the situation was being handled by a competent yacht service.

The early days of the new year belied this assumption. By the end of January, we were back in Lavagna trying to find resolution. We had obtained the name of a prominent and influential yacht broker named Pino Basilico, whose spacious offices were located at the Porto Vecchio in Genova. We set up a meeting in his office, and both Dominic and Angelo accompanied us. Basilico's view was that the year had expired and no one cared about the existence of the carnet because no one knew how to deal with it. His professional advice was to tear it up, forget it, and continue to lay the boat up according to law, as we had been doing. He pointed out the window to the yachts lying at berth and told us that no one cared about taxes or the import problems that we were taking so seriously. He ended by tossing the carnet into his wastebasket. Dominic and Angelo applauded this action and left with grins; to them it was a mission accomplished. Bill and I felt relieved, to be sure, but we did not feel entirely at ease with this solution and retrieved the documentation from the wastebasket. When we returned to Florida, we took it with us so it would not be on the boat.

It was also at this time that we met our first fellow Americans in Lavagna. For so long our elegant Stars and Stripes had flown uniquely amongst the rows of red, white and blue British and French flags; red, white and green Italian tricolors; the reds, blacks and yellows of Germany and Spain. Now we spied over on "F" dock a 60-foot blue sailboat with *Antipodes* – Las Vegas painted on her stern and Old Glory streaming above it. We wasted no time in making the acquaintance of the Murphys, who were happy to speak English with Americans somewhat conversant about Ligurian weather. They had brought their boat over by transport from Florida and had been working their way along the ports of the French and Italian Rivieras. They had been wintering in Lavagna and planned to stay abroad for an extended period of time. They had been in France legally for one year and were as eager as we were to get papers in order. Their stay in the EU could be extended for another six months if they had their papers stamped in Cannes.

A group had formed in Cannes that was trying to draft rules for foreign vessels visiting the EU. This labor must rival that of Sisyphus, since to date the problems have not been resolved. In fact, the waters have been muddied even more with the entrance of Malta to the EU. The four of us wound up driving to Cannes one day, and we returned triumphantly to Lavagna with a stamp admitting us to France for one year with a second year extension possible. While we were not sure what this would do for us, it was at least an official stamp – and that is more than we had been able to get from anyone in Italy. The fact that we had been granted this stamp with the boat not being anywhere near France seemed to be of no concern to anyone.

The Murphys proved to be a delightful and very useful addition to our lives. We were about the same age and had been married about the same length of time. Don had hearing problems; Kathy's mother had Alzheimer's disease. We each had two children, although they had grandchildren as well. Their travel goals were different from ours but that only added zest to our friendship. Kathy is one of those resourceful people who can find what they need wherever they go. Even though she spoke no Italian, she had unearthed facilities in Lavagna and Chiavari we had not even guessed at. They pedaled their bikes everywhere and had ferreted out all the best markets and discovered how to buy most of their medications very inexpensively and without prescriptions at the local pharmacy. They had even rigged up a television and satellite dish. They had some bottom work done at the port in Chiavari in the spring and sailed off to Sardegna as soon as the weather settled. Their goals included seeing the Adriatic, Greece, Tunis, and wherever the currents in their life might send them. These were not goals we had, but we were, and are, the grateful recipients of their lessons learned and freely shared.

The spring was happy and busy despite the wild weather and legal frustrations. We spent St. Patrick's Day in rainy Dublin with the parents of our son-in-law. En route back to Italy, we visited in England for a week. We tried to escape the horrible newscasts in England of the foot-in-mouth epidemic by leaving London for Greenwich. There we took pictures of one another straddling the Prime Meridian and marveled over the famous clock so authoritatively and fascinatingly covered in Dava Sorbel's book *Longitude*. We continued through the incessant cold drizzle to Southampton, where we haunted chandlery shops and purchased Admiralty charts. My favorite find was a British cockpit guide to marine rules. Regions A and B are referred to obliquely in one short sentence at the bottom of the back flap. It reads, "These buoyage conventions are in general practice. A few places follow different ones." Of course these "few places" include the United States of America!

We dived under the English Channel on the chunnel train, rented a car and explored a portion of France. (One of our goals is to boat on the canals of Europe; *Gatti* is low enough, with a draft shallow enough to make this a possibility.) By car we followed a section of the beautiful Midi Canal and watched boaters handling the locks. Lounging on the verdant banks, we found it easy to visualize ourselves in our floating home gliding lazily along beneath the overhanging trees.

We returned to Florida for the month of May to handle taxes and other complications of life, but we were keen to return to Italy. We were expecting another guest. The niece of Bill's post-retirement business partner was taking a cruise with her college-age son and their cruise ship was going to be anchored at Portofino for the Fourth of July. Could we maybe get together? You bet we could! We left Florida loaded down with flag napkins, flag soap, red, white, and blue bunting and streamers, a fresh, big new flag for *Gatti* and recordings of Sousa marches. We arranged early for one of those coveted spots in the quaint little harbor that are so hard to come by in the summer months.

July 3 dawned with clear skies and smooth seas. How beautiful Liguria can be under such conditions! I believe that nowhere else in the world is the sky so intensely blue. This was our first visit to another port, and we were excited. Our friend Frank had been down from his home further up the Riviera, and we had gone over by land to scope out our spot. Everything looked grand. There would be no need to use that beastly VHF radio crouching behind its shiny mahogany door. Angelo assured me that all I had to do was call Lorenzo on the cell phone when we approached the harbor. I don't much like the cell phone either, but I figured I could handle it with little difficulty. In addition, there would be no *cima a terra* docking that would require hauling up a heavy bow chain. The really big yachts that tie up there, secure their stern lines to the quay and use their bow anchors up front. We, however, would tie up to a buoy at the bow. Having examined the docking procedures earlier from the quay, we had all these things clear in our minds. I would hand Lorenzo a bow line and Bill would handle the stern.

Gatti skimmed across the gulf with enthusiasm, laying a frothy wake behind her on the turquoise surface of the water. We passed the seaport towns, their small, enclosed ports bristling with masts. Huge yachts and cruise ships lay offshore rolling gently, while their passengers flitted about in tenders and jet skis. Then, before us, the famous harbor tucked away among the mountains gracefully opened. We passed the cove where we had anchored before and slowly followed the narrow channel, along which were anchored at buoys the little fishing boats by which many people in the area make their living. Here also were beautifully crafted wooden Riva runabouts, rowboats, and pleasure boats.

And now the time had arrived. I dialed Lorenzo's number. *"Pronto!"* followed the first ring. *"Siamo i Gatti Felici,"* I replied, pretty stoutly for me. What followed was a torrent of instructions in Italian. My confidence evaporated like the morning dew. By good luck, Lorenzo was already underway and was obviously expecting us, if not prepared for us. Here he came on a rubber inflatable, standing upright in the bow with a line taut in his hand. He greatly resembled a man riding a dolphin. He motioned for us to follow him, and Bill masterfully turned the boat and backed toward the quay. Lorenzo zoomed under our bow, and I duly passed him the ready line. And then, to my everlasting discredit, I dismissed Lorenzo from my mind. Bill was tying up aft, and I had done my job. Oops! No, I had not. Bill was now calling to me to retrieve the bowline. Lorenzo had attached it to the buoy and was now returning the working end, or at least trying to. He looked at me with a mixture of pity and scorn in his dark eyes that was very disconcerting.

We had tied up in fine style, more or less, and we flopped on our deck to get our bearings and congratulate ourselves. The quay is generally crescent-shaped with the mountains beginning a pretty quick ascent all around it. Shops and restaurants on the ground floors of tall apartments and cobbled streets fill much of the area between the mountains and the sea. The houses climb the slopes. There is no auto traffic in the port area. Those who do arrive by car pay a king's ransom to do so in the parking garage hidden in the back streets. Most people arrive by bus or *moto,* the ubiquitous little motor scooters.

We found ourselves on the north curve of the crescent between the rocky little beach and the front curve that provides mooring for the big boys. (Perhaps "north" is not precise directionally. I tend to refer to "north" as up the Italian coast and "south" as down.) Above us towered Brown's Castle, with terraces of cascading flowers and trees. Next to us starboard were two other boats. One was a tiny, very ship-shape sailboat piloted by three men somewhat older than we. They had explored all the canals of Germany, Holland and France and were now working their way toward Greece. Next to them was a big new Azimut bouncing about like a giant plastic toy. It flew the American flag, but its passengers never deigned a glance in our direction. The occupants appeared to be a gentleman of our age, a young trophy wife and baby, and a couple of family members. The crew of two had living quarters at the stern, which they entered through a narrow hatch like prairie dogs.

We had arrived about midday, when even a popular spot like Portofino in July is quiet and lazy. It is a town we know well, but its appearance from a berth was so different and charming that we just sat on the deck admiring how beautifully the tall old buildings across the harbor from us blended together, adding to the natural beauty of the spot. Then around two o'clock the yachts began to arrive. Off Lorenzo would rush, erect in his horse-like boat, and beyond the harbor would run up to some leviathan and begin directing it with hand signals. It would turn laboriously and back down the channel to the quay. Anchors would run out with great crashings while uniformed crews rushed about like ants and the yachts backed to the quay. Again and again this scene was reenacted until the crescent was packed hull to hull with great vessels, their fenders rubbing and portholes aligned. We could no longer see the buildings across from us, obscured by this accumulation of tremendous wealth and ego. Powerboats, tenders, jet skis and the like were lowered from gleaming hydraulic davits, and the owners or charters began buzzing about the harbor and out to sea; posing next to Jacuzzis; or relaxing on deck while officious crew members served them frosty cocktails. What an amazing change in such short a time. Portofino had been transformed into Las Vegas. The charm these people had come in search of had fled before them, and they were not even aware of its flight.

Summer evenings go late in Portofino. The sun sets around 9:15 p.m. and it is about then that the tables are laid on expansive decks. The enormous bouquets of flowers are delivered, the candles lighted and the beautiful people prepare themselves for their evening in this exclusive place. The restaurants fill up with those who lack aft decks and private staff. The sounds of clinking glasses, rattling cutlery, and laughter fill the harbor.

The evening *passeggiata* was great fun for us. Locals wandered the quay looking at the yachts over their tall gelatos. Not wealthy themselves, they were still very used to this evening tableau and in no way awed. They looked at the boats with interest, not jealousy, and, as elsewhere in Liguria, they stopped and looked unblinking without embarrassment.

This is, after all, really their playground, and the yachts provide a constant change of scene. When they had worked their leisurely way around to *Gatti*, their reaction tended to change. Here was a beautiful old boat. Here were people, wherever they called home, who loved her and labored to keep her beautiful and seaworthy. Here were people they could relate to, people with a real Genovese sea spirit. Some complimented her in Italian. Some who spoke English asked about her history. As usual, *Gatti* had cut to the level of soul.

Portofino

Drawn by Rebecca Sankner

CHAPTER XXI

MORNING COMES TO PORTOFINO
JULY 4, 2001

'And for all this, nature is never spent;
There lives the dearest freshness deep down things;
And though the last lights off the black West went
Oh, morning, at the brown brink eastward, springs –'
Gerard Manley Hopkins, *God's Grandeur*

I lay in the dark before dawn, rocking softly in my bunk, gradually growing conscious of where I was. The mewling of seabirds flying in presaged a refreshing downpour of rain. As the deluge tapered to a shower, a spit and an end, I heard the American men on the sailboat speaking softly in the predawn quiet just outside my porthole. Their little engine sputtered to life, they gathered in their lines and headed out through the stillness of the harbor as the sun began to slowly push back the dark. Fully awake now to the day, I settled myself on the aft deck to watch day come to Portofino.

Before me lay the six enormous yachts. To their bows and our starboard lay the tiny fishing boats and slick Rivas motionless in their calm anchorage. Behind me and to port rose the wooded cliffs surrounding the village, forested with olives, oaks, pines, cypress and palms ranging from deep green to silvery sage. The verdant display was punctuated by color bursts of fuchsia bougainvilleas, snowy magnolias, rose, pink, and white oleanders, brilliant scarlet geraniums, lavender wisteria, and pink and blue hydrangeas. These slopes – unlike the sleeping town – were far from quiet. Hundreds of birds greeted the day with enthusiastic song. Before long the domestic sound of crowing roosters broke into the wildly beautiful birdsong. Meanwhile, the tall pastel buildings rising from the quay and the magnificent foliage-draped villas clinging to the mountainsides slumbered on, their wooden shutters flung open to the cool sea breeze of the night.

The church bell high above the harbor tolled its first round at 8 a.m. sharp, imperiously but melodically calling folk to their duties. Languidly the town began to rub its eyes and stretch luxuriously. First to appear were the crews of the yachts armed with hose and squeegee. Two dapper police women strolled by on their first round of the day, followed closely by garbage trucks that unceremoniously emptied the containers overflowing from the extravagances of the night before. Restaurateurs appeared, laconically putting out their tables, which their children then covered with fresh linens. Matrons set up Coca-Cola and other colorful umbrellas over tables of needlework artistically arranged and shopkeepers – for the most part fashionably dressed pretty young women – turned keys in the locks of the elegant boutiques.

Before long the yachts were weighing anchor, gathering in their flotillas of tenders and making their ponderous way out of the harbor. Most of the owners did not show themselves. A notable exception was a young woman who sat on an upper deck reading. Not once did she raise her head or look back at the little paradise receding at her stern. Now that the floating hotels were gone, we could see the town fully again and enjoy its frenetic flurry of life. The first ferries began darting in and out, with eager faces packed on their two levels. By 10 a.m. the daily cruise ship had dropped anchor in the sea beyond the port, and its tenders began their uninterrupted runs from ship to shore, swelling the crowds mixing colorfully around the quay. Shortly after the bell chimes of noon, new yachts were backing in obediently, following the hand signals of Lorenzo, the café tables under the brilliant awnings were full, and the day's laundry was flapping merrily from open, geranium-lined windows. The purring of motors, wash of water, clanking of chains, and babble of voices echoed from the slopes.

I, of course, did not remain immobilized all morning. Today was the Fourth of July and we were ready to celebrate with other Americans far from home. We were still in those days of innocence which have since been so cruelly poisoned. Up went the red, white and blue. Out came the Italian sausage hot dogs and fixings and, as our guests set tentative feet on our swinging *passerella*, out poured the strains of *Anchors Aweigh*! We ate, toasted the day with pink, bubbly Testarossa, strolled around the port and swam at the little beach until it was time for them to catch the tender back to the elegant cruise ship that waited outside, impatient to move on to the next tourist stop. That night Angelo, his two sons and pregnant wife came down on two tiny *motos* to have *gelati*. Bill joined them in their treat; I was already sound asleep after a day of early rising, party giving and non-stop blissful conversation in English.

The following day we spent hiking the promontory to San Fruttuoso. The promontory is really Monte di Portofino which juts out 3 kilometers into the sea and rises to a height of over 600 meters. It separates the Golfo di Tigullio to the south from the Golfo Paradiso to the north. Most of the Portofino promontory is a national park that has been left in its pristine state. It is covered with growth inhabited by *cinghiali* or wild boars, and a wealth of plant and animal life. In fact, developers use this proliferation of wildlife as an argument to clear the area of "dangerous" creatures. Pathways, some paved and others mere dirt trails, crisscross it from Portofino, Camogli, and San Fruttuoso. The paths, identified on a scale of difficulty, are mapped out by red dots unobtrusively painted on tree trunks and rocks. Our chosen trail was pretty difficult, characterized by treks along the steep cliffs, leapings on or over rocks and gnarled tree roots, and a steep descent to the church. Along the way we found yet another simple monument to the partisans. A small rock structure was identified as being a hiding place for weapons, and a simple plaque requested that the area be respected as it was sanctified. And it did indeed sit there untouched and undefiled by graffiti and trash. The early miles of the trail offered a number of glimpses of the port, growing smaller and smaller below us. From the height, *Gatti*'s golden teak decks seemed a long expanse with the Stars and Stripes fluttering at the stern. We spend so much time living aboard her that it is always a bit of a surprise to see from a distance how big she really is.

We arrived at the cove on which the Abbey of San Fruttuoso di Capodimonte is located about noon, having survived a terrifying last couple miles of what seemed a vertical trail. We even arrived there upright when it had many times seemed so probable that we would roll in tattered and bruised. We celebrated our accomplishment with a delicious meal made of simple ingredients at a small restaurant on the beach, from which we could see the industrious ferries shuttle sun-lovers in and out. A few yachts better versed in anchoring than we rocked at either edge of the narrow inlet. During the trip in which we had first docked outside the harbor at Portofino with our new windlass, we had tried to anchor in this cove as well. Even though the day had been fine and the seas calm, the waters were fantastically deep and the bottom very rocky. Our expertise was not up to the task, and we had ruefully given it up.

There are many days when the church cannot be reached by water because of wind and tide. Even if one successfully anchors in the cove, the steep, rocky sides of the inlet do not permit landing. One must take a dingy or ferry to the small beach area on which the abbey sits. The Benedictine abbey was built sometime around the 11th century and had first caught our attention that wonderful Thanksgiving Day that we had run *Gatti* down to Lavagna from Genova. A remarkable ceremony is enacted here each winter as divers descend to the Cristo degli Abissi, positioned 15 meters under water. This icon represents the patron saint of divers and can be seen from the surface when the sea is still. Today was a calm, fine day, and several boats and hikers had shown up. While most were sunbathing, we toured the church and caught the last ferry of the day. The return trip was certainly shorter and less hazardous and exhausting than going; in short order we were deposited on the Portofino pier, not far from our own boat.

It wasn't long before the restaurants began to fill and the deck dinner parties to begin as on the night before. This time we joined the throng at one of the seaside restaurants. We had been so conscious of tourists and cruise ships that we were startled when during our meal a gentleman stopped at our table and inquired, "Aren't you on the boat from Naples?" After an initial denial, we suddenly remembered that Naples, Florida, was our hailing port and replied in laughing affirmative. How much fun to be recognized as unique in that throng of people!

The next morning we bid farewell to Lorenzo, who had forgiven me when I apologized for my mishandling of the buoy line. All I had had to do was tell him in my halting Italian that it was my first experience and his dark eyes had warmed and all was forgotten. He waved to us as we left his very special town, and we whizzed back across the Gulf of Tigullio in high spirits. Bill expertly maneuvered us between *Bo Drum* and *Rachele* and I ran off the wobbly, swinging *passerella* with a line and secured us. Bill went forward with the slimy, smelly line dangling from the boat hook and pulled our bow line and chain tight. We had had a grand, exciting adventure and generally had handled ourselves with a degree of competence that belied how much ignorance we still had to overcome.

CHAPTER XXII

ON ITALIAN SOIL

'In the elder days of Art,
Builders wrought with greatest care
Each minute and unseen part;
For the Gods see everywhere.'
John Logan, *The Builders*

Shortly after our Portofino adventure, we had *Gatti* pulled. It was time to repaint her bottom, and we wanted to make some mechanical modifications. When we bought her, she still had her original fresh water tank. It had been totally useless to us because Jerry had installed a pump without enough power to pump the water out. This had not yet been a real problem for us because up to this time we had spent most of our nights at dock, but it was a stupid situation that required fixing. Bill had designed a rectangular tank rather than the cylindrical one that took up so much room, and Dominic located a man who would make it for us. We also removed the cheap plastic black water tank that had been installed under the settee. It did not leak in any way but when the boat was closed up, a very distinct and unpleasant odor developed. Dominic was to have a black water tank manufactured after the fresh water one was completed, but this never happened. The holding tank was not really a problem either. Not only do European ports not use them, but there are no facilities for pumping them out. One has to go out to sea to empty them. This situation will surely change in time, but for the moment the holding tank was not a pressing problem.

Before the boat was hauled, we moved everything off into a storage box. Although the Italians referred to the area as a "box," it was really more like a medium-sized storage unit. The story of box rentals in Lavagna is not a happy one to recall. The first box we rented constantly dripped from both ceiling and walls and, having endured this for the first year, we told Dominic we needed something better. The something better was a fair way from our slip but was midway between the slip and the boatyard. We paid a year's rental for this box and for that entire year we had to share it with two other people. At the time we unloaded *Gatti*'s furnishings we had exactly half the box to work with and then only after we had repacked the stuff that was already there. As usual, I was furious and Bill was philosophical, if annoyed. He had a good relationship with Dominic and having access to his office was a valuable commodity. And since we did have room for our things after the repacking, it seemed a small thing to be annoyed about; there were much more important things to be enraged about.

One of these was the legality of the hauling. Our friends the Murphys had taken their boat to Chiavari to have her bottom painted and bow thruster repaired. Because *Antipodes* was U.S. documented, the port put in a call to the *Guardia di Finanza,* who came by and bonded it for a $250 fee. The boat was closed and hauled and the work was done. For an additional fee, the Finance folk came back again and released it when it was put back in the water. This bonding process solves the international problems of a boat being on foreign soil as opposed to foreign waters. It relieves non-European Union owners of paying the 20 percent Value Added Tax (VAT); days out of the water under these circumstances count as days "laid up," which translate into valuable additional days permitted in European waters. We thought we had arranged for the same process.

Bill started *Gatti* up and we turned down the fairway to leave the port and run over to Chiavari. Suddenly Dominic shouted, "No, no! We are having the work done in Lavagna. It is better here." Why does one hire a yacht service if not to provide guidance in conforming to local requirements and locating talent? So we turned back to the Lavagna yard where we were expected and *Gatti* was lifted out on the largest lift, with all due concern for her movement and positioning. We were pleased until Dominic slapped his temporary registration number banner on her and hauled down her flag. What was this? We are a U.S. documented vessel. Where were the *Finanza* people? No need, we were assured. Lavagna was a private port; Chiavari was public.

We were nervous and unhappy the entire 10 days *Gatti* was on land. The carnet problem still haunted us despite all the assurances that it was not important. We knew it was important, and we knew that our boat needed to be bonded when she was on Italian soil. As it was, all we could do was work as fast as we could and pray we would get back in the water before we were detected by the authorities. We were especially concerned at this juncture because some of those EU vessels that had flown U.S. flags illegally were at that very moment impounded in the very yard in which *Gatti* now quivered.

A grueling time had begun. We rented a hotel room near the port, and I am sure the owners tried to keep the other guests preoccupied each evening when we staggered in. We were surely not representative of happy Italians on holiday. Every morning we would get up early and share strong *cappuccino* and *focaccia al Recco* with a crowd of dock workers at a local open air café. Then we would fetch our tools for the day from the box and climb aboard our very hot boat, where we slaved all day without ceasing. At evening we would lock up the tools and drag our filthy selves, bone tired and coated with gray bilge paint, back to the hotel. There we would collapse in a big, welcoming tub, in which we would later wash our clothes. We would then drape them out on the balcony to dry overnight.

And what was this work that left us so grungy and exhausted at day's end? The horror of it almost defies description. While others worked on our shafts and other mechanical work in the lazarette, we cleaned and repainted the bilge. This in itself was not so bad aside from the heat and the small working space. There was even a certain satisfaction to applying the fresh gray bilge paint and leaving formerly mildewed, algaed and unpainted spots glistening like new. But there was no fun around the water tank. The tank was cylindrical and huge. It did not fit through the hatch. It was stoutly secured and affixed by rusty hoops and screws. It weighed a ton. It had not been touched since the boat was constructed in 1952.

For a few days people would arrive, sent over by Dominic. "We are here to remove the water tank." They would climb aboard, take a look, scratch their heads, and leave, never to be seen again. Our frustration and anger grew. Finally one afternoon the floodgates burst. We would have to take the tank out ourselves with what inadequate tools we had. It was obvious the hatch had to be enlarged. With his cordless drill, Bill made a perforated line. With a hacksaw blade he laboriously connected the dots. After hours of this senseless, yet necessary, labor, the wood of the enlarged hatch was lifted out, to all appearances having been gnawed out by a rat of considerable

155

proportions. Bill could not fit below with the tank there and so I, albeit claustrophobic, squeezed myself in. We hammered, sawed and swore at the fittings that held the steel tank firmly in their corroded grips until at last they gave way before our persistence. We then pulled and tugged and chipped away at the muck that held it glued to the bottom. When it at length loosened, we maneuvered it to our enlarged opening, and by late afternoon it was sitting on our aft deck high above the pavement of the boatyard. Bill had gone off on an errand when yet two more Italian young men climbed the ladder and hopped over the rail onto our deck. "We have come to remove the water tank."

"There it is," I said. "Remove it."

They looked so confused that I deigned to add in my best Italian, "We waited and waited and finally my husband and I removed it ourselves." They looked at the huge tank, the hatch and me. Then they looked at each other. Then they got ropes and lowered the tank next to the foot of the ladder far below and left without another word.

Bill returned and looked at the progress in astonishment. I tried again this time in English. "I waited and waited and no one came, so I did it myself."

"You did not," was his matter-of-fact response.

While on the subject of our aft deck, it might be added that our beautiful teak would never fully recover. Workmen in grimy boots came and went and, try as we would, we were not able to fully protect the wood; our "yacht service" people turned a deaf ear of unconcern. This attitude was particularly peculiar because we have never had anyone else in Italy come aboard before they insisted on removing their shoes. This protocol applies to guests as well as workmen.

After the tank removal, the truly awful part of the job began. It was hard to digest the fact that while Jerry had done remarkably fine work on restoring the boat, he had never touched beneath the water tank. There we found 50 years' worth of caked, horrible dirt and debris. It had cemented closed the weep holes in the supports designed to let bilge water flow back to the pump. Of course, Jerry had not installed a pump aft either. Bill's concern was that we would find dry rot and other wooden boat diseases beneath all this corruption. Day after day we crawled down into the cramped hold with spoons, screwdrivers and other tools strong enough to break through the compacted dirt and small enough to shovel it into the containers we carried down with us. It was beastly hot and miserably unpleasant. At times I would be wedged in so tight between beams and ribs that only whimpering aloud provided me the outlet to prevent my going crazy. But gradually we uncovered all the wood. Everything was healthy and firm. We scrubbed and cleaned away the last residue and repainted the entire area with gray bilge paint. It became a joke each time we entered the little hardware-chandler shop across the street. *"Più fume grigio?"* This was the smoke shade of gray we were using. We fortunately completed the job before the stock was depleted.

An interesting aspect of the pulling was that the Navtex suddenly took an interest in life. We couldn't decide if it was the fact that we were perched up high or if stations were just being brought on line. The Toulon station was coming in loud and clear, with messages that were primarily military warnings. However, we did hear from Malta about a suspect vessel that might be carrying illegal immigrants, and we even snared a garbled weather report from Oslo. We were so excited to be getting anything, though, that we kept all the geographical and information areas enabled. We were even tuned in for iceberg warnings. Having once broken its code of silence, the Navtex continued to function in this mode even after we were back at dock.

At last all was completed. We painted our way out of the cabin, leaving the floor a sleek gray, and checked out of the hotel, to the proprietors' immense satisfaction. All the work we had wanted to do was complete. We had been aboard to oversee all the work that was done and were satisfied with it. We had touched or painted almost every inch of wood in the vessel and found her sound. The bottom had been repainted and needed a day or two to dry properly. This bottom paint had caused us a great deal of trouble. *Gatti*'s bottom had been a beautiful shade of deep aqua with an emerald boot top. We wanted the same color, but it seemed a shade not popular with Italians. At last a few cans were found in Chiavari; enough to do the job.

We climbed into our rental car and headed off to France for a respite. We waved to *Gatti* sitting high on her supports with her unique aquamarine paint drying in the hot sun. How sexy she looked out of the water with her sleek architecture on display.

We meandered along the Cote d'Azur, stopping in to visit the stylish ports packed with yachts, and wandered the sun-drenched beaches. We drove into the mountains and stayed in petite hotels in small towns that served delicious dinners. We avoided tourist spots; this was midsummer and the country was bulging with vacationers. We found Paris so cold we had to buy sweat shirts. We relaxed, recuperated and began to feel like human beings again. Then we turned in the car that had proven to be such a godsend for two months and luxuriated on a Eurostar train back to Chiavari. We arrived in port to find *Gatti* snuggled back in G56 between her good pals. Dominic had actually gotten her back in the water and tied down as promised.

CHAPTER XXIII

THE TIDE RISES, THE TIDE FALLS

'There was never anything by wit of man so well devised, or so sure established, which in continuance of time hath not been corrupted.
The Book of Common Prayer, Concerning the Service of the Church

Many things in life appear perfect at first glance, and it is only after familiarity has worn through the shine of newness that flaws appear. Prince Charming may trumpet a deafening snore; the pure white sands of a beach may be alive with sand fleas; a boat that appears perfect may have a water tank that has not been moved for 50 years; a yacht service may be discovered to be serving itself very nicely to the exclusion of its clients. We were increasingly being forced to admit to ourselves that this was the case with Dominic and Angelo.

Dominic had originally opened the office at the port with a franchise to sell Carnavale boats and provide yacht service. Later Angelo had joined him as a partner. Both were in their 30s, married, with children. Both were of small stature and full of vitality. Beyond that, the comparison ended. Dominic was hyperactive – always rushing about, taking cell phone calls on the run, lighting and snuffing cigarettes. He purchased every new gadget to hit the market regardless of expense and was constantly buying and selling expensive automobiles and motorcycles. Seldom at home, he spent his free time gallivanting about the countryside at mega-speeds on enormous Ducatis, clad in fashionable leather gear from top to toe. He was always moaning about the difficulty of keeping food on the family table. He placed this "difficulty" on the trials of the workplace rather than the extravagances of the paterfamilias.

Dominic had such difficulty keeping his mind focused on any one subject for any length of time that more than once I congratulated myself for never having met him in the classroom. For a period of time his interest turned to expensive watches, which he bought, sold and hoarded. While we were never totally satisfied with our arrangements, at the outset the situation was workable. Bill used the office and had fun being there. While many things were not attended to as they should have been, we did get a number of things done, such as acquiring the *passerella* and windlass. The electrical work and yard work were coordinated by the office. But gradually things began to fall apart. Even the Carnavale boat manufacturer withdrew Dominic's franchise. Boat sales became the focus of the office and any pretense of "service" fell by the wayside.

Angelo was a very different sort of man from Dominic. He was a family man, thoughtful and quiet, but also teasing and fun-loving. The father of sons, he happily shared parenting and often had his boys with him. Angelo was calm, patient and intelligent. He was always generous with his time to unravel some bit of Italian grammar for me, and his understanding and ability to explain really impressed this language teacher. He was honest and could not look you in the eye if he were saying anything devious. While in two and a half years we never met Dominic's family, we saw a fair share of Angelo's. Both men had additions to their families during our stay, and we presented them with baby gifts, in addition to always bringing goodies from America on every trip. We always received thank-yous from Angelo's family.

The office itself was a strategically placed end unit. Across from it were the marine store and the Oasis restaurant. It had lots of nice window space, all of which was covered by white sheets. A small entry area sprouted green mildew, and a display of tattered, dirty marine flags hung disconsolately from a line above the doorway. Two long cement flower pots across the front of the entry bloomed fragrantly with cigarette butts. Motorcycles were massed about the door. Within, chaos ruled. Papers and magazines were piled everywhere. When a computer was belatedly introduced, it was initially used to display naked women, and the office became a gathering place for adolescent-minded grown men. This phase passed in time, and Angelo undertook to conquer useful programs. Dominic's interest was passing, since he could not sit still long enough to accomplish much.

Over the time we were there, the physical scene around the office gradually improved. I took charge of the flower pots, and before long this frustrated gardener had them overflowing with spider plants, bright geraniums, and the colorful cyclamen that seem to bloom in Liguria more lushly than any other place on earth. Slowly the public responded and gradually my daily collection of discarded cigarettes diminished. Angelo removed the sheets from one window and with his considerable artistic talent created a very attractive nautical display. He then carved out an office space for himself and became truly adept with the computer. Bill first did digital photography of the boats that were for sale, and before long Angelo was doing this for himself. The entry was painted and the bedraggled flags torn down. But while the physical scene improved, the functioning ability of the office deteriorated.

Besides Dominic and Angelo, there were two other notable characters attached to the office on and off. The first was Pigra, whose function was said to be boat cleaner. This young woman was mortally afraid of falling off boats and seemed to have an abnormal aversion to water in any context. She did air *Gatti* out and dust prior to our arrival on two occasions, but while boats all around us were being washed weekly, ours never was. The other character was a somewhat-beyond-middle aged man named Beppe. He first appeared in the role of sailing instructor but never seemed to get far beyond his early morning cup of brandy or his initial three students. He disappeared for awhile and then reincarnated as a supposed computer expert who would also serve as financial clerk. We were blessedly spared the outcome of this experiment because we were leaving as it began.

Another character we got to know well through the office, although financially unconnected with it, was Giuseppe. Giuseppe at 40 was one of those guys who makes a woman snort derisively in her heart. He thought he was the cat's meow to be sure. He was certainly not a bad looking man and had even at one time been one of the *carabinieri* – a group that surely employs some of the most attractive men on earth. It was probably the conscious tossing of his flowing mane of dark hair, the shirt opened to the navel to reveal gold chains and crucifixes on the bare chest, the tattoos and flashy watches that detracted from his looks. He was well-built and could be charming, but his sexual monomania rendered him obnoxious. He roared about on a black Ducati motorcycle and was, quite predictably, divorced. He was remarkable in two areas. One was his linguistic ability. He had a number of girlfriends during our time in Liguria and each left a definitive, if temporary, mark on him. When he was seeing the

Australian girl, he became fluent in English, which was a nice advantage for us. But when she left and the Majorcan took her place, any vestige of English evaporated and Spanish flourished. Giuseppe's second area of expertise was his craftsmanship. He was a carpenter who specialized in teak decks. He had a passion for perfection and worked very hard at his trade. It would be difficult to find anyone of any age who could build a finer deck than Giuseppe, and he was very kind in helping Bill find wood for various projects and allowing him the use of his tools.

One of the most frustrating things about Dominic's office was the fact that communication was a real problem. Dominic and Angelo knew English fairly well. Dominic spoke it the most fluently, and Angelo could read the language well. I had been studying Italian for some time and was proficient in reading and writing. What I needed was the chance to improve my conversational ability. In the office not only did no one speak to me in Italian, but they spoke the Genovese dialect, which I had a lot of trouble understanding. True, it was not the duty of a yacht service to supply language instruction, but there seemed to be a conscious effort to keep us uninformed. Even after the office got a computer, I would send e-mails in flawless Italian that were never answered.

The fact is that Ligurians in general were not disposed to be helpful linguistically or in culture sharing. When I tried to use my Italian, they would either look uncomprehending or speak in English. This was a surprise because I had never encountered this attitude in other parts of the country. My experience had been that delight and encouragement were shown when I tried to communicate. We had also found that people in other sections of Italy were very proud of their local customs and eager to introduce outsiders to the fun. Every event we attended in Liguria I learned about by reading the local newspaper daily and ferreting out information.

For example, Recco has a giant celebration every year on Sept. 7-8 called the *Sagra del Fuoco*. People flock there from far and near to wolf down the wonderful *focaccia al Recco*, a tasty combination of this specialty bread and cheese, and view the world-class fireworks. Recco is a small town tucked away between the beach and the mountains and, like many of the towns in the area, it has a *torrente*. This is essentially a riverbed that falls from the mountain heights to the sea. In the summer it is bone dry, but during rains and snow melts, it carries vast amounts of water gushing through town. In

September, fireworks are embedded in the dry riverbed from high up the mountain to the sea. When they are ignited, "bombs" explode one after the other all the way down the *torrente*. When the beach is reached, a remarkable fireworks display illuminates the heavens. Some of the most famous pyrotechnic experts in the world are hired to choreograph the display. Dominic lives in Recco and on the day of the big event, we told him with great excitement that we were taking the train up. He looked vague and allowed that he had no idea this was the day of celebration. We knew this was not true since he then let slip that his wife had called and told him the traffic snarls were horrendous. This was only one example of our feeling that we were being left out of the loop somewhere.

In short, before we had shipped *Gatti*, Dominic had promised us he could handle everything. The more time that passed, the less he seemed able to do. We had many needs aboard that were not met. With every trip we made from Italy, we left our boat documents for Dominic to turn over to the *capitaneria*, or port captain who keeps such documents on file. He had not once done so, resulting in our having no paperwork to verify the dates the boat had been laid up. Every trip we had made was tinged with hysteria. One time, the day before we left, Dominic had run up with a form to be filled out and returned at once to the *capitaneria*. We rushed about taking care of it only to find it still on his desk when we returned months later. We were uneasy about the carnet, the illegal pulling, and the lack of documentation that we were there legally. Our yacht service that was being handsomely paid to smooth our way was keeping us in a state of constant anxiety.

Added to the legalities and frustrations with the yacht service were port concerns. When we first arrived, the port appeared big and quite grand to us. It had not taken long for the honeymoon to end and for us to see behind the scenes. The port was 20 years old and had been poorly maintained. Originally it was designed with an upper level of gardens, playgrounds, pools, fountains and a swimming pool from which one could enjoy a sweeping view of the gulf beyond the breakwater. This level was now derelict. Graffiti covered the walls. The empty swimming pool had weathered years of non-use and was barricaded. The pools and fountains were corroded and slimy with algae. The plantings were brambles and weeds. The waters from above leaked down into the storage boxes below.

The *capitaneria* was at the end of our pier. It was a sort of tower painted with horizontal black and white stripes, the upper windows sheathed in mirrored glass. At least a portion remained so sheathed; plywood sheets covered missing panels. We had no idea when they had vanished, whether they had fallen, or who, walking below, might have been taken out.

Many of the docks were barricaded and posted as being unsafe. The one functioning restroom was clean and had lots of hot water, but none of the toilet stalls closed properly. Locks, long gone, had been replaced with chains long since ripped loose. The gremlins of Huntington Harbor had visited Lavagna as well. Only three showers worked and, while this was often no problem for me, in the summer long lines formed. There were no controls to limit bathroom access, and Bill and I both experienced lovers coming in to shower together in both the men's and women's facilities. The bathroom facility at the other end of the port could not be called functional. There was no hot water and the men's toilets were simply holes in the floor. The funny thing was that it was very difficult to get the port office to part with keys for these facilities. We managed to beg one but were refused a second one. It took a month or two for us to discover that they were readily obtainable at the local hardware store for a few *lire*.

The port was bankrupt, and slip owners were charged a huge assessment for repairs. It was only after we had rented our slip for the second year at a sizable rent increase that we were told the owner had not paid his assessment and was not supposed to be using his berth. Dominic one day came rushing up in his typical hyperactive fashion and breathlessly warned us that if anyone should ask, we were friends of Mr. Pollino and had not paid any rental. This was ridiculous; Bill could not even pronounce the man's name, we would not understand the question as it would undoubtedly be posed in Italian, and my ability to answer, let alone lie fluently in any language, would be sorely taxed. We had never met the man or even heard his name before, and we clearly would not be party to Dominic's machinations.

Many owners had opted not to pay the assessment because it was unclear who actually owned the port. The Italian government leases ports to approved parties for agreed upon numbers of years. Lavagna had a 20 year lease which was up, and everyone was confused as to what was to be done next. In the end a new lease seemed to have been obtained by a consortium led by an Italian who lived in Monaco and Miami. "Mafia!" spat out Dominic.

Whoever he was and whatever his connections, the port did begin to improve slightly. It was the new management that had required paperwork detailing our flagging and length of stay, which had rattled Dominic earlier, before one of our departures. Even though the jetties began to be slowly repaired, most of the other activity had no follow-through. Our paperwork was never required from Dominic. The old weeds were pulled out on the upper level of the port and thousands of bright flowers planted. However, since no watering system was installed, they lived but two happy weeks. A convenient Bancomat, or ATM, was installed in the outer corner of the *capitaneria*, but no eye was cast up to the impending crashes from the upper levels. A lady was installed at a small table shaded by an umbrella outside the restroom door. A basket for tips was on the table. I suppose she did cut down on the number of intimate showers and dog baths, but no investment was made beyond the front door.

In mid June the Murphys sailed to the island of Sardegna for a stay. We took one of those Moby Dick ferries I had seen in Livorno over to the port of Olbia, along with a little rental car. We drove down the coast to the charming port of Ottiolu, where *Antipodes* was berthed. We were enchanted by the place and asked the port captain to look into the possibility of our wintering there. The office staff researched the documentation problem for us and concluded that we would need the paperwork we lacked in order to stay there. We needed documented proof that we had been laid up the requisite number of months since our entry into Italian waters. The only written documentation we had was the carnet, which showed our arrival on Thanksgiving Day, 1999. We headed back to Lavagna frustrated and angry; a few days later the Murphys sailed to Rome.

When we had first arrived in Italy, one day I had been leafing through the glossy boating magazines in Dominic's office. I saw an ad for a new port that was being constructed in Ostia, not far from where the old Roman ports of Claudius and Trajan had been located. The artist's conception lay before me in full color, and I fell in love. At the bottom of the page was an Internet address. Bill had tried to contact the address several times in the intervening months without success. I commissioned the Murphys to see what they could learn. They had no sooner arrived in Rome than we received an e-mail – "We are at the new Porto Turistico di Roma at Ostia. There is a man here at Terzi Yachting who has resolved our documentation. We are legal for one year." Information for contacting this magical place followed. But we wanted more than long-distance contacts. We still had the car, so we hopped in and headed for Rome on June 27, 2001.

As usual, our impulsiveness reduced the opportunities to get much done. The Murphys were gone for the day, but *Antipodes* looked right at home in the harbor. Terzi Yachting was not yet open, but the port was there in all its splendor. We hurried down to the port office, where two attractive and enthusiastic female employees loaded us on to an electric cart and took us on a tour. What a fabulous place! The port area was brand new, and the development company had a 50-year lease. Everything was fresh and gleaming and deserted. There were maybe four boats on the side of the harbor designed for big boats, although a fair number of smaller craft lay at dock on the other side. Most of the shops, cafés and offices on the wharf had not yet opened, but colorful signs gave notice of the tenants and opening dates.

By the time our tour was completed, the Terzi office had opened. It was being manned by Mrs. Terzi and her teen-age son Gianluca. The office was spacious, bright and orderly. A white rug lay before the big wood desk and Gaugain-inspired art work enlivened the fresh white walls. A copy of *Moby Dick* lay on a second desk along a far wall. Polished wood floors glowed warmly and thriving potted plants enjoyed the light through sparkling glass windows and door. We were offered refreshments from the espresso machine and refrigerator located in a back room. Gianluca spoke more English than his mother, and we were able to ascertain that this office could indeed handle any paperwork that was needed. This entire visit was very exciting. In the first place, Paola Terzi and I liked one another at once and we could have predicted right then that we would become good friends. In addition, both mother and son understood my Italian and encouraged me to express my thoughts. They did not laugh or even smile at my many errors. They acted as though everything I said made perfect sense. I felt tremendously pleased that my language studies had not been as useless as I had come to feel further north.

We left Rome and stopped near Siena to visit hot springs that we had discovered during the summer of port hunting. Terme di Petriolo, improbably located in the middle of a forest, is reached by a winding country road. We soaked and dreamed and planned. I was hooked. What I wanted more than anything else on earth was to own my very own slip within easy reach of my favorite city. The stock market was still paying good returns, and Bill set his mind to figuring the best way to come up with the $87,000. Since the purchase price was stated in *lire*, the sum sounded even more awesomely high – 157,000,000 *lire* before the 20 percent VAT tax. My check would have read *centocinquantasettemilionilire*.

After much soul-searching, and begging combined with cool calculation and research, we decided buying a slip would be a good investment. We had British friends who owned a slip in Spain, and they were convinced that buying water in the Mediterranean was the best investment that could have been made in recent years. Their slip had appreciated dramatically, and the fact that Mr. Pollino's rental had reflected this climb, gave our desire a good financial rationale. In addition, a continued rental was not at all assured. Despite its dilapidated state, the Port of Lavagna was packed to the gills. Abetted by all these convincing arguments, we began to try to contact the Port of Rome in earnest. And yet we tried without success. We called; we e-mailed; we faxed. No response. Finally we e-mailed the Terzis. Could they arrange the sale? Since that is their business, they were able to do so quite handily.

On July 10 we took a break from the bilge work in which we were still engaged, and returned to Rome, where we met Alberto Terzi and his employee Mario. They could indeed handle the slip purchase as well as supply us with appropriate documentation on our arrival. We returned to Liguria and continued the work that we felt was necessary to get *Gatti* to Rome in good shape. The Port of Rome would before long have a good boatyard, but it was as yet incomplete. So even though our toils with the water tank and associated problems were long and arduous, we had exciting prospects to keep us motivated.

CHAPTER XXIV

HALCYON DAYS OF SUMMER

'Believe me, my young friend, there is
nothing – absolutely nothing – half so
worth doing as simply messing about in boats.'
Kenneth Graham, *The Wind in the Willows*

The months of July and August 2001 were packed with work, fun, and big plans. Throughout the year many events are staged by the small seaside towns, particularly during the summer. From the Fish Festival the second Sunday in May in Camogli when an enormous pan, 14 feet in diameter, is heated on the beach and fried fish is provided free to all comers to the Fire Festival in Recco in early September, many delightful diversions occur everywhere in the area. We enjoyed frequent fireworks displays and concerts in the cool evenings after the hot main star of the day had closed his burning eye.

The days that spanned our return from our Portofino July 4 celebration to July 20, when we pulled the boat, were halcyon days at the port – days so full of relaxation, enjoyment and companionship that one wished they would never end. Most of the boats were now occupied by happy people – mostly Italians – on holiday. The grocery shelves were routinely bare and every café and restaurant in town bulged with diners who poured out of the doors and on to the streets. Here tables and umbrellas were set up behind hastily erected barricades of terracotta planters, overflowing with geraniums or potted with shrubs, wound all around with tiny white fairy lights. Flower bouquets hung on the walls beside each shop door and lines of people craving hot *farinata* or cool *gelati* twisted down the *caruggi*. These narrow little alleyways have served as streets since medieval days, during which time they simplified the dumping of hot oil on invaders' heads. Tiny balconies come very close to touching one another's railings high above the middle of the street in some areas of this warren. But now there was no need of oil other than perhaps the dozens of varieties of suntan oils that can be found along the Italian Riviera or one of the hundreds of varieties of olive oil. Now the balconies served only as strategic sites for viewing the fun. Chatter, laughter and music filled the warm, languid nights. All the hotels, so dismal and shuttered during the winter, were now full to bursting.

Many of these vacationers came to Lavagna not for the port but for the long beach that stretches south to the little town of Cavi, midway between Lavagna and Sestri Levante. On every available spot of rock or deck, sun worshippers lay, their bodies almost visibly bronzing. On every available spot of sand, a lounge was erected, with a color-coordinated umbrella sprouting next to it. The wild, windswept beaches we knew had been tamed and regimented. Every section had become a small business empire. Signs such as *Fantasma* or some equally exotic name popped up; ropes delineated the business boundaries. On the streetside, long rows of little cabins had been put up for changing, cooling off, showering and snoozing during the mandatory rest of the early afternoon hours. Between these structures and the sea the brightly colored lounges were laid out as closely together as possible. They are rented by the hour, day, week or however much lucky time you have. There are also sections of free beach, but these are obviously not as desirable as having your own reserved spot in the midst of a city of people.

There was never a dull day or night the entire month of July. A miniature train track was laid out at the port and squealing children rode 'round and 'round while indulgent parents waved from the sidelines. The weather was blissful, with warm days and very cool evenings. *Rachele*'s people arrived and stayed on board; *Bo Drum*'s people were frequent visitors. The couple across from us moved aboard with their mammoth shaggy black Newfoundland. He relaxed under a little umbrella on dock by day and clambered clumsily over his *passerella* to fill up the cabin by night. A young British couple had moved their brand new Azimut boat three slips down from us. An American couple in a unique sailboat designed on the plans of a Chesapeake Bay schooner arrived.

These pleasant additions translated into dinners and shopping with English speakers and cool wines and creative *antipasti* on various decks. We discovered the wine shop in Chiavari had concealed in a back room huge vats of various local wines which could be purchased at ridiculously low prices – bring your own bottle or place a deposit on one of theirs for 500 lire. We discovered that the legendary July sales in Rome were also legendary July sales in Genova. During these days it would have been hard to imagine that clouds were forming below the horizon or that evil was being plotted anywhere.

We came back to Lavagna from our French holiday the second week of August to an altered port. It was deserted! Gone was the shaggy dog and his floating home, *Mirande*. Gone was the elderly gentleman who had so patiently untangled my fingers and instructed us in knots, gone with his wife in *Hoka Hey*. Gone were even *Rachele* and *Bo Drum*. The colorful umbrellas had been withdrawn from the streets. The few restaurants that remained open refused to fire up their pizza ovens before 8 p.m. if they could be induced to do so at all. *Ferragosto* had struck and brought along with it, its own special sweetness. The south end of town was bustling still with beachgoers and the hotels were full, but the port looked like a downtown parking garage at 7 p.m.

Ferragosto, August 15, marks the important religious holiday of the Assumption of Mary as well as the first real day of summer vacation. It is one thing to spend a few days or a weekend at the beach. *Ferragosto* is something else entirely. Most Italians have a month of vacation and receive a special paycheck before the big day. Every year they hit the roads in enormous numbers, cluttering the *autostrade* and killing great numbers of themselves in the rush to get to holiday spots. These spots are the mountains, the coast, or the boat. The boats leave for the islands primarily – Sardegna, Corsica, Capri, the Arcipelago Toscano, Ischia, Ponza, and the other idyllic havens that dot the waters around the peninsula. Families and friends generally go to the same spots year after year, where they relax, resolve international as well as national political problems, and catch up on gossip.

Those few of us who remained on our boats in port enjoyed the open water around us. A couple we assumed had just bought their boat, *Caroline,* was moored five slips down and across the jetty from us. Every day they maneuvered out to sea in a most amateur fashion, and every evening when they returned we helped to catch them and get them tied up. This was a very rewarding ritual for us. We were amused; we learned a lot by their mistakes; we followed their steady improvement; we were the lucky recipients of their tasty homemade

171

wine. We loaned utensils and tools back and forth and became real back-porch neighbors.

We gradually got our belongings moved out of the storage shed and back on board. How nice it was to tuck extra anchors and canvas down in our glossy fresh gray bilge. We had purchased Thermapeutic mattresses for our bunks and took advantage of the terrific sales in Genova to dress them smartly in Frette linens. We had bought a tiny washing machine that we set up down below in the lazerette. Laundry had been a very expensive item for us because there were no self-service coin laundries in all of Lavagna. We had to hike the long way across the bridge to Chiavari with our wash to a laundry where it was done for us, and we paid dearly for the service. Seasoned boaters who came to the port assured us that this was a unique situation, but we thought the washing machine would pay for itself in convenience as well as outlay over time, even when we were in other locations. The Candy was a little wonder that heated its own water and did an admirable job on the clothes. It did an admirable job as well of developing our upper body muscles as its energetic centrifuge required a strong presence to hold it in place.

August 14 found us enjoying Lavagna's big annual festivity like old timers. We had attended the celebration of the Fieschi wedding the year before with Nicole and Ciarán, but we had not understood the event well and thus had missed out on much of the fun. In 1200 A.D. two great houses had been united in the marriage of Bianca de' Bianchi and Opizzo Fieschi, and the event had been celebrated with an enormous cake that required 18,000 eggs in its recipe and fed hundreds of the common folk. Each anniversary the event is commemorated with a huge medieval display and reenactments. Parades fill the streets with music, marching, flag hurling, and authentic costume. Pitch-fired torches blaze in the ancient iron rings set in the massive stone walls of buildings (so that is what they are for!) and luridly light the tiny cobblestone *caruggi*. A "bride" and "groom" are elected from the young and beautiful of the region to rule over the festivities and ride on horseback side by side in their fabulous wedding clothes. A giant cake is no longer baked, but lines form everywhere to purchase pieces of the delectable specialty pastry.

Most fun of all are the tickets sold in advance of the big party. Pink and blue tickets are sold to the appropriate genders. On the tickets are various pictures, symbols, numbers and such. One blue and one pink ticket bearing identical symbols are printed. The night of the party, one pins on the ticket and wanders through the merriment looking for a "match." We understand that many friends are made in this way and that even weddings have resulted. Many young people sported several tickets in the hope of improving their odds. This year we understood the event better and scouted out good seats long before the parade began. It was easy to imagine, sitting by the great carved *ardesia* church doors with the ancient bell tolling above us and costumed people playing medieval instruments around us, that we were actually waiting for the original Fieschi wedding party to arrive.

Later in the month we went to Rome by train and with the help of Alberto Terzi and Mario, we put a 20 percent deposit on our slip. This wonderful chore was right up there with making a selection in a gelato shop. Here was a brand new port, sparkling clean, its long docks with their modern electrical and water connections practically empty. The elegant little shops were still not open, but now stock was being arranged behind gleaming windows.

We sat in the sun outside the Maremosso Café and weighed the delightful options. We could essentially choose any slip we wanted in the fifteen meter section. Should we be close to the wharf or at the end? Should our aft deck face the rising or setting sun? Did we want to be on "O" dock and enjoy the activities of a restaurant or did we want to be as quiet as possible? In the end we elected to buy the next-to-the-end slip on "P" dock. "P" is the longest dock in the marina and afforded us a view of the fairway, a straight visual shot through the harbor entrance, and a glimpse of the Tyrrhenian Sea beyond. Since in Lavagna we had not been able to see the sea for the height of the breakwater, this seemed to be a desirable feature. The pier was "T" shaped, so that the very end slip had a concrete jetty running down the starboard side of a docked vessel. While this would be convenient for maintaining *Gatti*'s never-ending, demanding brightwork, the view from my bunk would not be ideal. In addition, there was a slip that ran along the outside of the "T" at which a really big yacht could tie up and overshadow us. The other advantage to our selection was that the water and power box that served both slips was behind this end slip rather than ours. Having it directly behind us would have made ingress, egress and docking more difficult. We had already encountered enough difficulties with our *passerella* without adding more problems. The fire extinguisher was three slips down as was a handy ladder going down to dinghy level. The rising sun would pour through our fore hatch, and we would dine aft in the evening with the setting sun.

This momentous decision having been made, we got down to planning. We would move *Gatti* Sept. 15. Nicole and Ciarán scheduled a two-week vacation around this plan, with stop-overs at Portovenere, Elba and Porto Ercole on our way down. We could finally visit by sea all those enticing ports we had investigated by land three years earlier. In January, when our tax picture was more advantageous, we would complete the slip purchase. We would not be charged rent and Terzi Yachting would care for *Gatti* for about half of what Dominic had charged when we were absent, and nothing when we were aboard. Many of the slips had already been sold, but very few boats were in residence yet. When the port was full, which would undoubtedly occur before very long, we could lease out our slip when we were out exploring. We hoped to do a lot more sailing in the calmer waters of the central Tyrrhenian Sea than we had been able to manage in the unpredictable and often violent Ligurian Sea.

Another thing we really liked were the dock workers or *ormeggiatori*. We were familiar with these people in Lavagna but had never quite understood their job. They were obviously port employees, always around the docks checking on security and helping out in bad weather. Many mariners called them by radio when they were approaching their berths to help with the treacheries of mooring. We didn't know if there was a charge for this service or not. Several *ormeggiatori* at this port ran about in new white inflatables and hung out amiably at the Maremosso. When a boat came in, the tower called them, told them what slip to go to, and there they were waiting when the vessel arrived. Another inflatable would roar away to the harbor entrance and lead the vessel to the appropriate berth. We watched them work with a very long sailboat that was battling a strong offshore wind. Docking was complicated further by the fact that there were no other boats docked nearby to help hold the craft in place. But the cheerful young men hopped on at the stern to secure lines, while others nudged her bow with the inflatable. We could live with this kind of help. We approved enthusiastically of everything we saw.

We went back to *Gatti* to relax until our family arrived. The only perceptible difference from the earlier days of summer was that Dominic had grown distant. He did not approve of Rome or Romans, or anything not Ligurian for that matter, and he certainly did not relish losing clients who had caused so little trouble. He dourly warned us of crafty Romans and scheming thieves. But we paid no attention to his negativity, and the days flowed smoothly by. We were drawing to the end of our Ligurian stay and savored everything around us with that sharpened sense of appreciation one feels when he knows that a well-loved place is being left behind.

CHAPTER XXV

SEPTEMBER 11, 2001
DISASTER AT HOME AND ABROAD

'Turning and turning in the widening gyre
The falcon cannot hear the falconer;
Things fall apart; the centre cannot hold;
Mere anarchy is loosed upon the world,
The blood-dimmed tide is loosed, and everywhere
The ceremony of innocence is drowned;
The best lack all conviction, while the worst
Are full of passionate intensity.'
William Butler Yeats, *The Second Coming*

The morning of Sept. 11, 2001 broke in dazzling splendor. It was a day promising unlimited possibilities and was especially exciting because we were driving to Milan to pick up our daughter and son-in-law. After Nicole's graduation from law school in New York, Ciarán had been accepted into the MBA program at Stanford, so this trip they were coming from California via New York. We certainly remembered well how tiring that jet lag could be. They had a two-week vacation and, surely, during that time we would have seas calm enough to get *Gatti* to her new slip in Ostia and still have lots of time to play and explore along the way.

We arrived at Malpensa, the airport outside of Milan, predictably early, as though our eager anticipation could move a plane along more rapidly. The flight was equally predictably late. We sat at the airport Autogrille drinking cappuccino, willing the plane in, and idly listening to two American couples seated nearby who were awaiting their departure. At least to the male members, this visit to Italy had been less than pleasurable. They alternately played and threw down again a hand-held electronic game and swore at the time, creeping by as slowly as the Italian approach to life. Obviously their flight had also been delayed, and they had learned nothing about relaxation during their vacation.

But time does move even when it seems otherwise, and it was not long before we were collecting our family and heading south to the port. They chatted in the car about their new job, studies, and California lifestyle. They had changed planes in Newark, not so far from their old apartment in Brooklyn. With great nostalgia they noted how beautiful New York was from the air, how majestic were the Twin Towers, near which they both had worked, how much they missed the Big Apple and hoped to perhaps return there to live and work one day. The trip to Lavagna went quickly and happily, and we arrived at *Gatti* shortly after 1 p.m. The port was quiet except for locals eating and chatting at the Albatross and Oasis restaurants. The sun was bright and warm and *Gatti* swayed gently to a soft swell. We stretched out on teak lounges on the aft deck with chilled local Vermentino wine, utterly contented.

At 2:30 Dominic's hysterical voice broke our serenity. Dominic is hyperactive even by Italian standards, and we were not greatly alarmed to see him running down the jetty shouting demonically. "Bad news! Bad news!" he burst out breathlessly as he bounded over the *passerella*. Okay, Dominic, what is being overblown this time? The blackwater tank won't be done on time? By now he was catching his breath and looking very much like a bird that has flown unexpectedly into a glass window. It was as though some celestial probe were sucking all the English he knew out of the top of his head. "America is at war! New York and the Pentagon are attacked!" Like so many millions of people at that awful time, none of this news immediately sank in. It was the assassination of JFK all over again. We could feel those stupid smiles spreading across our faces. What was wrong with this crazy Italian? But Dominic's distress was all too real. "Come over to the Oasis. We have a T.V." Then he leaped back on the dock and ran off.

Ciarán called his politically astute mom in Dublin while we pulled in the BBC on our shortwave radio. Slowly the awful truth took focus and our daughter dissolved in tears. I was the first to arrive at the Oasis, where everyone in port had gathered. Grouped at the tables were all the people we knew from other encounters – the *ormeggiatori*, waitresses, café owner, mechanics. No one spoke: All eyes were glued in disbelief to the horror unfolding live before our eyes. I was greeted with a quiet respect and solicitousness that were very moving. A place was cleared for me before the big-screen T.V. English subtitles were turned on. I watched the second tower slowly slide into the billowing clouds of smoke and debris. The Italian commentator's voice was tearful as he cried out again and again, "*Non esistono più! Non esistono più!*" (They are no more!)

Before long, the four of us sat among our Italian friends, all of us stultified before the repeated images of jet airliners making wide and deadly curves, collapsing towers, burning buildings and cheering Middle Eastern people that flashed before us. Who could these people be, and why were they so joyous in the face of such destruction? The Italians in the bar before long began putting these horrifying events into a local perspective. One could not truly expect an Italian to be stunned mute for long. "We have the military at Pisa and La Spezia. NATO is very close to us. What if they attack us next?" No one knew who had attacked or why, if the conspiracy were world wide or no, from what quarter the next horror would be reported. All we knew for sure was that the world had taken a nightmarish turn. American airspace had been shut down, and who could begin to predict the future when the brain could not even digest the present? My mind wandered off to one of those byways brains follow when the mental load becomes too weighty. I wondered where those malcontent Americans from the Malpensa airport had been diverted. For sure they would not be back in America this night.

Our next few days unfolded in similar fashion to those of people around the globe. The sea had become as stormy and uncertain as the political scene, and we sat at dock, gleaning what news we could from our radio. Our compatriots back at home on American soil seemed to be traumatized in such a profound way that no one was really able to support anyone except by sharing mingled griefs and fears. The nation and all of its citizens were reeling.

We fared somewhat better by being in a land that had been physically untouched by this particular act of terror but was well acquainted with terrorism. The people of Italy also have hearts and sympathies that know no limits. We tied a black veil to our flagstaff and many Italians, even those we had not seen before, made the long walk down the jetty to inquire after our family and friends and express their condolences. Our American friends at the port returned from a trip to Rome and Sicily to find a bouquet of flowers on the stern of their sailboat. In a way we had a mother's comforting love around us. The Italians grieved, but they had not been damaged as

179

Americans had. Not knowing what to do with their grief, they tended gently to the Americans in their midst. Even the restaurant owners sent us home after dinner with little goodies – a loaf of bread or a bottle of wine. These many little kindnesses balanced us and gave us a security far from home that exceeded any that was being found at home.

Nicole and Ciarán spent a lot of time on the computer. Their friends in New York sent out e-mails letting people know they were all right. A young couple honeymooning in Italy wondered when they would ever get home and how their funds were going to hold up. Slowly we started functioning mentally again and making plans. We were more eager than ever to get to Rome, and the weather seemed to be improving. If nothing else, we had to do something productive and keep ourselves busy. On Saturday, Sept. 14, we had dozens of bottles of our favorite mineral water delivered to the boat, and we laid in the necessary supplies. We planned to leave the next morning for the first leg of our 200-mile trip.

Sunday dawned with weather not great by any standard but passable for the Ligurian Sea. We checked in with Dominic's office. Angelo had made reservations for us at the charming port of Portovenere, and the port personnel had agreed at both locations that the weather was improving and would get better and better as we sailed south. Portovenere, at the opening of the Gulf of Poets on the south side of The Cinque Terre, represented a cruise of about 30 miles along the magnificent coastline. And so we set sail. This time we pulled in our heavy spring lines. We did not intend to return to G56. We waved gleefully to our staunch neighbors *Rachele* and *Bo Drum,* only recently returned from their month-long August vacations. I pranced happily about the deck as we headed out of the port we had called home for so long.

Out of the harbor we found the waters in the Gulf of Tigullio to be rough enough, but after passing the point at Sestri Levante, the waves grew larger and routinely broke over the bow. There was a strong naval presence out here in the Ligurian Sea, which did little to comfort us. Were terrorists about to attack here too? We had bumped and crashed our way through this unpleasant sea for about 10 miles when I went below to set things in order. The drawers below our bunks had uncharacteristically worked their way out. But what I discovered in the cabin was every boater's nightmare. Water was pouring in at our starboard bow. Ciarán left his post following our

180

track on the colorful plotter and also came below. He then gravely went to get Bill.

While we inspected and discussed our problem, a voice came over our radio. There was a large Italian naval vessel a couple miles out to our starboard with two or three sailboats frolicking fairly close to it. This ship requested in Italian and English that the vessel at such and such a position tune to channel seven. Here we were taking on water, the radio was barking out a demand, and I stupidly had no idea of our position or if we were the vessel being identified. I turned to the plotter to obtain this information and, horror of horrors, our colorful Ligurian coast with the bright blue track we had been laying down as we traveled to our first waypoint was now the gray land mass of Labrador, and we were leaving a black track over dry land. This was all too much for me. Our bilge pumps were doing a great job, but we had no idea what had happened to us. There really was no choice aside from returning to Lavagna. In this situation I recognized concretely for the first time how lack of experience can lead to panic and panic to tragedy. I resolved that I would not go to sea again until I was much more competent. But there were cooler and more experienced seamen aboard than I, and we turned back north. Once we had turned, the waves were with us and much less water came in. We reentered our harbor and tied up ruefully back at G56.

The damage to *Gatti* was this. We had struck something in the water, which had torn off six feet of the plank along the chine on our starboard side and done some minor damage to the hull on the port side. When the boat was at rest, she did not leak but moving forward she scooped in the sea. If she were on plane, no water came in. The world seemed so turned on its ear that we almost believed we had been targeted by terrorists or had rammed an Italian submarine. What had NATO done to our GPS that it showed we were in Labrador even now when we were back at dock? In any event, there was nothing to do but to pull poor *Gatti* yet again and repair the damage.

We had to pull her at Lavagna this time because we did not want to leave the harbor. The pulling was a nightmare. Dominic refused to call the *Finanza* people again, and she was lifted out with a small crane rather than the large one we had used before. A ghastly cracking sound echoed from her hull as she was lifted from the water. She was propped up right next to where boats were pulled out and returned to the water, so that the entire time there was work going on only inches from us and boats being swung all around us.

Dominic again insisted that since this was a private port, his registration number would legalize *Gatti*. However, the fact that he taped over her name and hailing port defied all this gibberish.

Then there was the issue of insurance. In retrospect maybe we should have paid for the repair ourselves and let insurance do what it would. We needed four estimates, and the insurance company set up two of them for us with *cantieri* at the port. Once the specter of insurance showed itself, our status at the port changed. Dominic suddenly became very conscious of money versus service and friendship. He pushed a carpenter who was his friend and had done a little work for us in the past. Another carpenter came down from Carasco, a mountain town above Chiavari, to present his opinion and bid. The *cantieri* at the port were good places, but the close relationships of people living in a small town made any bidding an exercise in futility. Everyone knew what everyone else was offering, and everyone was bidding high because of the insurance aspect. We were especially impressed with one of the *cantieri*. The gentleman at this boatwork was very kind to us and saw to it that supports under the boat that had been carelessly and incorrectly placed were adjusted. He advised us to store *Gatti* for the winter in his well-equipped indoor facility. We could return to America and get our thoughts and nerves in order. His establishment would do expert work and in May she could go back in the water and head for Rome.

We had had to lease G56 through May, and Dominic had promised that he would sublet it after we went to Rome and return our rental. If he did this, the storage at the *cantiere* would not have cost more than we had already laid out. In fact, Dominic already had a boat he had just sold set up in our G56. We were ready to have *Gatti* put in this *cantiere* until Dominic's incompetence landed us in trouble again. She had been illegally pulled and could not be taken into the shop under such conditions. She would have to be put back in the water if for only an hour. The *Finanza* people would be called, and they would bond the boat. She would then be lifted again and work begun. This was more than either the boat or we could take, and so we agreed to have Dominic's friend, Mr. Bucaccio, do the work. With the insurance appraiser, we showed him exactly what was to be done and what materials were to be used; all the details were outlined in a written contract.

Despite all this confusion, we tried to make a decent vacation for Nicole and Ciarán, who had arranged to be in Italy for two weeks and could not return to the United States yet had they wanted to. We rented a car and went exploring. We had a good time roaming through Italy, but we were very conscious that we were homeless nomads. The trip was surreal, and when we found ourselves in a good authentic Mexican restaurant in the heart of Bologna, we indulged freely in margaritas. Nothing seemed weird any more.

When the young folks left, we drove back to the boat and lived aboard while the final negotiations were worked out for repair and the actual work began. Unlike our experience in Marina del Rey, we were not supposed to be living on board. Each night a security truck would drive through and beam lights around the area. The first night we hunkered down in our bunks and wakened early so we could get to the restrooms before workers arrived and spotted us. Just before sunrise we peered over our gunwale and prepared to make our descent. This same maneuver seemed to be reflected on half the boats in the yard. Heads poked up furtively and feet swung noiselessly over railings, seeking a foothold on ladder rungs. Not a word was spoken or a sound made as the ship rats scurried to the ground and dispersed into the predawn dark. No, this was all very, very far from the advice we had received in the retirement seminar.

CHAPTER XXVI

TO AND FRO

'Many a green isle needs must be
In the deep wide sea of misery,
Or the mariner, worn and wan,
Never thus could voyage on.'
Percy Bysshe Shelley, *Lines Written Amongst
the Euganean Hills*

In early October we headed back to Florida via New York. Like many other Americans abroad, we felt at a loss. We had no concern for our safety but our families were concerned for us, and our Italian home was once again illegally in the Lavagna shipyard. Too much had happened in too short a time, and we felt awash. Would the tide ever turn in our favor again? It felt as though the earth were deluged and the whole world as we had known it destroyed. Would there ever be a rainbow and a dove for us or anyone else?

Our plane was almost empty, and everyone had a chance to stretch out over unoccupied seats to sleep during the long flight. There was no happy chatter such as one generally hears on planes to and from Italy. As we approached New York, there was no sound other than the muffled roar of the engines. Past the New York skyline, down the runway at Newark airport, not a syllable was breathed. Noses were pressed to windows, eyes were moist with tears. On another continent lay our injured boat and brand new empty slip. On this continent lay a country wounded and confused. As we continued on to Florida and our condominium door, surrounded everywhere by American flags and posted slogans, my mind drifted again and again to Antony's warning to Octavius in Shakespeare's *Julius Caesar* – "This is a mourning Rome. This is a dangerous Rome."

It was hard to settle down in Florida, even though we were exhausted. The extreme nationalism, the imminence of war, the nightly television news of gloom and doom were distressing. We went to California to check in with doctors and visit our children and friends. We brought Jerry up to date on *Gatti* and admired the progress he was making on *Joie,* his new old boat. We visited with Doug and had dinner with Paul. Doug had gathered up some goodies for *Gatti* including a 10-pound zinc plate which we had been unable to locate in Italy. Zinc is used as a sacrificial metal on boat hulls and propellers to protect them from corrosion in the water and while it is used on boats everywhere, we had not been able to find the size we preferred. Doug had suffered a dreadful recurrence of cancer, and his long, wavy blond hair had fallen out. Not to be outdone though, this irrepressible man had donned a baseball cap with his pony tail attached behind. We had a wonderful visit with no intimation of the truly awful time he had had or the surgeries and pain that lay just ahead of him. In short, this was to be the last time we would see this remarkable, caring human being. His tide ebbed well before its time. But all this was unknown to us at the time and would probably have been more than we could bear.

We visited Nicole in Palo Alto and Charles in Sacramento. Charles decided to relocate in Florida and we returned East with a focus at last. We rented a house for him, Bill flew out and helped him drive cross-country, and on Christmas Eve we celebrated his settling in. Nicole was spending Christmas in Dublin but thought it would be fun to celebrate New Year's Eve in Rome. Now, there was the first happy thought that had crossed our minds in many weeks.

I sent an e-mail to Mario in Alberto Terzi's office. Lo and behold! We got a response. This was the first successful communication between the United States and Italy we had ever had. It is true that we had spoken to Dominic a time or two by telephone, but he had e-mailed us only once and his written Italian was awful. This time we received a return communication couched in such elegant Italian that it brought tears to the eyes of my new Florida tutor. "This is an educated man. This is a very good person!" Mario's news was as welcome as his laudable syntax. He could arrange for a very nice apartment at a reasonable price in Trastevere near his own apartment. Trastevere has always been a favorite quarter of Rome for us, and we decided to rent the place for a week.

We spent Christmas in Florida with our newly settled in son and other family and then boarded yet another plane back to Italy. We had taken our Italian cell phone to Florida with us, and we reactivated it on the train between the airport and the Trastevere station. Our daughter answered the phone. *"Ciao, bella!"* How good it was to hear her, happy in this wonderful place. We arrived and found her comfortably ensconced in a cozy, warm apartment overlooking one of the narrow streets of the quarter through a mass of cheerful cyclamen potted on the windowsill. No sooner were we settled in than Mario came to see us with Paola and Alberto in tow. Nicole and Ciarán had been here for two days and Mario had seen to all their comforts. Now it was our turn as well. We were presented with wine, champagne (our favorite Veuve Cliquot!), beans, sausage and a towering panettone cake – all the ingredients necessary to create a true Roman New Year's feast. Despite the gifts we had always taken to Dominic and Angelo, they had never given us a gift in return.

We were overwhelmed with the kindness of these new friends. New Year's Eve found us again in Piazza del Popolo under magical fireworks and fountains of frothing champagne. The world was beginning to feel more comforting. How many, many centuries had this very piazza seen wars and celebrations come and go? And yet it remained a constant, surviving the worst that humans could devise. Maybe the troubles of the last year could really be behind us, and we could look forward again hopefully.

On Jan. 1 we made our first withdrawal of brand new euros. We would in some ways miss the old *lire* with their pictures of famous Italians. I had always been impressed that an educator, Maria Montessori, was featured on a bill. Other denominations recognized giants in the arts and sciences in addition to the politicians we have come to expect on our own currency. But the designs on the euros had been well thought out; the bills were clean and new and the conversion so easy. All the money was crisp, uncirculated, and of lovely different colors; it gave us the feeling of being players in an international Monopoly game.

The children returned to the States via Dublin, and Bill and I went down to the Port of Rome to discuss paying the balance on our slip. Our lawyer had been in communication with Alberto, and it seemed better for us not to close the transaction for another couple months, until the port had complete clearance from the Italian government. So instead of writing a check, we were driven to the Terzi home for an elaborate *pranzo*. Alberto and Paola, their son Gianluca, Mario, Eraldo, who works in the Terzi office, and his wife and daughter all sat with us around the long table. Course after delicious course was served, and we were accorded all the benefits and attentions of guests of honor. We toured the beautiful home and yard and, when we met the five cats, we knew we had serendipitously stumbled upon kindred spirits. This was our first meal in an Italian home, and we felt very special. The openness, warmth and friendliness were in stark contrast to our Ligurian experience. These were people who had opened their home to us, not the conniving, underhanded folk the Ligurians had warned of so darkly. Despite the language difficulty, we really had no trouble communicating and had lots of fun in the process.

After this remarkable dinner, we took the train up to Lavagna and collapsed in our boat, which had been returned to G56 only days before our arrival. She was warm and dry. The bilge pumps never came on, and the repairs appeared to have been done well. We visited our insurance agent in Genova. Luigi was concerned about the quality of the work. He had purposely looked Dominic up at the big international boat show in Genova in November and had not been impressed. Whatever had transpired between them had made Luigi very skeptical. We paid Dominic in full for the work. Because he had insisted on pulling the boat under his registration number, we had to pay the 20 percent VAT tax on an already greatly inflated repair cost and an inordinately long stay in the boatyard. Our slip had been "sublet" during this time, but Dominic was not yet ready to give us that money. He reminded us that we had leased the slip through May, and there would be more money due to us, depending on when we moved to Rome.

As fate would have it, January weather was remarkably good. "Let's go to Rome tomorrow morning," Angelo suggested, adding that he was free to go along with us. That was terrific news. We gassed up and prepared for departure. We were actually going to leave Liguria behind. We would no longer be at the mercy of Mr. Pollino and his climbing rents. We would no longer be buffeted by the winds and rains of that fickle sea. We would be near Rome, the city we had wanted to live in 12 years earlier. Equally exciting was the fact that we would have a friend along who knew the waters and was fun to be with.

CHAPTER XXVII

ARRIVADERCI, LAVAGNA
JANUARY 18, 2002

'Once more upon the waters! Yet once more!
And the waves bound beneath me as a steed
That knows his rider.
Lord Byron, *Childe Harold's Pilgrimage*

Goodbye, *Rachele*! *Ciao*, *Bo Drum*! *Ci vediamo*, *Hoka Hey*, *Squalo Bianco*, *Caroline*, and *Freemantle Spirit*! The predawn morning was bone-chilling cold as *Gatti* slipped her lines or, rather, we pulled her heavy-duty lines and springs aboard. This time we would not need them again at that slip. She slid gently out from between her neighbors of two years and turned into the fairway. The low throb of her engines was all that broke the stillness. A few bright stars shone in the black sky, and our wake left a white path behind us as we sailed out into a Gulf of Tigullio surprisingly smooth for January. The port lights left behind gradually blended with the town lights, Lavagna became recognizable as a city and then began to recede into the darkness. Now the lights of Portofino and Rapallo sparkled in the distance behind us and the promontory became smaller as we approached and then passed the point of Sestri Levante. The seas picked up as the lights diminished. Tiny points of light identified houses perched high on the cliffs and clusters of lights showed where small villages crouched. As terrestrial lights thinned and dimmed, celestial points of light increased. Constellations etched the void and an occasional meteor made a spectacular flight earthward.

I was enjoying this display above me when Bill turned his attentions to the forward bilge. Our starboard repair could scarcely be called that. At just about the same point we started taking on water during our first attempt to go to Rome, we were taking it on again. The three of us had conversation there on the black, heaving sea under the cold unconcern of the stars. Should we return to Lavagna again or press on? Angelo called Mr. Bucaccio at home. He rose from his warm bed to assure us that there was no problem. "It is a bad job," Angelo insisted. Mr. Bucaccio refused to accept this assessment, and I could almost see him shrug in his cozy, dry pajamas and shuffle back to his covers. We were facing 200 miles, but we all felt the boat was basically sound and the weather was propitious. Angelo knew his sea and climate well. All three of us wanted to go to Rome. Bill and I could not see the sense of another expensive pull in a boatyard that had proved incompetent. The problem seemed to be water pushing in at the repair when the boat was underway. At rest, there was no leak and at high speed the leak became negligible. We were sure the wood was sound, if unsealed. Angelo called Dominic and reported events. Dominic decided for some reason to drive down the coast and keep a check on our progress. And thus it was that we continued on our southern course with our spirits greatly dampened but feeling a degree of confidence in a well found vessel.

We sloshed on through the dark with *Gatti*'s lights now being our only illuminations – the neon green of the radar screen; the white lights of the autopilot, fluxgate compass and other helm controls; the gray light of the handheld GPS; the bright spectrum of colors on the plotter/sounder that was tracking us with a red line; the yellow light from the radio. The radio made the only sounds other than our subdued voices, the rush of the sea and the drone of the engines. It spouted out a weather report that informed us there was fog over the Tuscan coast. While this alarmed me, Angelo assured us that such a weather pattern keeps the seas calm and his prognostication proved correct.

The sky was beginning to brighten as we passed the Cinque Terre towns, perched like aeries on the craggy peaks. Next we glided by the island of Palmaria and the lighthouse on the little island Tino, just beyond Portovenere. We were crossing the opening to the Gulf of La Spezia when the sun rolled into view. Such a sun! It was blood red with a ring of fog banding its upper third. It looked like a big red rubber bladder at which Gandolf might have blown a smoke ring. It was a sun that to all appearances had not risen but rather had been flung into the sky directly in front of us. There was a sort of horrible fascination in that sun of such unexpected color and consistency. So awed were we by this phenomenon, that we did not notice when the plotter went berserk. Its bright display of color had become gray. Our tracking line had become black. Most disturbing of all, we were tracking across Ecuador.

"Angelo, what has happened? The last time we came down, the plotter sent us to Labrador. When we left today, we were back in Italy. And now this! What is wrong?"

Angelo was fascinated that we found ourselves in South America, but he was not unduly surprised that our plotter was out of whack. Between the NATO base and the Italian navy stationed at La Spezia, this scrambling of signals is a common practice. He assured us that all would return to normal within 50 miles and, indeed, we were not far down the Tuscan coast when we were returned to our correct course on the plotter, the gray of Ecuador giving way to the bright green of the Italian peninsula. This experience confirmed the lessons of our advanced navigation class. If we had not plotted a dead reckoning course on our chart, we could have truly panicked. The best equipment is not infallible and the highest scientific advances are not givens.

Gatti had never been on a long enough run for us to chart her fuel consumption with any certainty, so we did not yet have a fuel consumption table. We took frequent measurements and began compiling the data necessary for any vessel that depends on fuel. We pulled into the big port at Viareggio to fuel up because gas pumps are conveniently located there, and we wouldn't have to worry about refueling for a while. Besides, the famous Carnival parades were due to kick off in a few days, and I hoped to pick up a news release. But this plan was frustrated when we found the fueling dock deserted and both the gasoline and diesel pumps shut down. It was unclear if this was because it was winter or the pumps were being altered from *lire* to the brand new euro. We pushed on to Livorno, where we checked our fuel level again. Dominic called on the cell phone to report that he was in Livorno himself and gasoline was available. None of us wanted to go into the complex, busy port unless it was absolutely necessary. Our fuel situation was really quite positive, so Angelo called ahead to our next possibility, Piombino. The fuel dock here did indeed have *benzina verde,* and an operator would be sent out to service us at 12:30 p.m.

The run from Livorno to Piombino was excellent fun. Our spirits were actually rising. We had left the Ligurian Sea behind at La Spezia and now were in the waters of the Northern Tyrrhenian Sea. It seemed we would make it to Rome after all. At least the threat of

Lavagna was far back in our wake. The island of Capraia was a vague shape far out at sea, and Angelo told us of wonderful vacations spent there with his wife and sons. By the time we got to Piombino, the sun was brilliant and warm. The air was fresh and clear, and the island of Elba stood off boldly and invitingly to our starboard. The port of Piombino is actually a pretty bad place. Big factories throw out clouds of dirty smoke and nauseating fumes and ferries shuttle back and forth from Elba. It is not a place where a yacht is welcome unless in extremity. We did not go here, but rather to a brand new port called Marina di Salivoli, just around the bend from Piombino. Both ports are located on land that juts out to shape the northern shore of the Bay of Follonica. It was hard to imagine that such a delightful port as Salivoli could exist under the shadow of the other.

We tied up at a fueling dock that was not yet manned even though it was the appointed time. Dominic pulled up in his car about the same time and jumped aboard to examine our leak. Of course, now that we were not plowing through the sea, water was not washing in. His jaw was set, and he seemed to think the repair was fine despite Angelo's violent protests. By this point in our adventures we had become pretty good Italians as far as patience goes, so we dined on delicious sandwiches made for us by the Albatross Café at the Lavagna port and soaked up sunshine until the fuel attendant finally showed up. *Gatti* has two tanks that hold 100 gallons each, so the fueling itself took quite a while.

The sun was still bright when we headed out again, but there would be no further pleasures in the day. The waters in the Bay of Follonica were rough, and we were drenched with icy spray. The air was cooling rapidly, and we were getting cold. By the time we passed Argentario, the waves were knocking hard against us. Argentario is the mountain – once an island – that houses the ports of Santo Stefano and Ercole. We had wanted to visit these places by sea, but now all we wanted was to get past. Day was closing down. We were sopping wet and cold beyond what I could have imagined the body could survive. We had to keep our speed up and plane to avoid taking on water at the bow, and *Gatti* quivered and recoiled under the merciless poundings of the waves. By the time we were passing the busy commercial port of Civitavecchia it was very dark. The merchant vessels and cruise ships made the channel look more like a Los Angeles freeway than anything else. There were so many lights and so much traffic that we all had to keep a sharp lookout despite the misery we were in.

We had decided as far back as Argentario that we would not make it to Rome this day. Angelo was now in unfamiliar waters, and we might as well have been Columbus teetering on the edge of the world. It is not prudent to navigate at night under these conditions, so we had called ahead to the port Riva di Traiano and secured a transit slip. This was the new port we had looked at two years earlier, and we were not opposed to stopping there. It was hard to locate at night, with its narrow harbor entrance almost parallel to the coast and menacing rocks encroaching on both sides.

But locate it we did and navigate it we did. Dominic was on the dock and helped us tie up. Angelo jumped off to connect our electric line and water hose. We did not have the right connection for the water hose because we had carelessly left the fitting on the pipe back at G56. The polarity was reversed and, when Dominic plugged in our power line, the breaker was thrown. This is a common problem in Italy and easily remedied with a little manipulation of the wires. "There is something wrong with the power on your boat," said our good friend Dominic, who had been caring for our electrical needs for more than two years. With those words of comfort thrown carelessly over his shoulder, he and Angelo jumped into their car and were gone.

We were all exhausted cats, pummeled beyond further action. *Gatti* sagged at her lines. Bill and I stripped off our sopping garments. We could do no more than climb in together in my bunk under every cover we possessed and shiver against one another until sleep numbed the hunger and the anger. Slowly our bodies warmed somewhat and began to repair themselves under the blanket of unconsciousness.

Gatti lays a Ligurian wake between Doug's davits and below her passerella.

CHAPTER XXVIII

ALL ROADS LEAD TO ROME

'Hurry! We burn
For Rome so near us, for the phoenix moment
When we have thrown off this traveller's trance
And mother-naked and ageless-ancient
Wake in her warm nest of renaissance."
Cecil Day-Lewis, *Flight to Italy*

We wakened to a sunny day and felt our spirits revive a bit. The day before, Angelo had called Terzi Yachting and said we were en route and would arrive around noon. Alberto was a bit surprised, since we had planned to let him know some days in advance of our departure, but he assured us that he could have everything ready. Since it was a run of only about 40 miles down to Porto di Roma, we had time to wander around a bit. We paid our bill at the port office and had a cappuccino at a pleasant but empty café on the wharf. The port was a true disappointment in view of the promise it had shown at our prior visit. A surly woman guarding the restrooms denied us entry to shower. Most of the shops were vacant or closed up tight. Admittedly, January is not prime boating season, but one would have thought that a port so far removed from the closest town would have offered a few more services. The wharf might have been deserted, but the harbor certainly was not. We were grateful that a transit slip had even been available. This port that had been so empty two years earlier was now crammed with vessels.

Warmed by our coffee if not a shower, we started *Gatti*'s engines and headed out the narrow harbor mouth, this time sickeningly conscious of the sharp rocks that flanked us. Down the coast we roared on a calm morning sea, with a bright sun thawing our hearts and old, arthritic joints. Past the black sands of Ladispoli we slid; past the popular beaches and exclusive seaside villas of Fregene and Marinella. The expanses of sand and relatively flat land seemed strange to us after our time in the shadow of cliffs. Before long we were passing the Fiumicino Canal, the Isola Sacra, and then the Tiber River pouring into the Central Tyrrhenian Sea. Just beyond the river, rose the breakwater of our new home with masts poking above it and flags of many nations fluttering behind.

The time for action now faced me squarely and inescapably. I, of course, had had the radio out and tuned to the calling channel the entire way, but now was the time that I would have to speak to it. I picked up the microphone and for the first time depressed the button. "Porto di Roma. This is *i Gatti Felici* coming to *Posto* 665." My Portofino experience had shown me that it would be some time before I tried my marine introductions again in Italian. I released the button and a clear voice speaking English came over the radio.

"*I Gatti Felici*, this is Porto di Roma. There is some work here. Wait outside the harbor and we will send *ormeggiatori.*"

The work involved a little dredge diligently clearing the channel. We waited a minute or two before two young men appeared in a spotlessly clean white rubber dinghy. We followed them through the harbor entrance, past the fueling dock and brand new control tower with all its windows intact. Now we were in the basin with the pebble beach and we turned to port. Past "N" dock, past "O" dock where the Murphys had moored. And here was "P" dock, home to only four boats moored away down at the quay. A wind had begun to blow in from the west and docking actually was pretty difficult. There were no flanking neighbors to nudge between or finger piers. But the *ormeggiatori* knew their business, harbor and winds. They also knew how to deal with inexperienced female sailors. We had no lines at the dock and so, rather than catching a line, I had to throw ours off. Our northern lines were very heavy and fat, and my aptitude very slim. One of the *ormeggiatori* asked permission to jump aboard, and he took over at the stern. Other young men on dock caught and secured the lines in a way unfamiliar to us. We tied up to strong iron rings fixed in the side of the jetty rather than the bollards we were used to. Meantime, the dinghy pushed against *Gatti*'s bow and held her in place until our bow line was carried forward and secured.

No sooner were we in place than Mario and Paola came rushing down the long, empty dock and greeted us with warm hugs and kisses. Mario ran off to get the hose attachment we had forgotten in Lavagna after he ascertained that our electrical connection was the correct one and the polarity not reversed. Now here was a place that understood these matters! We were then left to our own devices for a while to get ourselves in some order. This was quite necessary because we had many items stowed and lots of wet clothing. Mario returned with Alberto later in the day, bringing stamped documents that legalized our presence in Italy. For the very first time we held in our hands documentation with our names and information stamped by the port captain. Bill was listed as the *capitano* and I as a *marinaio*. I began to protest that I was a navigator rather than a simple sailor, but no one seemed to care. In fact, all that it gained me was that thereafter Bill was referred to as *comandante,* which made me feel even more lowly. *"Complimenti!"* pronounced Alberto looking approvingly around our elegant little saloon. Gianluca brought out homemade pastries from his mother – yet another taste of her truly magnificent culinary repertoire. How dreadful one day can be and how blessed the next! It may be we need the low tides to make us exult so in the high ones.

We had nine days before we were to return to Florida. We had daily attentions from a real yacht service. We signed and filed our documents. Alberto climbed into the bilge with us for an inspection and acquainted himself with our electric system and other aspects of the boat he would be responsible for in our absence. He paid careful attention to our "repair." We became acquainted with the *ormeggiatori,* who were always on hand to be helpful. If the truth be told, there were very few boats to be tended to. While the lower half of the port where the smaller slips were located was filling up nicely, there was only a handful of yachts on our end. We had one bout of gale force winds during which we worried that we had as yet only one bow line rather than two and deemed it prudent to put out a starboard line. We enjoyed having the empty slips around us and the feeling of being on the open sea, but at this point we regretted the absence of *Rachele* and *Bo Drum,* who had always held us firmly in place. The *ormeggiatori* saw us struggling in the wind with this line and rushed to our assistance.

We rediscovered the friendly staff at the Maremosso and feasted on cappuccino and *cornetti* every morning at our new café. It took a few mornings to adjust our thinking from the Ligurian brioche to the sugary Laziale *cornetto.* Paola's brother-in-law is an airline pilot who speaks excellent English, and one evening we three couples went to an old restaurant in the Alban hills outside of Rome for a true Italian dinner. Under braids of garlic and peppers, balls of cheese and shanks of prosciutto, we dined on local specialties. Afterwards, at midnight, Alberto drove us through the now deserted streets of Rome. Past their old home on the Aventine, past the Colosseum and other historic landmarks we raced and had our own private tour by a bona fide Roman under the magic of the city lights.

We rented a car and drove up to Genova to renew our insurance. We then dropped down to Lavagna and met with Dominic, Mr. Bucaccio, Angelo and Giuseppe. We were assured that all would be made right with *Gatti*. They would contact Alberto, come to Rome and take the boat out. Our slip was being "sublet," and Dominic would return our lease money when we returned after the lease year ran out in May. As usual, we delivered little gifts all around, this time some toy *carabinieri* vehicles for Angelo's sons and a Roma soccer shirt.

It was now January 27 and the first night of *Carnevale* in Viareggio. We had written an article about carnival the previous year and this very Sunday it was being published in our hometown newspaper, the *St. Petersburg Times*. What could be more natural than to attend? Viareggio is famous for its enormous animated floats whose messages are often allegorical in nature and truly thought-provoking. We were interested in how world events would be reflected in this year's themes. As it turned out, the terrorist attacks in New York occurred at a time long after the float topics had been decided on and construction was well underway. Thus, the political commentary suffered somewhat but, since the parade theme celebrated the opening of a huge new float construction facility and museum in the city, it was as grand a show as always and well worth the pinch it put in our travel preparations. It was late at night when we stumbled into our bunks for a couple hours of sleep.

It was the next day that we were to return home, so early the following morning we set out bags of Ligurian goodies brought back for Mario's and Alberto's families. Food is delicious throughout Italy, but we will always be partial to Ligurian olive oil and pesto. Focaccia, farinata and vermentino wine cannot be matched elsewhere. Italians are great gift givers and the beautiful wrappings are generally as special as the contents. We did not have the materials or skill to do so well in this department, but we did our best. We then drove to Leonardo da Vinci Airport in Fiumicino, only a few miles from our slip. What a pleasure that was, even if we did miss our turn and take in a few miles of unintended *autostrada* in the process. It sure beat lugging baggage to Chiavari, changing trains in Genova, detraining in Milan, and taking the bus to Malpensa! We boarded our plane and snuggled down with a sigh of relief. We had accomplished a great deal more in these four weeks than we had expected to. As the plane climbed westward into the heavens, we passed over our port. We couldn't see her, but we knew *Gatti* was safely moored in her very own slip with caring people around her. She was celebrating her 50th birthday in this year of 2002, and she had a 50-year lease in a wonderful new home. While the world was shaping up as a hostile and unpredictable place, we found comfort in those numbers.

CHAPTER XXIX

A PORT FOR ANY STORM

'Wise fear, you know,
Forbids the robbing of a foe;
But what, to serve our private ends,
Forbids the cheating of our friends?'
Charles Churchill, *The Ghost*

February, March and April we spent at various projects back in Florida. We began tearing things apart in the condominium with an eye to remodeling. In the fall we had bought a 1954 Chris-Craft Riviera runabout. It had seemed idiotic to live near the water on this western peninsula with no boat at all when we lived on a yacht on our eastern peninsula. To even consider a carefree new fiberglass boat was unthinkable. *Bubbles* was the name of the boat we purchased. We at once set ourselves to work stripping her down, removing her engine to be rebuilt, sanding and recaulking. Our son was working long hours at a new job, but it was fun to have him nearby again. We corresponded regularly by e-mail with Mario and were assured all was well with *Gatti*. Paola and I corresponded by regular mail; I had not yet induced her to try e-mail. Since she could see *Gatti* at dock from her office window every morning, I was doubly reassured. Paola got a toy poodle puppy named Teo for Valentine's Day and Gianluca got a parrot named Paco. I worked hard on Italian and, before we knew it, May had arrived and we could go back to our boat.

Our Genovese lawyer, Terzi Yachting, Porto di Roma, the notary and ourselves had agreed that we would consummate our slip purchase on May 4. We had had euros transferred from our British bank to our Italian bank in Lavagna and now arranged for them to be transferred to the branch office in Ostia. When we had first brought the boat to Italy, we had converted dollars to euros at a very advantageous rate and felt more confident than ever that we were making an excellent investment. Time was to prove us right, as the euro jumped from 85 cents U.S. to $1.30.

Our flight landed at Fiumicino May 2, only two days before the big transaction. Paola had asked for our flight information, but I had not provided it. A good thing too! It was a terrible flight, complicated by a skin biopsy I had taken from an ankle a day prior to departure. We flew out of Atlanta, which historically has always been a disaster for me. We sat on the runway for three hours on this occasion, I in a center seat, unable to move or lift my throbbing foot. By the time we reached Paris, just about everyone on board had missed connecting flights, and there was more delay. By the time we arrived in Rome, my foot was so enormously swollen that we took a taxi to the port. It cost a great deal more than it should have, but we were too weary to care and too anxious to get back on board. The taxi situation proved to be an ongoing problem that we finally resolved with car rentals and rides from friends. The taxi drivers at the airport are interested in fares to Rome and do not consider nearby Ostia worth their while. A bus runs from the airport to the downtown Ostia bus and train station, but it is an exhausting undertaking for tired and laden international travelers. It is extremely frustrating to live so close and yet be so far.

We were hobbling with our luggage out our jetty when the *ormeggiatori* appeared. With smiles they handed our bags aboard and ran to the office to get our key. Massimo told us that Alberto had had him run the engines every couple weeks and that our pumps had been checked routinely in view of the leaking. *Gatti* had never before experienced care like this from a yacht service and neither had we. At our cabin door was a whimsically decorated little wooden crate packed with wine, cookies, candy, canned peaches, crackers – in short, a grand repast for exhausted travelers. Paola had seen to every delicious detail. We pulled up our *passerella* and collapsed. We understand that Mario made a trip over to see to our needs, but we were oblivious to this additional kindness.

Pain and exhaustion were somewhat assuaged when the big day arrived. Paola drove us to the bank where, after some delay, we were given our cashier check. Then she dropped us off at the port office, where Mario served as one of several witnesses as the notary read aloud all the facets of the contract. There we all sat around a long table as she droned on and on in English. If it was boring to us, it must have seemed interminable to the Italian-only speakers. All of us then signed multiple copies, checks were passed out and Posto Barca

665 became the personal property for 50 years of the Happy Cats. On our way back from the port office to *Gatti*, Mario bought a round of *prosecco* at the Maremosso and we toasted the occasion.

Bill and I trotted out to look at our purchase with new eyes. We walked around our space of concrete jetty, checked more closely our two big mooring rings and our power/water box. We looked down into "our" clear aqua water at "our" little schools of fish darting back and forth. Our little blue sign affixed to the side of the pier between our two *anelli* with the "665" might as well have said "Harper." We examined our location again. Was this really the best slip? We had had so many options in this empty end of the port. But, yes, this indeed was the best. The fire hydrant was close but not in the way. Ditto the dock ladder. The power/water box was off to the side rather than directly in the line of fire of our *passerella*. Only one slip in from the fairway, we would be able to watch the traffic when some developed. We could see obliquely past the control tower to the harbor mouth. Yes, it was perfect and it was ours. We had a home to winter in without worry and a spot that one day people would want to rent in our absence. No one could blow up our water.

One thing and one thing only was not perfect. As we paced our pier, dried seagull droppings crunched beneath our feet. Because there were hardly any boats on our jetty and we were alone at the end, the seagulls of Ostia had decided the place had been constructed with their convenience in mind. Actually, since it had been their undisputed place long before construction, they had something of a point. When we returned this time *Gatti* looked different. All of her canvas had been removed, including her bimini, because the seagulls had made such a mess on it that it had to be sent out to be cleaned. Not only was this an expensive proposition, but the canvas that was reinstalled shortly after our return lacked any semblance of impermeability.

And so the Seagull War was declared. The birds were as determined to hold what they considered their own as we were to claim it as ours. During the course of the battles, both sides developed a keen appreciation for the enemy's intelligence. I felt like David Copperfield's Aunt Betsy driving away the donkeys. As twilight fell each evening, the big fat white patrol bird would fly over to see where we were. At the schreeched go-ahead, the flock would settle around us mewling and chattering. We would chase them off and they would take to the air, throwing the most astounding insults at us over their wing tips. Later in the night they would return. Sometimes they would make it all night but not often. Seagulls have an inability to stand wing to wing for long without making a rude comment or cracking a joke at which the others either grumble or hoot. Their cackling would generally awaken us and off we would go on deck, waving towels and pajamas. The quiet of the night would be shattered by their flapping wings and imprecations. One morning I heard a scratching sound on the deck above my bunk. I was not a graduate of Huntington Harbor's "H" dock for naught. I knew the sound of bird feet when I heard it. I poked my head quietly out of the hatch and there was *Il Duce* himself, apparently working at loosening a screw in the rail. It was only gradually that he became aware of my presence and, lifting his beak, we regarded one another silently eye-to-eye. Then, having gotten his wits together, he flew off.

To give them credit, as much as they hated us, they never to our knowledge came back on deck or defecated on the boat. A biology teacher once told me that birds have no control over their elimination. This is untrue. We have many times witnessed vengeful behavior along these lines, and we know what we know. They could have made life much more unpleasant for us had they truly wished it. As long as we were alone on the end of the dock, we kept up our vigil and every morning hosed down the pier. What an incredible pile of garbage those fowl would leave behind – shells, bones, skulls of tiny animals, pieces of cloth, fur and fruit. The gastrointestinal system of a seagull must be made of cast iron. Within a couple of weeks a few more boats had come to the dock, and we all shared the onus of patrol and cleanup. Complaints were lodged at the port office and finally the gang pretty much surrendered.

The days passed pleasantly. The port filled up with enormous charter boats and private yachts from around the world. We kept our flag chart handy so we could identify all the countries of Africa, the Middle and Far East, and other spots that were really foreign to us. There was always action across the fairway where the big boats tied up parallel to the breakwater. The crews would come in on the yachts and work at cleaning and scrubbing for a couple days. Then deck furniture would come out and provisions would be delivered. Finally one day the flowers and topiary plants would be brought on board, the crew would don flashy uniforms, and a vehicle would arrive with the guests. Sometimes they would arrive by van, sometimes in fleets of black Mercedes. Sometimes they would head out at once and be gone for a week or so; often they would stay in port for a day or two and be chauffeured into Rome for some sightseeing before taking to the sea.

If the port became boring, 77 cents and 45 minutes would get us from the port gate to anywhere in Rome we wished. I think there is no place better to wander on the face of the earth. It would take more than a lifetime to know the city well with her layers and layers of civilizations. There were mornings chatting in Italian with Paola. There was Ostia Antica close at hand with summer productions in its ancient amphitheater in the cool of the evening under rustling and fragrant umbrella pines. There were exhibitions and concerts at the port as well as throughout the entire country and auto trips to relaxing thermal pools. There were train trips to Sicily and Brindisi and shopping in Firenze. There were dinghy trips up the Tiber and friendships forged with other boaters. And then there was Dominic.

In the spring prior to our return, Dominic had called Alberto as promised and made an appointment to come down to look at *Gatti*. He had not appeared and that was all anyone had heard from him. Alberto suggested that we contact our Genovese lawyer.

"Bill won't sue him," I said. "He is a friend."

"Oh. He is a friend," Alberto replied, and the matter was dropped.

However, the matter was not resolved. We asked Dominic and Angelo to meet with us and drove the long way up to Lavagna. When we arrived, Angelo was not around at first. We asked for him. He rushed in and out quickly, without looking us in the eye. Dominic had no problem looking us in the eye, though. Yes, he realized the boat repair was not satisfactory, and we should bring *Gatti* back to Lavagna, where the work would be made right by the esteemed Mr. Bucaccio. Yes, our slip in Lavagna had been sublet from January through May, but he did not feel he owed us the $4,000 in rent that we had already paid and he had collected a second time. We had paid $10,000 for an incompetent repair job managed by our yacht service and now we were being robbed of money over which there was no question of ownership. A man we had considered a friend sat there like a stranger. On his desk was the animated rubber shark that belted out *Mack the Knife* that we had brought him from Florida. Clicking away was the printer we had given Angelo for producing his photos. Outside the cheerful cyclamen tumbled over their planters in a riot of color. All about us were little gifts we had presented over the months out of friendship. Yes, this was Dominic's office all right; this person looked like Dominic, but he treated us with a contempt and coldness we could never have imagined.

To say we were deeply hurt does not begin to describe our distress. What was there to do but leave? We considered suing him for a while and our lawyer held a letter for us while we pondered. But, in the end, there seemed little point to the exercise. We had been excited about our move to Italy and had been foolish enough to trust people we did not really know. We have noticed that many Americans are like that. We are happy, joyful puppies abroad, exuberant in our delight at all we find. We lack a certain cautious reserve that it would be wise to cultivate. But if we have the reserve, we must sacrifice the exuberance, a portion of the joy in all we are discovering. It is a choice that must be made, each to the detriment of the other. This acknowledgement is as sad as growing up and leaving our innocence behind. Bill and I have pretty well over time chosen to keep the joy, holding to the conviction that most people in the world are good and fair. This is not to say that we pay for things far in advance any more, neglect to check our receipts more carefully, or take everything at face value.

Low tides are a bit like that. Sometimes trash and ugliness have been cast into the concealing waters and are not apparent to us until the sea curls far back on itself and exposes what is hidden in its depths.

CHAPTER XXX

ADVENTURES ABOUND

'I am in Rome! Oft as the morning ray
Visits these eyes, waking at once I cry,
Whence this excess of joy? What has befallen me?
And from within a thrilling voice replies,
Thou art in Rome! A thousand busy thoughts
Rush on my mind, a thousand images;
And I spring up as girt to run a race!'
Samuel Rogers, *Rome*

Life at the Port of Rome was very different from what we had experienced in Lavagna. For the first summer there were very few boats, and we enjoyed a camaraderie with our small number of neighbors and the untenanted expanse of water around us. A couple other wooden yachts – Italian Biagliettis –were docked there, so we were in good company with our unending sanding, varnishing and deck sealing. One of these boats was owned by a young couple who had recently purchased their *Freesie*. They slaved happily all summer, cleaning, stripping and varnishing every inch of the yacht inside and out. Their plan was to sail to the island of Ponza on the summer solstice for the grand fireworks that mark the day of the island's patron saint, San Silverio. The big day arrived and those yachts which had not left earlier, headed south to the Pontine Islands. But poor *Freesie* had a problem with one of her engines, so the magical midnight hour struck for fireworks in Ponza and she was still moored to "P" dock. But all her problems were eventually ironed out, and the day soon came that she sailed out of port with the proud young couple standing at the helm of their little kingdom.

Another wooden Biaglietti was owned by an older gentleman of considerable taste and breeding. He frequently hosted intimate dinner parties on his spacious aft deck. He laid his table with snowy linens, set out sparkling crystal goblets, and poured his wine from bottles chilled in elegant sterling silver coolers. All the little specialty shops had by now been stocked and opened, and we could browse lazily during the day. At night the parking lot bulged and swarms of people meandered along the wharf, shopped, stopped for aperitifs, licked gelatos, or stole kisses on our pebbled beach. Boat shows, auto shows, beauty contests, local produce shows, art and sculpture exhibits and concerts all added excitement and style to our lives without our having to even leave the port.

Parking for the public was limited to spaces outside the security gates of the port. A young man with a *moto* stood sentinel here and collected parking fees in between flirtations with attractive young women. As the popularity of the port grew, parking became a big problem for the adjacent neighborhood. But not for us. Our slip purchase included our very own numbered parking space within the gates behind the shops, so we actually owned a piece of dry Italian soil. We had a placard to place on our dashboard when we had a car and a magnetic key that would unlock the gate. No vehicles were permitted in the shopping and dock areas other than electric carts, so the whole area between the store fronts and the water was actually a half-mile-long piazza open to the sea. We had a second magnetic key that admitted us to "P" dock and the modern, clean showers that were not accessible to the public. We enjoyed a privacy on deck that had eluded us in Lavagna. *Passeggiatas* here were taken along the quay and not out on the jetties.

Behind the secured parking fences were two marshy ponds – leftovers of what had been the typical topography of the region. The Pontine Marshes, which provided Romans of many centuries with horrendous malaria outbreaks have been, for the most part, drained by large ditches and pumping stations that crisscross the region. These two ponds were re-created by the company that developed the port and donated to LIPU, a non-profit Italian bird organization, as part of the deal. In its first year, the area attracted 250 species of birds, and we were all enthusiastically looking forward to even more. The pond water is surrounded by grasses and other tall growth within which blinds are cleverly hidden. It seemed as if every week more and more people arrived clad in camouflage attire and carrying binoculars to take part in the tours. Migrating birds from Africa find it a haven of rest after their arduous journey and join the ranks of many local denizens. Local headlines proclaimed the exciting news of a swan nest billowy with goslings. We were able to go by the

LIPU office and hold baby owls, ducks and the like as well as make ourselves useful. Since its founding 13 years ago, we have worked with and supported the Torre Argentina cat colony in Rome. Now we had good work to attend to in our own back yard as well.

Granted, we no longer enjoyed living on the edge of a picturesque medieval Ligurian town. The tenements and high-rise apartments of Ostia towered just behind our port; most could be called nothing better than just plain ugly and rundown. We missed our strolls into town, our visits to little family-run shops, and our mini hikes over the Entella River bridge to Chiavari. I missed the church bells by whose chiming I had unconsciously begun to organize my days. But we were finding cosmopolitan living and its conveniences seductive. We could hear English in many places and, even though the ease of communication was beginning to cut into my Italian fluency, I was often too lazy to care. We could use any number of local Internet businesses if there should be a problem with our computer on board. We could even find peanut butter at international food shops. Something was lost and something gained in the transition but our move had been, on the whole, very good. On days that I was most frustrated by the squalor of Ostia, all I needed to do was raise my eyes to the balconies to find my spirits raised as well. Many of these were tiny Gardens of Eden. Flowers, vines, herbs, and even vegetables and trees were carefully tended to and blossomed far above and below their small plots. The balconies of Ostia would make a fine project for a budding photographer.

After the canals were dug and land drained in the late 1800s, Ostia began to develop. A great period of neoclassic architecture blossomed and during the twenty-year period following 1919, the city became a showplace, drawing the talents of some of the greatest architects of the day. A good highway and trains brought sweltering Romans to the cool seaside. Elegant bathing establishments were built along the beach. Most notable among these was the beautiful "Roma." Situated in the sea on a magnificent pier, its huge domed top and graceful wings made it a focal point for the area. As it was also a superb focal reference for Allied bombing, the Germans blew it up in 1943. The town suffered grievous losses in 1943-44 as the beautiful new rail station and other sites suffered the same fate as the Roma. This devastating period was followed by the proliferation of the enormous apartment complexes that now give Ostia an ugly feel in some parts. But one has the sense that the Ostia of today is again trying to find itself. It has a great deal to offer and one hopes that good things can be renewed and developed. The construction of our port and recent upgrading of the beach area are positive signs. Ostia is due for a renaissance.

By far the greatest attraction of the area is its magnificent beaches. The coastline that stretches from Anzio to Ostia is characterized by natural dunes and wide, wide beaches. The sand has a high iron content which makes it unlike the sugar-white sands of our Florida home, but it is soft and fine and so deep that it is often difficult to walk through it. Sand bathing is a popular pastime here. One can just snuggle down in the warm, soft stuff and feel renewed.

From our port through town lie 10 kilometers sporting about 50 bathing establishments very different indeed from the seasonal ones we had come to know in Liguria. Many are nightclubs and have big pools, tennis courts, and gyms. A few are even survivors of the neoclassical period. Beyond these membership-only facilities lie the most beautiful free beaches, some of which are part of the State reserve of the Roman Coast. They are reached from the coast road by walking across long boardwalks through the dunes. Many of these beach areas have a small restaurant, bar, and shower area. These conveniences are fenced off from the precious dunes which support an amazing array of vegetation, some of it endangered.

Ostia Lido is Rome's beach, the two being connected by the Via del Mare, and the traffic can snarl to the point that helicopters are at times required to untangle it. On summer weekends, thousands of beachgoers park along the berm of the coast road as well as packing the city streets. One weekend, ambulances could not negotiate the road because so many people had parked there. More new buses have been assigned to serve the area, but it is never a good idea to visit the beach on a weekend. It is much better to sprawl out on one's deck during those frenetic days and then, during the week, go down to one of the beach restaurants and dine on fresh seafood and cold wine in the peace of the long summer evening. There is much to commend life in Ostia once one has sorted it out.

The Ligurians pride themselves on having been a real hindrance to ancient Roman subjugation. We now found ourselves right in the middle of Roman history. Sites are named after Aeneas and his wife, Lavinia, as well as all the Latin authors and history-makers my Latin training had made so familiar to me. In fact, Pliny the Younger had a villa not far from where our boat is moored today. The ruins of Ostia

Antica are a short way up the Via del Mare. This very first Ostia was constructed at what was then the mouth of the river and its commercial success derived from rare saltpans located there. The city is believed to have been founded in the fourth century B.C. and in its heyday had a population of 50,000. The city covered a huge area, much of which has yet to be excavated; but what is there is amazing. It is lovely just to stroll through this countryside of meadow grasses, reconstructions, ruins, and imaginings.

An amphitheater was built here, courtesy of Agrippa, the son-in-law of the Emperor Augustus, in which various entertainments are presented during the summer. We attended an evening performance of Aristophane's *The Clouds*. We wandered along the ancient road to the theater and climbed the worn steps to a tier of stone seats. The umbrella pines whispered and fanned us as the actors strutted on the stage, wearing big, authentic Greek masks. The appreciative, quiet audience came well supplied with picnic baskets filled with wine and cheese, and, most importantly, cushions to sit on. Rock concerts are staged here as well, so there is entertainment for every taste. While this original Ostia is no longer a living community, the town of Ostia Antica still is. It was a suburb of the old Ostia, but reached prominence in the early Christian era. In fact, it became a diocese as early as 313 A.D. A castle and palace are only part of the wealth of history to be found here. Much of our summer was spent discovering historic sites right in our own backyard as well as in Rome and her environs.

Aside from the few residents on our dock, other boats tied up in transit. A rare American would arrive by trawler or sailboat and stay for a couple days or a couple months. Porto di Roma is wonderfully situated for exploring the country, and car rentals right at the port were reasonable and convenient for boat people. None of that 30-minute train trip to Genova for a car! All the boaters we met made interesting acquaintances and a few became real friends. People who live on boats differ from the rest of humanity. We noted a real propensity toward imperious male captains and submissive mates and an unmovable determination that their way of life, type of vessel, and so forth were the only intelligent options in life. But this extreme was happily offset by open-minded people enjoying the freedom of the sea and discovering our marvelous Earth. While all the people we met were polite and helpful, we soon learned to distinguish those with whom we shared values.

The Murphys were such people, and we have maintained our friendship as they have moved through the Adriatic and Ionian to the Black Sea and back. Now we found ourselves meeting more people like them. One couple had brought their trawler from California to Antwerp and spent time working their way south in the rivers and canals of Europe, passing a fabulous winter in Paris near the Bastille. Joan is a great cook and their little boat sported a veritable garden of herbs and flowers on its upper deck. John is a diver and their terrific dog, Tipper, brought great joy to those of us who were petless. Another couple, from New Orleans, spent roughly the same months on their sailboat *Marbella* as we did on *Gatti*. They had wintered in Genova, and we shared memories good and bad of the region. We also shared a passion for the Ligurian food that we missed so much. Whenever one or the other of us went to visit Genova – which we did with some regularity – it was understood that goodies were to be brought back to Rome. Mary Lou and Phil were a semi-retired nurse and doctor respectively, and it was also reassuring to be able to run medical concerns by them every so often. In addition, Phil was an electronics and computer wizard, and we benefited greatly from his expertise. As with the Murphys, we met up with them in various places both by boat and car and enjoyed touring together.

A British couple who lived in Monaco docked behind us one propitious day. We now had another boat at the end of our pier. They had recently purchased a large Sunseeker power yacht and had brought her on her maiden voyage from Monte Carlo to Rome. They had previously done a great deal of sailing on much bigger vessels they had owned, complete with crews. But now they had decided it would be more fun to travel on their own. They had obtained licenses and gone to it with gusto. We enjoyed sharing our newly acquired navigational skills together as well as restaurant discoveries and the like. Lance and Nikki love the Pontine Islands, which lie north of the Bay of Naples. The island of Ponza has been their Utopia for years, and they have close connections with the people there. Since Ponza is a fairly easy run of 60 odd miles from Rome, they frequently would leave *OceanS* at our port for weeks at a time when they flew home to tend to business. In future times we would benefit from their Ponza ties and be able to occupy coveted slips in the charming harbor whose size is not commensurate with its popularity among the rich and famous.

Another interesting family we met early that first summer were the Italian owners of a prominent shipyard along the Tiber. A boat and dive show was being set up along the quay and the "100 Sails" regatta was going to be launched for the first time from our spanking new port. As part of the festivities, a large boat tied up at our jetty at the long slip on the very end. This was the first time anyone had docked there, so that fact alone added some excitement to our day. But this was not just any old boat. This was the venerable *Pietro Micca*, one of the last working steam tugs in the world. Built in 1898, the shiny red steel tug still tows other vessels around the Mediterranean. Many of these are charter yachts that over-winter inexpensively in Tunisia. It is cheaper to have them towed north in the summer than to pay a crew as well as fuel costs. *Pietro Micca* is owned by the Giua family and is very much a family member. No expense is spared on her maintenance and, when she is not out working, she can be found visiting various Italian ports educating the public on environmental issues. Her home dock is on the Fiumara, very close to our port, and she was visiting because she had been invited to signal the start of the regatta.

Even though *Pietro* was considerably older than *Gatti*, the Signori Giua, Senior, were highly appreciative of what it takes to keep an old girl in her prime. They complimented *Gatti* and us, we shared a glass of wine in our saloon, and we were treated to a tour of *Pietro*'s engine room, where the fiery light from the furnace glinted on polished copper engine parts. In the end, we were invited to join a group of journalists, dignitaries and celebrities who chugged out of the harbor to start the regatta. Actually we did not chug at all. We glided more smoothly and quietly through the water than any gasoline engine could have propelled us.

As we exited the harbor, we blew out a long blast of steam and a toot from our tall red stack to the control tower and the hundreds of spectators who crowded the quay and breakwater. We started the race with another great blast and munched a superb Italian lunch while colorful spinnakers ballooned out all around us. Dinghies bristling with television cameras and photographers circled us and begged for sandwiches and beer, which were expertly tossed their way. At the close of this remarkable afternoon when we arrived back at "P" dock and *Pietro Micca* had been secured with her heavy hemp lines, we scurried down her sturdy gangway and over our own little latticed one. The next hour or so was one of those rare times in which one feels truly rich and completely satisfied with life. The wealthy, the beautiful, the influential of Rome passed us as they left the big tug and continued down the pier to the quay. They looked at us, now relaxed on our aft deck, as though we were the luckiest people alive. We could not have disagreed.

Aside from meeting companionable people that summer and learning our way around our new home, we squeezed in other fun as well. We had purchased rail passes in the States, and now we tried to put as many travel days as possible to good use. We took a night train to Paris and went up to Firenze for a day of shopping. We headed south to Palermo at the far end of Sicily primarily to procure some famed *pesto palermitano* for Lance and Nikki. We filled their order, as well as getting some for Paola and ourselves. We had never heard of it, let alone tasted before, but this was to be only the first of many treks in its pursuit that we were to make over time. It can be purchased from a colorful vendor in the heart of Palermo's old market and is worth a trip from anywhere on the planet. From Sicily we went to Brindisi, the southern end of the Appian Way.

Back home at the port, interesting activities were still underway. Our shipyard, or *cantiere,* was developing at a fast pace. An enormous aqua blue lift was constructed, and serious boat work was commencing. One morning over cappuccino at the Maremosso we watched as a film crew set up shop on an older 60-foot Biaglietti. Reflecting shades and cameras were set up on board and hoards of *carabinieri* and police arrived for coffee and to shake the hand of the famous Italian actor who starred in a weekly television show of the police action variety. Behind the shop area, a police van pulled up with three huge German shepherds kenneled in the back. We thought it prudent to get out of the way so we went back to *Gatti* and watched the action from deck.

The Biaglietti was moored at the wharf on "Q" dock, just down from us. The van hid itself inside one of the brand new *cantiere* buildings. A big police boat and two neon orange inflatables concealed themselves from the camera behind our starboard side. At a given signal, sirens began to scream, lights to flash and engines to rev. The three boats went tearing by us to the side of the Biaglietti. At the same instant, the van came screeching at top speed out of the cantiere with sirens and lights going. The dogs leaped from the van, over the rails and onto the deck at about the same instant the boat cops were leaping on from the water side. This scene was enacted again and again to our great delight. From where we sit today it is hard to remember how empty the port was for that filming. There was lots of open water for those boats to speed through. Today the scene would look very different indeed.

In addition to being entertained, I was planning some entertainment of my own. Bill's 60th birthday was approaching. I enlisted Paola's help in planning a surprise, envisioning perhaps renting the Maremosso for the evening. But Paola would not hear of such a thing. She insisted on throwing a party at her home as a birthday gift from Alberto and herself. I contacted friends throughout Italy to show up at her villa and, although our daughter could not come from California, our son was able to come. Crafty planning was involved in collecting Charles at the airport and hiding him on a friend's trawler for the day. I then had to convince Bill to stop by the Terzis on our way to dinner.

The results were fabulous. We rang the bell at the locked gate at the back of the spacious backyard and were admitted. Lighted torches guided us to tables laden with all kinds of enticing foods, wines and Cristal champagne. Bill at first thought we were interrupting a party and, as the realization slowly dawned on him that this was his party, friends began appearing. First to make an appearance was Frank, who had driven down from the Riviera with a friend. The surprise was perfect and, when finally our son strolled out the door, Bill was totally overcome. We will always treasure this as one of our best nights in Italy. Wonderful people opened their home and hearts to us, and we were able to celebrate with friends we had not seen for some time and who had gone to considerable lengths to be with us.

Yes, these were undoubtedly heady days that summer. Life was unfolding around us like an exquisite flower, and only one worm threatened to eat away at all that perfection. In late May an attempt was made to deliver an ominously official letter to us at my sister's house in Florida. We had used her address before we had moved to the condominium. Because the document had to be signed for by us, it had not been left with her and she did not know what it was about. We had a very sick feeling, though, when we learned it was from an Italian governmental agency. In went a frantic call to our lawyer. "We think the carnet has surfaced! What should we do?"

"Do nothing yet. Do not have the document picked up until we can confer with one another." In the end, of course, it had to be picked up, and our son faxed the contents to the lawyers. Where were we? Had we sold the boat? The carnet had to be satisfied, and it had to be satisfied in Genova. The law firm began working on a resolution, and Bill and I began chewing our cuticles, all the nails having long since been devoured. While negotiations ran back and forth between the lawyers and port authorities, we tried to amuse ourselves and take our minds off our anxieties.

Gatti meets *Pietro Micca*.

Gatti on sea side of port.

CHAPTER XXXI

EXPEDITION ON THE TIBER

'Those graceful groves that shade the plain,
Where Tiber rolls majestic to the main,
And flattens, as he runs, the fair campagne.'
**Ovid, *Metamorphoses* (*Book xiv*, *Aeneas Arrives
in Italy*)   Sir Samuel Garth, translator**

The Tiber – or Tevere – is a river of legend and paradox. It was into its tawny flood that evil Uncle Amulius floated the infant twins Romulus and Remus in an attempt to wipe out the true heirs to the throne. This villainy was thwarted by a mother wolf that lifted them from the raging waters in her gentle jaws and carried them back to the cozy lair of her natural cubs. The paradoxes of the famous river were evident even then, as helpless babes were saved from the murderous ferocity of a human relative to be nourished by a wild beast. The tributaries of the Tiber had long since carved out the hills that the twins would later select for the location of a great new city, and it was on these same hills that Romulus killed his brother Remus and established the city named for himself alone. This probably shows that no matter how good a beast's intentions may be, wolf milk is not the preferred nutrition for human infants. Brotherly love and fratricide added to the riparian paradox.

While the Tiber provided a means of commerce and connection to the Mediterranean and lands beyond, it also provided protection from hostile approaches from the sea. Originating in the mountains near Florence, the river makes its way 210 miles to Rome. Much river traffic existed pretty far inland in ancient times, with marble being barged upriver all the way to Orvieto. The 20 additional miles of river from the city to the sea were navigable by seagoing vessels. Thousands upon thousands amphorae of oil and wine were unloaded at Testaccio, where over time a great hill of broken pottery rose. This famous landmark is today at street level home to stables, a nursery, restaurants and car dealerships. It is topped by churches, ruins and lush vegetation.

Little ports lined the Tiber's banks within the city, catering to military, commercial and ferry traffic. With the exception of the very wealthy, who could afford houses with strong and tall protective walls, people lived on and tilled the land right down to the river banks in soil made fertile by seasonal floodings. But these same floods also worked great hardship on both farmers and wharfmen alike. Three or four times each century enormous floods were recorded that wreaked havoc on the city at large. Throughout Rome today one can see stones set high into tall building fronts recording the height of the water in such and such a year. While the river served both as a fresh water source and as a sewer carrying off refuse to the sea, that ample flow also bore logs and solid debris which were – and still are – swept down and endanger sailors. Few blessings in life come to us unencumbered with mirror curses.

While the Tiber today is certainly a major geographic component of Rome as it sweeps through town in great curves, it does not provide the focal point that the Seine does for Paris, for example. In 1900 huge travertine walls were erected to contain the floods. Today in downtown Rome one must look over the walls along the tree lined *lungotevere* that follows the river's course at street level or pause on one of the many bridges that span the river to view it well. In several areas, flights of stairs provide descent to the quay, where one can stroll along the river's edge. So despite being so far below street level, the Tiber is very accessible and also very beautiful. Lovers from around the globe bask in the sensual atmosphere. For years civic groups have been trying to improve the health, beauty and potential of the river, and within just the last two years ferry taxis and dinner cruise boats have begun carrying riders from Tiber Island upriver. Educational tours, which go downstream from the Marconi Bridge to Tiber's mouth and concentrate on historic sites and environmental concerns, have been started. While to many the Tiber may appear yellow, muddy, or just plain dirty, to true Romans it is *Il Tevere Biondo* or "blond" Tiber. The sentiments here are not unlike those expressed by Americans who deeply love "Old Man River," our own paradoxical Mississippi.

We had felt on relatively intimate terms with the river within the city of Rome because we had visited frequently over the years. So it came as some surprise to us one day when Alberto casually asked if we had been up the river in the dinghy yet. It had never occurred to us that such a thing could be done, but the seed having been planted, we couldn't wait to sample the fruit. Alberto himself was familiar with the river up as far as Testaccio and advised us to take lots of fuel for *Gattina* and lots of water for ourselves. From our slip in port we are able to see the masts of sailboats skimming above our breakwater as they sail up and down the river and it is really surprising that we had not ventured up there on our own inspiration.

Very early one June morning as we tried to get our minds off carnet troubles, we loaded up the suggested necessities along with bread, cheese, olives, wine and the cell phone. It was still very cool, the seas were calm and there were even four magnificent swans floating regally before the control tower. Out in the Mediterranean, we were accosted by a *carabinieri* boat and had to explain that we were a tender and not a solo vessel. Otherwise we would have been required to be flagged and have our insurance documents on board with us. It took no more than two words of my Italian to assure the officials that we were *stranieri* or foreigners. This term hurt my feelings a bit, but given the circumstances, I got over it. The amusing thing about the whole incident was that these *carabinieri* were docked a pier over from us and had an office at the port. Many mornings we had *cappuccini* and *cornetti* at the Maremosso at tables adjacent to theirs. I guess it pays to look busy.

Having handled this confrontation, which took place before our long breakwater fronting the sea, we scurried around the edge of our port and entered the Tiber's mouth. The river flows down through Rome and eventually empties into the Tyrrhenian Sea from two mouths, so to speak. The mouth we turned up is the one that runs along the side of our port. It is called the Fiumara Grande and is the natural riverbed. The more northerly mouth is a canal dug back in the Imperial Age of Rome. Between the two "branches" lies a large piece of land roughly rectangular in shape called the Isola Sacra, or Sacred Island. On the canal side of the island is the bustling little city of Fiumicino. The branches join together at a point above Fiumicino called the Capo Due Rami. The term "fiumara" derives from the Italian words *fiume* (river) and *mare* (sea). Despite the strong flow of the river, the waters are also affected by the tides of the Tyrrhenian and are brackish. There are times when weather denies egress or ingress to the river; the mouth is shallow from transported silt and awesome, enormous waves can build up quite quickly. The mouth of the Fiumara can be a very dangerous place indeed on occasion.

We were at once surprised by the strength of the flow even in June and appreciated Alberto's caveat to have lots of fuel. Our eight horsepower Honda was being positively gluttonous. On either side of us, the banks were lined with ramshackle but functional homes, whose main feature was a great net at the river's edge. These hung picturesquely over the water from tall, rickety racks, and the whole scene in the cool purity of early morning was one of serenity and simple beauty rather than the squalor and poverty they present on the land side. Off to our starboard side we could see the Tor San Michele, designed by Michelangelo for Pope Pio V. This tall octagonal stone tower was completed by Giovanni Lippi after Michelangelo's death and was used as a defense from sea attacks up until 1807. We actually can see this tower much better from the port than from the river because the Tiber has changed its course numerous times in its long history, and the tower no longer sits at river's edge. Unfortunately, although the tower appears to be in magnificent repair, it is fenced off and visitors are not welcomed.

Marinas now flanked us on either side. Some of the boat yards were long and narrow, hugging the banks on one side and shouldered in on the other by the high levees that protect the Isola Sacra from flood. The majority of the yards were tiny operations camped on the river bank. The most modern development was the new Porto Romano, a community of condominiums and the Tevere Yacht Club, built around a lovely harbor which we had actually seriously investigated before buying our slip at Porto di Roma. Its sparkling swimming pool and brilliantly green lush lawns set it apart from the decidedly less pristine works around it.

Above and below this characteristically out-of-place, up-to-date area, decrepit wooden piers staggered along the water's edge. Boats moored there were rafted four and five abreast, only some of the over 3,000 boats moored along the river. Other boats rose on the dry land beyond the docks, propped up on all kinds of supports, from old logs to steel barrels. They filled the spaces between buildings that looked as though they should have collapsed long ago. There was activity everywhere and we, having visited these yards from land-side, knew that those old buildings housed artisans, tools, equipment and know-how to correct any ill a ship of any construction might suffer. We knew that in that massive structure of rusted metal at Tecnomar rested entire mahogany trees sliced into enormous timbers.

There would be a time when *Gatti* would be a winter guest here. She would be housed in that tall carpenters' shop and have her stern sheathed in the venerable mahogany that lay aging there at this very moment. Competent artisans would repair her cruel wound so poorly tended to in Lavagna. We passed our good friend *Pietro Micca*, the steamship, and discovered where the "*Gattofelice*" of literary fame was moored. This was particularly exciting for me since I was at the time improving my Italian and learning more about boating in the Mediterranean by reading the book of the same name as this boat. The author is Nino Codagnone, and Alberto had given me an autographed copy of the book because he was amused that our boat names were so similar.

Near Tecnomar the river was narrowed by an island that appeared to be constructed of weeds and reeds. We could not see the opposite bank of the river any longer, although we knew that little yards filled that side as well. After *Gatti's* future repairs would be completed, she would spend two weeks in these river waters, rafted with five other vessels across from this apparent island of reeds. We would discover that there is more to the island than meets the eye. Called Isola Boacciana, it supports a few cottonwoods and related trees and a medley of bird voices choruses there 24 hours a day. Most delightful would be the evening cuckoos and big swooping bats with their voracious appetites for equally voracious mosquitoes. We would also discover the difficulty of climbing over boat decks to reach our own and having neighbors tramp across ours. We would become aware of the constant flow of flotsam that catches between those moored boats and must be knocked loose and set adrift every couple of days. But on this June day we did not have intimate knowledge of life on the banks of the great river, so we did a lot of marveling and surmising.

To our starboard now we could see the Tor Boacciana. This stone tower was standing sentinel at least as far back as 1190 because it is described in records of the landing of Richard the Lionhearted. It is presumably located on the site of the Ostia lighthouse of antiquity. It stands crumbling amid brambles and climbing vines that seem intent on loosening one stone from the other. Or perhaps it is those same tendrils that hold the poor edifice upright. In any event, unlike the Tor San Michele, it is readily accessible to anyone willing to scramble through the suffocating vegetation. Just beyond the tower is the first bridge crossing the river, connecting the cities of Ostia and Fiumicino. The bridge is low and, while it is an essential for the bumper-to-bumper insane land traffic, its construction had to have caused great financial loss to the boat works along the upper river banks.

Up we chugged past the point called Capo Due Rami, the fork where the Tevere divides into the canal and the Fiumara through which we had just passed. We were now in the Tiber proper, and the change was dramatic. There was no development whatever. We curved around the broad meadows of the ruins of Ostia Antica to our starboard, and then we could have almost imagined ourselves in the time of the Republic. Trees and tall grasses lined the banks. Occasionally a stone ruin poked up through the vegetation. A distance from the river we could see the living town of Ostia Antica, where stands the renaissance castle of Julius II. Originally located on a bend of the river, it guarded the approach to Rome. The record flood of 1557 cut through the river meander and isolated the castle one kilometer from the water.

We continued upriver passing the suburban towns that march along the river to Rome, A commuter train connects them all from Ostia on the sea to the metro stations in EUR, the Basilica of St. Paul, and Piramide. Occasionally we could see or hear this busy little commuter that runs frequently all day long and into the night. Otherwise, the only way we knew we were passing these urban centers was by the huge drains gushing treated water into the river. In one spot where the flow was not so strong, we became aware of bubbles all around us. It felt a little like moving through a river of Coca-Cola. Little bubbles fizzed and sputtered about us. Looking below the surface, we could see big bubbles rising from deep down. We had been jokingly told not to put our hands in the water if we wished to withdraw them with flesh still adhered to bone and were happy to comply with this advice.

But not only did pollution bubble up from the deep. A sharp outlook had to be kept for sundry items coming down on the river surface. Much of what hurled down on us were brush and tree parts, ranging from branches to large tree trunks. But some of the detritus was manufactured, heading to sea to be cracked into by some unwary vessel or cleverly submerged until some low tide would reveal its ugliness. The strangest manmade item we dodged was a floating refrigerator. This was a full-size unit with the door open. Whatever provided flotation was, and remains, a mystery to us. All of these items, natural and otherwise, of course end up in the sea, where they can travel great distances and become a major danger to navigation. When our Navtex became fully functional, we received almost daily warnings of floating perils. These would include tree trunks many meters long, lengths of PVC pipe, lifeboats, vessels adrift, chests, cetacean carcasses, and an occasional mention of, yes, refrigerators. It was very possible that some similar solid item hiding just below the waves of the Ligurian Sea had brought grief to *Gatti*. One would suppose it would be sensible to try to corral these hazards before they reached the point where the Fiumara and Canal part company. But for reasons obscure to us, no efforts appear to be made in this direction.

Before many more minutes in our upriver voyage, we passed under the modern bridge that carries the Grande Raccordo Anulare, or circle road, around the city of Rome. The roar of traffic intruded on our solitude briefly and then was left behind. Higher up the stream we passed a few houses with fishing piers and a couple of quaint, floating cafés. Otherwise there was nothing but silence broken only by a bird or two or a leaping fish doubtless in search of any available oxygen. The quiet was again suddenly fractured by the roaring, honking and general cacophony of Roman traffic, and we could see beautiful classical buildings beyond the banks beside us. This was EUR, the section of Rome that Mussolini had sought to develop as the new city center. As fast as it had appeared, it dropped from sight and although we knew we were now well into Rome, a stranger never would have guessed it. No noise of the feverish traffic above filtered down to us.

We continued under the busy Marconi Bridge but had to abandon our pilgrimage before we reached Testaccio because a small dam blocked the way. Had the water been higher, we might have negotiated it but, as it was, we were 17 miles from *Gatti,* and the day had become hot. That water Alberto had advised us to bring along was being gulped as quickly as *La Gattina's* fuel. We later learned that in our ignorance we had passed an Etruscan portico and a place where the ancient Romans had changed oxen teams that pulled the boats and barges up against the powerful flow. The tour boat that now operates from the Marconi Bridge downstream points out these and other fascinating places.

We ruefully turned back and fairly flew with the current. It was easy to see why Romans for centuries had moored mill-barges in the middle of the current; the rapid flow provided hydro-power to grind grains into flour for bread. We tied up briefly to a willow tree overhanging the bank and, while we ate lunch, called our son in Florida. It is a strange and wonderful world that allows one to be isolated on one of the world's most famous rivers in the midst of ruins centuries old and to talk in person to a child a continent and ocean away. Our children are gradually getting used to the idea that the parents they knew as regular, staid individuals may contact them from some pretty bizarre places. It is a rare and wonderful thing for a parent to be able to do and a fair retribution.

This time when we reached the Capo Due Rami river fork, we ventured down the canal. The canal was built by the emperor Claudius who constructed a port in 42 A.D. More than 3,000 ships navigated the Mediterranean at that time just in the pursuit of food imports for the Roman population, which numbered close to one million. According to the Roman historian Tacitus, a terrible storm in 62 A.D. was responsible for destroying 200 ships in the port. A fire ensued, which destroyed another 100 ships along the Tiber. Between the reigns of Claudius and Trajan, the Tiber continued to deposit silt, undergo periods of flooding, and move the river bed about. Trajan began work on a new port further inland in 106 A.D. The result was an hexagonal port with each side measuring 350 meters.

Today the location of Claudius' port has been swallowed by Fiumicino Airport, and Trajan's port can be visited only under restricted conditions. In the future, knowledgeable friends would give us a special tour of the port, but that was the future; this day a place that had so much allure to a yearning old Latin teacher was closed to us. The canal is an active commercial area, so we did not venture down too far in *Gattina*. The upper part is well developed, with the lawns and gardens of exquisite villas running down to the river's edge. A few very modern and efficient boat yards are also located in this area; they become grungier, less efficient, and less modern as one continues downstream. The canal eventually becomes a frenetic center for commercial fishing boats, no place for an eight-foot dinghy. The city of Fiumicino lies on either side of the canal and is best visited by strolling along the quays where fresh catches from the sea can be bought or one can view the fishing vessels from the comfort of a café table.

We turned around into the fierce current again, went back up the canal to the fork, re-entered the Fiumara and, racing now on a current excited by its proximity to the sea, were dumped into the Med. We motored around our breakwater and entered our port, where *Gatti* was waiting impatiently and a little out of temper at having been excluded from our adventure.

The popular Tiber flows around the Isola Boacciana.

CHAPTER XXXII

AT LAST

'The ship is anchor'd safe and sound, its voyage closed and done.
From fearful trip the victor ship comes in
with object won.'
Walt Whitman, *O Captain! My Captain!*

Despite our amusing ourselves with trips and adventures, the shadow of the carnet blocked a great deal of our sun and deeply worried us. When we had first brought *Gatti* into Italy, our lawyer had made a copy of the document, but since no one had known what to do with it, it sat in our file in his office. But now we knew what had to be done: The official letter in Florida spelled it all out. It stated unequivocally that *i Gatti Felici* would have to return to the port of Genova for the issue to be fully resolved. Initially Alberto was concerned about this, fearing we might be impounded, so he used his considerable influence to have the matter handled in Rome. All to no avail. Italy has been a unified nation since 1861, but Liguria is one region, Lazio another, and never the twain shall meet in many circumstances. No, the carnet had to be satisfied at the point of entry and, yes, Bill and I had better show up there physically on *Gatti* with money and proof of her being laid up.

The specter that had shadowed us for three years was now a menacing reality. Even had Dominic still been a friend, he could not have provided the verification we had constantly requested. Our lawyer advised us to reconstruct our comings and goings. So for two weeks we celebrated birthdays, explored the Tiber and in between tried to decipher passport stamps and determine our months in Italy and in the United States. Only someone with a smudgy passport several years old can fully appreciate this challenge. But we managed it and, in the end, we had a credible record of when the boat had been in use and when untenanted.

Only then were the proper port personnel contacted by the law office, and we at last stared reality full in the face. The authorities appeared to recognize that we were a harmless retired couple, without a lot of good sense maybe, but harmless all the same. Sometimes it is a good thing to be viewed as a happy, innocent puppy! It was possible to get the carnet taken care of and ourselves on legal footing, but we would need to go to Genova with the boat and do it soon. *Gatti* had not yet been repaired, and still leaked at the bow when underway. While she did not take on water at dock or while planing, we knew to our sorrow what happened at other times. We also knew that she was basically sound despite the leak because she had been carefully examined in the boatyard and we had had additional screws put in at the waterline.

We rented a car and drove the 250 odd miles to Genova and met with the port authorities. We had our questions answered satisfactorily even if the answers themselves were unsatisfactory. We were in trouble, but not deep trouble. We had not sold the yacht; we had not tried to deprive Italy of tax dollars. No one wanted to be punitive. We just had to show up and prove that what we said was true.

It was understood by all parties that weather was a factor, but we were urged to try to resolve the matter as expeditiously as possible. Our nerves also demanded a speedy resolution. To have this issue hanging over us until the following September was unthinkable. It was accepted that we had laid up the boat lawfully to the degree anyone understood the concept, but we had to have the last page of the carnet signed off at the same port that had signed us in. It was suggested that Mr. Basilico could be useful in handling this. Our jaws fell. Was this the same Basilico who had thrown the carnet into his wastebasket and told us to forget it, that no one cared about it?

The importer we were dealing with was nonplussed at our story and told us that of all the people at the port, Basilico was the one who should have most appreciated the gravity of the carnet. Not only was he a yacht broker of some renown, but his brother held a prominent position at the port. In any event, it became painfully clear to current authorities that we refused to deal with a man who had already caused us so much uncertainty. Against all odds we had actually located the right man to help us and, worse than helping us, he had, for whatever reason, chosen to mislead us.

Another problem was that we did not have the original carnet document in our possession in Italy. Our lawyer had a copy, though. We left with clear instructions for the first time during our Italian experience. The importer would find someone other than Basilico to handle the problem. We would take a copy of the carnet to our local *carabinieri* office and swear that we had lost the original. This would make the copy legally acceptable. We would round up €700 and arrive at the Magazzino di Cotone at the old Port of Genova on *Gatti*.

After actually speaking to competent people and knowing exactly what to do, we drove back to Rome and got *Gatti* ready. We took our carnet copy over to the *carabinieri* office at the port. We were greeted by a handsome young man nattily dressed in his Armani-designed uniform with the bold red stripe down the leg. He spoke no English, but we managed to make our needs known. He doubtless knew our predicament well in advance, as everyone else at the port seemed to know and sympathize. It is a frightening thing to fall into the clutches of a bureaucracy, which perhaps Italians understand even better than Americans. The officer invited us in to sit in front of his desk while he got things in order. With the greatest care and precision, he arranged shiny blue sheets of carbon paper between three forms on a clipboard. Italian technology is as advanced as anyone's, so we looked at one another wonderingly, trying to remember when we had last seen carbon paper. Apparently this was a normal exercise for the officer, who did not appear to see anything amiss. All was handled neatly, professionally and efficiently, and we signed the top sheet. We then took one copy, attached it to the carnet copy, and met the first requirement.

We had made a reservation at the Port of Genoa before we left. We were not about to tie up at the suggested pier of the Magazzino di Cotone. It is an interesting pier supporting long buildings that used to be cotton warehouses. Today these house restaurants, chandleries, video arcades, shops and ... Basilico's office. Instead we went to the pier on the other side of the beautiful aquarium that is built out over the old harbor like a long blue boat.

Since we could not make it from Rome to Genova in one day, we decided to make another reservation at the little port near Piombino where we had fueled up with Angelo. It is a good mid-way stop. Making the reservation was an interesting feat in itself. No one believed there was any port except the commercial one at Piombino. But we knew we had stopped at a different, delightful port just around the bend.. We looked in our *Pagine Azzurre*, the Blue Pages that annually update details about every port in the country. No mention of our port there either. Alberto looked at us as though we were hallucinating.

About this time, our old friends the Odinos on their good ship *Odino* sailed in from a disappointing trip to Greece. They had spent two weeks at a slip a short way down from us earlier in the season, and we had greatly enjoyed their company. They are a French couple who speak excellent English and have visited the States numerous times.

The Odinos have a sailboat and unlike many other people we met with sailing craft, actually move about under sail for the better part of their travels but, like ourselves, they prefer to stay in ports rather than anchoring out. When they had stopped at Porto di Roma the first time, they were on their way to holiday in Greece. They might have stayed longer except that the steam tug *Pietro Micca* tied up at the end of our pier. Their big, bewhiskered cat, also called Odino, took great exception to the hissing and smoke-belching of our new neighbor and kept slithering past our stern on his belly doing his own hissing and obviously intent on either catching or driving away the intruder. To preserve feline sanity as well as their own, the Odinos had moved on southward.

They had found no docking available in Ionian Greece, and so they were now on their way back to Menton to await the arrival of a grandchild. And, yes, they planned to dock at Marina di Salivoli on the way back as they had on the way down. Yes, of course, our shadowy port existed, and Odino pulled out his new revised edition of the Blue Pages to prove it. We dialed the number provided; a real flesh-and-blood person spoke to us; and a slip was reserved. How many times we have encountered this regionalism! One would think that at least in the boating community where waves wash over arbitrary political divisions, a measure of unity would exist. But at least we now had met the requirements of docking and fueling. We gathered money, passports and boat documents and surveyed the heavens and seas.

By now our Navtex was working overtime, to the point that we had had to stock up on the heat-sensitive paper it printed on. At 0900 and 2100 hours every day we got a printout from the Rome Meteorological Service covering pertinent Italian seas. We had by now blocked out other stations, including Oslo and the iceberg reports. It listed current conditions and outlooks as well as storms under course or predicted and general meteorological situations. Usually the reports were reasonably accurate. In addition to weather, Navtex was providing us with daily updates on military operations, dangers to navigation such as traveling appliances, lighthouse and buoy reports, and various other bits of information that might prove to be of importance to the mariner. The reports were printed out in English sometimes fractured to the point that we almost fractured our ribs with laughter, but that is really an unkind comment, particularly in view of my fractured Italian. The wording was sometimes very funny, but the information was certainly understandable and valuable. In addition, the search and rescue messages sent out on this remarkable system have resulted in the saving of lives that might otherwise have been lost at sea – from wealthy yacht owners, to ferry passengers, to illegal aliens piled into shallow little boats. We had been receiving enough messages on the Navtex since leaving Lavagna to feel secure with the system on board.

Now our little unit was printing out current reports that the weather would hold for four or five days which should give us time to complete our mission. A mistral was blowing through the Gulf of Leon which would eventually hit the mountains surrounding Genova and bop, as usual, between islands and coast for several days. All torpedo firing and associated war games were restricted to an area around La Spezia. Yet predictions, as we well knew, were iffy at best in the Ligurian Sea. We had been trapped there enough to feel a strong dread.

We called over to our tower by radio and were informed of the best time to fuel up. The tower and fuel dock sit on the same side of the port entrance as our slip, and we could see a fair amount of summertime activity going on. The difficulty was not so much that there were a lot of boats fueling as the size of the yachts filling their enormous tanks. When we finally tied up at the dock, we were the only vessel there, and we told the attendant to fill both tanks with *benzina*. We went about our chores of closing hatches and portholes and then prepared to relax on the dock in the warm sun while the fueling took place. Fortunately, before too long, Bill realized that we were not being fueled with *benzina* at all, but rather *gasolio*. *Benzina* is gasoline and *gasolio* is diesel fuel, and to confuse the two is to ruin expensive engines.

The poor gas attendant shut off the pump and ran to get a hand pump, returning with a couple other men to help him. For the next half hour they laboriously pumped out the diesel fuel. Everyone was apologetic and relieved that *Gatti*'s tanks had been so low. Yes, everyone had heard us ask for *benzina*, but in Europe so few boats our size use gasoline that habit interfered with hearing. Afterward, the fuel attendants told us always to ask in future for *benzina verde* and be sure that the nozzle inserted into our tanks was green. *Benzina verde* is simply unleaded gasoline but saying the extra word might jog the attention of the next gas pumper. We have taken this advice seriously and have avoided a repetition of this error.

Early the following morning we slipped our lines and headed out of our safe port. We left our heavy spring lines at our dock as a kind of personal assurance that we would be back soon. It was not a joyous departure. We were going a long and expensive distance back to a place we had been eager to leave. A leisurely trip in fair weather in a boat that had been properly repaired would have been all right, but the current conditions were unsettling. It had taken us so long to escape to Rome that I feared I might not get back for a long time. The port personnel had some question as to whether or not we would make it out of our own waters. A large swell was sending spray over our mole and, as we were told later, water broke over *Gatti*'s bow and foamed about us as we headed out into the open sea. But we sailed with best wishes and prayers for *buon vento* and were waved off with smiles. I don't know how much they may have doubted our competence.

We had not had *Gatti* out since she had come to Rome. I know I entertained a lot of doubt about myself. We had made 30-mile runs along the Pacific coast and we had come from Civitavecchia to Rome by ourselves, but this was a 250-nautical mile trip up a busy coast in unsettled weather to a commercial port. There were just the two of us, and I had little experience in handling such a big boat. I would be responsible for look-out, getting Bill things he needed, updating our dead reckoning chart, and other chores unassociated with the helm. I was concerned about the boat as well. Pino, the port diver, had cleaned her bottom prior to our departure and reported the wood in good condition, but a sizable section of it had no paint and here marine growth was luxuriant. Those unsatisfactory workers in Lavagna had either neglected to repaint her after the last "repair," had not put her back in the water before the anti-fouling properties in the paint died, or had used junk paint.

The trip went better than expected. We had proper charts with our dead reckoning drawn out. We had our plotter, on which we had set waypoints, and an electronic chart that provided us with a visible track and pertinent information on points of concern such as fishing areas and military zones. The sounder assured us that we had meters and meters of water below us. Information was exchanged between the autopilot and plotter. We had our handheld GPS, a magnetic compass in addition to a fluxgate, and a hand-held compass for taking relative bearings. The blips on the radar screen were no longer meaningless neon sparks, but valuable bits of information which, put together with our other input, provided us about as much certainty as one can expect at sea.

We had learned a lot since our first Coast Guard class and, although we were not experts in the actual use of some of the equipment, we understood it and became more expert by the mile. It actually became fun to put to practical use much of what we had learned in a theoretical sort of way. Additionally, our radio was on but there was little conversation this trip. We listened in as some anglers discussed lunch options and the British captains of two charter yachts compared notes on the best anchorage off Elba. The weather even cooperated to large extent. All around us the skies were overcast and, for the most part, we could not glimpse the Italian coast 12 miles to our starboard. But for the two days required to reach Genova, the sun shone above us from a clear hole in the sky. It almost felt as though we were in a Renaissance painting of the Annunciation or a venerable religious work in which golden light is shed on some saint or other. A feeling of peace and security began to warm me as it appeared we were really being watched over.

Up the Laziale coast we moved, past the sandy beaches of Santa Marinella and Fregene. It being summer now, we could make out the gaudy colors of lounges and umbrellas. Past the port Riva di Traiano, where we had spent such a frozen, exhausted night six months earlier. We traveled past the bustling port of Civitavecchia, but this time it was morning and we did not have to contend with the vocabulary of maritime lights.

We moved out of the region of Lazio into Tuscan waters. The Maremma stretched out flat and green far inland before it mounted into rolling hills. By the time we rounded the promontory of

Argentario, the sea was kicking up considerably. A lot of ferries and pleasure boats are always carrying people between Porto Ercole, Santo Stefano, and the offshore islands of Giglio and others in the Tuscan Archipelago. The weather had apparently not dampened anyone's spirits, and we had to maintain a sharp lookout. Scheduled vessels such as ferries have the right of way, and it seemed we were the give-way vessel in every sighting. The radar screen became a truly valuable aid and was fairly jumping with green blips all about us. Now we had slid past Mount Argentario and crossed the Bay of Follonica, which had so cruelly buffeted and drenched us when we had come down in January with Angelo. Its disposition was not much improved, and so with gratitude we pulled up to the fuel dock in charming Marina di Salivoli.

We took on fuel, docked without a hitch, paid for the night and made a reservation for the return trip home. At the port office we were accosted by two policemen who asked to see our passports. Because we had left them on the boat, the pair followed us back to the dock. This was all a little unnerving because we already were dealing with our share of legal problems. We produced our documents, but they declined our invitation to come aboard. Everything was apparently in order, we answered the typical questions about *Gatti*'s age, etc. and graciously accepted their *complimenti*. Apparently the Italian name with the American flag had caught their attention. This has been the only time in any port that the police have shown the slightest interest in our yacht with its foreign flag. It would appear the security systems of the world are seriously flawed. These, however, were not our concerns – we were tired to the bone. We went below and fell into a deep, well-earned sleep.

At dawn we stole as quietly as possible from the slumbering harbor and continued northward through relatively quiet seas with only anchored fishing boats and an occasional passing military vessel for company. All along the way, yachts and charter boats were securing anchorage in whatever lee spots could be located. Only a fool takes a mistral lightly. We moved past the commercial port of Livorno, where I had spent a frustrated night on *Cielo di San Francisco*. We passed Viareggio, where we had enjoyed Carnevale and been unable to find fuel in January. Already we were back in true mountain country, with the alpine peaks glistening white with marble. Past Massa and Carrara, where the creamy white marble is loaded onto ships in monstrous chunks or huge slabs; past the Gulf of

La Spezia, where we had to now pay close attention to the military boundaries and submarine zones marked on our paper and electronic charts; and then we were out of the Northern Tyrrhenian and back in the Ligurian Sea. Our plotter, which had been tracing a red track from our slip in Rome from waypoint to waypoint, continued to do so; for the first time it did not ship us off to Ecuador, Labrador or other unlikely terrain. Now the rugged mountain peaks rose directly from the waves and foam broke over rocks jutting out of the sea. Above us hung the familiar towns of the Cinque Terre, and before long we had rounded the point of Sestri Levanti and could see the breakwater at Lavagna across the Gulf of Tigullio. It seemed strange to race past the town, the mouth of the Entella, Chiavari, and finally the promontory of Portofino.

This was no longer home. We had loved it there and we still felt a kinship that will never leave us, but we felt no sadness in leaving it in our wake. Having rounded the towering promontory and passed quaint little Camogli nestled on its other side, we were now in essentially new waters. True, we had made the run down once with Dominic at the helm, but that had been so long ago and had seemed more like an enchantment than a journey. We had never ventured north of Camogli since our arrival in Italy, even with Angelo. We knew this coast well from train and car and hiking trail, but we had never navigated it. The little towns were, if possible, even more charming from the sea. Their tiny, rickety matchstick-like stairs, bolted into often sheer rock faces, worked their jagged way down the craggy slopes to tiny beach areas snuggled between towering rocks. There is absolutely nothing that can prevent a Ligurian from accessing the sea.

Our heavenly sun was becoming more and more obscured by clouds as we approached the large basin that defines the old port of Genova. The ancient harbor is not really all that large, but it supports a tremendous amount of divergent business. Several piers and marinas stretch into the water, and the harbor itself seems folded into the heart of town. It is a fascinating area, but one that is not well developed for the typical tourist. Waterfront bars and restaurants and heavenly bakeries flourish; so do prostitution and drug trafficking. A traffic-crammed raised highway, the Soprelevata, skirts the entire commercial waterfront, whose construction destroyed the courtyards of beautiful palazzos which used to grace the harbor. It reminds one much of the old Embarcadero of San Francisco that used to obscure the view and beauty of the San Francisco waterfront. It was removed after an earthquake. While nobody would wish such a calamity for Genova, the fact remains that the harbor would be much lovelier with the elevated roadway gone.

Of the several marinas in the basin we had selected the Marina Antico Porto for a number of reasons. Phil and Marylou had wintered here; it was next to the renowned aquarium built out over the water; and it was not the Magazzino di Cotone, where we could scarcely avoid running into Basilico. Having by now a nodding acquaintance with the radio, I called the marina number and was gratified to hear a clear English response. We were expected and while we awaited the promised *ormeggiatori*, Bill edged *Gatti* smoothly into the harbor, unruffled by ferries, tugs, and sightseeing boats. In fact, the only irritant was the wind-sailors who flitted about unaware of any law of the sea or personal survival.

We were passing the long pier that supports the old cotton warehouses when the *ormeggiatoris'* inflatable arrived and led us to a conveniently located slip in front of the port office and in full view of the attractive aquarium. No sooner had we hooked up our water and power and called the importer to say we had arrived in port and would report to his office early the next morning, than a huge wind arose, violent lightning strafed the port, roaring thunder shuddered our hull, and the skies split open, torn by their oceans of rain. This storm was one of the worst we had ever experienced during our entire Ligurian stay, and it seemed inconceivable that such fury had been lurking so close to us on the open sea and harbor entry. It was a terrifying thought and once again confirmed the reality that nothing must ever be taken for granted at sea. While we are all too aware of being undeserving of divine gifts, we are nonetheless grateful for them.

The following morning we caught a cab, which navigated its way through the confusions of the harbor and the Cristoforo Colombo Airport and deposited us at the office of the importer who was handling the affair. Here we were; here were our boat documents; here were our passports; here was the carnet copy and the sworn statement of loss; here was the money. All of this was swept together by the authorities, not without a little amazement. I don't think they had expected us to come through with such dispatch, and I also think it proved to them that we had indeed been trying very hard for a very long time to straighten out the carnet. We were introduced to the customs representative who would go and look at the boat and get the carnet signed off. It was agreed we would go and visit the aquarium while he went about his business; he would call us on our cell phone when he was finished.

We had never visited the aquarium in all our months of living nearby. Our car rental agent at the Porto di Roma had been shocked to learn of this serious oversight, for the Italians are justly proud of the aquarium. We promised that this trip we would go for sure. "No, you won't," he had smugly observed. "If you didn't go when you lived so close, you won't go when you have so much on your mind." This was a challenge that obviously had to be met, so we purchased our tickets and went inside. No sooner had we stopped at the first exhibit than the phone rang. It was the custom's officer asking us to meet him at the boat. We got our tickets stamped so we could re-enter the aquarium and charged over a bit apprehensively. What could the problem be now? Why did he need us so soon? We tore around the corner of the marine office and were greeted with a smile. All was in order, the carnet was signed off, and our nightmare was over.

We were issued exit papers from Genova to Malta. No one really cared whether we went to Malta or not. The Italian government was pleased to stamp that we had left Genova and both they and our own U.S. Department of Commerce probably toasted one another across the sea now that this thorny little nuisance had been resolved. The essential but elusive stamp had been obtained. The cats were legal; the cats were free. The cats returned to the aquarium with light hearts and took pictures from the windows of the beautiful old boat moored below them. Souvenirs had to be bought for the Europcar staff to prove we had kept our promise. When we returned to America, we received the Department of Commerce's documents closing the carnet. As far as both countries were concerned, the carnet had been satisfied. As far as we were both concerned, we never wanted to hear the word again.

The immediate meteorological disturbance had blown itself out the night of our arrival and while the mistral was now bearing down upon us, the weather south of us was not too bad. We had spent two nights in Genoa and now were miraculously free to go home. For the third time we were going to try to escape the Ligurian Sea. We were up and ready to go the third morning after our departure from Rome. We were first at the fuel dock, eager to be on our way, and as we waited for the *benzina verde* to flow through the green nozzle into our hungry tanks, we chatted with a couple on a trawler who were planning to go to Sardegna that day. They subscribed to a German weather service and kindly checked with it on our behalf. It appeared that if we did not tarry, we should be able to outrun the storm that was headed in our direction.

We headed down a coast that was by now becoming almost familiar. We passed the lighthouse at Portofino; crossed the Gulf of Tigullio with a sigh of mixed nostalgia and relief; passed the area where we had collided with whatever had been in the water and where we had discovered with Angelo that the repair had not been done; and approached the active military zone off La Spezia. Weather conditions do not seem to deter the Italian military from its various maneuvers, and our Navtex delineated the areas where torpedo firing was to take place. Once again our plotter stayed true to our location, perhaps because the Italian military is not really interested in luring vessels into range. Dominic and others had told us tales of entering these zones at night and being accosted by high speed naval vessels issuing warnings and also of seeing eerie lights deep in the waters below them. We wanted none of this excitement and thus kept an extremely close eye out. So close an eye, in fact, that we spied a very strange black rubbery-looking object sticking out above the waves. Whatever it might have been, it ran along side us for a fair distance as we skirted the military zone. Very odd things occur in these Italian waters; we began to question seriously what we might really have struck on that first ill-fated journey.

We continued south, passing a fair number of military vessels, giving them a wide berth, and receiving no communications or apparent notice. Bill had been watching a faint blip on the edge of our radar screen as I kept my lookout. I spotted something far ahead on the hazy horizon that looked for all the world like a large sailboat crossing our course. Now classroom training would come in handy. We had plenty of time for tracking because it was so far away. Out came the maneuvering board, and we began to calculate the other vessel's course and speed. It became clear at once that this was no sailboat. It was very, very big; very, very dense; and was moving very, very quickly on a course 180 degrees from ours. If security may seem lax in tourist ports, the same cannot be said of military vessels on the high seas. When we were still over a mile apart and had begun our turn to starboard, the oncoming vessel made radio contact. As we passed one another port to port, I could see through my binoculars several sailors, also with binoculars to their eyes, waving to us. They must have wondered what that antique American yacht was doing out on a day like this. For our part, we were awed by the enormous size and speed of their craft. It bristled with armor, tall towers, antennae, and big, fat radar domes. All this prickliness, I suppose, accounts for my having thought it a sailboat.

We continued on our way without further incident until we were approaching Marina di Salivoli. The run was lovely. We had our documents and were blissfully legal; we had our charts and electronics, and they were functioning flawlessly; we had knowledge, and we were using it with textbook results. Enter Salivoli. Since I had by now gained at least a modicum of self confidence, I picked up the radio microphone. "Marina di Salivoli. Marina di Salivoli. *Qui i Gatti Felici*". No response. By the time we had tried to rouse the port personnel several times, two other boats had arrived, making similar requests for a response from the operator. *Niente*. So much for my self-confidence.

The harbor is not large and the entrance commensurate to its size, but finally, in desperation, we entered without receiving clearance. Unlike Porto di Roma, at least it is easy to see vessels that might be about to exit while you enter. We tied up at the fuel dock which occasioned no great comment. We were fueled up but informed no reservation was on record and no slips were available. It was suggested we go back to the next inlet to the north to find harborage for the night. I may be a neophyte navigator on the high seas, but I do my homework, and I knew that the spot indicated would be impossible for us. It was open to the elements, it had only mooring buoys, and a storm was behind us.

We declined this generous offer and put in a call to somewhat snooty Punta Ala, a modern port and condominium development across the Bay of Follonica. They thought they could perhaps accommodate us but never called back with confirmation. In the end, a kind man who had a small fishing boat surrendered his slip to us for the night and moved to something smaller. For the record, one of the other boats that had been calling on the radio and was trying to come in was a French sailboat three times *Gatti*'s size. It was also finally accommodated. After all, a big storm was coming and shelter was essential. We backed gratefully into our spot, paid our rent at the office, and fell into a well-deserved sleep. With any luck we could actually be home the following evening.

Before dawn the next day we prepared as quietly as possible and in short order were out on tranquil waters. Picturesque fishing boats floated on a pink sea under a pink sky as we made our way across a Gulf of Follonica that was slick and tamed, no doubt resting up for the fun times the mistral promised. It wasn't until we reached Argentario, across the broad gulf, that the water kicked up and it was clear the storm was gaining on us. But *Gatti* scented home and plunged bravely on like a horse headed for stable, spewing foam fore and aft, her letters of emancipation stowed safely below. After all, she couldn't afford to slow down, or she would start taking on water at her wounded chine. And what horse does not charge ahead with the barn door so near?

We left the Northern Tyrrhenian Sea and found ourselves at least in our own waters. We plunged past the beautiful seaside resorts, their colorful umbrellas now closed against the impending storm. We approached our home port as dark clouds lowered over us, but the sun valiantly held them off from our bow. Past the canal at Fiumicino we rose and dipped. Past the lighthouse on Isola Sacra and through the muddy effluence of the Tiber, *Gatti* cut. And then we were at our own breakwater, the international flags snapping straight out in the stiff breeze. The waves were beginning to lash against the rocks and wall in piles of pearly foam, but our harbor mouth was open and inviting. With confidence and the pride one feels in overcoming dreadful fear, I pressed the button of my VHF microphone.

"Porto di Roma… Porto di Roma... Porto di Roma. *Qui i Gatti Felici.*"

"*I Gatti Felici* ! Hello!" came back the voice in English, clear, fully comprehensible, and warm with welcome.

"Porto di Roma, *i Gatti Felici* requests entry to the port to berth at *posto sei-sei cinque.*"

"That is possible; I will call the *ormeggiatori.*" I put down the microphone and moved out to tie on fenders. A voice rang out of the radio, "*Ormeggiatori, ormeggiatori, i Gatti Felici* is home."

And here sped the little dinghy with Massimo and Pino waving and shouting, "Did you have a good voyage? Were you successful?"

Oh, yes, indeed: *i gatti felici* – all three of them – had truly come home.

EPILOGUE

'Tho' much is taken, much abides; and tho'
We are not now that strength which in old days
Moved earth and heaven; that which we are, we are;
One equal temper of heroic hearts,
Made weak by time and fate, but strong in will
To strive, to seek, to find, and not to yield.'
                              Lord Tennyson, *Ulysses*

The boat has been in Italy for over six years now. Over time we have fallen into a comfortable pattern only marginally affected by the terrorist fallout. We spend the months of May, June and July in Italy and return to the States for our own *ferragosto* in the warm waters of the Gulf of Mexico during August and part of September. American travelers to Italy must obtain a visa if they plan to remain in the country beyond 90 days. We had not bothered with this formality until recently. But with increasing travel restrictions, we have now obtained a visa and *residenza*. We can now live there year-round if we wish. Mid-September through early December finds us back on board. This is the time of the boat shows, including the world class event in Genoa. We have been invited to participate in antique boat shows, and this is something we look forward to doing. Although every New Year's Eve we long to be at Piazza del Popolo, we seem to get there less and less. It is very cold on the water in the winter, and we seem to feel it more acutely now that we are in our 60s. Family gatherings are important and it is difficult for working children to find the time or money to join us there. In addition, we are now grandparents.

When we returned to Rome in the fall of 2002, we contacted the Giuas who own the steam tug *Pietro Micca* and a fine *cantiere* called Tecnomar. Their experts came over to the port and determined what was needed to bring *Gatti* back to prime condition. In November we motored up the Tiber, where she was pulled and housed in a workshop. We lived aboard for a few days, once again perched up high above dry land. If nothing else, we had learned that before work is begun there must be a very clear communication of exactly what that work is and what it will cost. Knowledgeable men removed planking while we were there to assess personally what needed to be done, and we agreed on repairs. Paper work was filed properly; we did not pay a VAT tax and were given lay-up credit.

Over the next months, while we were home in Florida, superb craftsmen repaired damaged areas (including a rib that had cracked the last time the boat had been pulled), replaced the boat's cracked transom with aged mahogany planks, painted her hull dazzling white, put good anti-fouling paint on her bottom and got her back in the water promptly. We were in telephone and e-mail communication through the entire process even receiving photos of the work in progress. At long last the new water tank with an appropriate pump was installed. When we returned in May, we found our yacht gleaming in the warm sun, rafted to four other boats in the tawny Tiber. We enjoyed this delightful river life for two weeks before revving our engines and returning to our slip, which had been uninhabited all winter. Tecnomar arranged for mechanics to come to the port and give our motors a well-needed servicing.

June 21, 2003 found us docked in the port of the island of Ponza along with our friends Lance and Nikki on *OceanS*, Phil and Mary Lou on *Marbella*, and some of the wealthiest people and finest yachts in the world. *Gatti* was magnificent with her fresh paint and varnish, a bright new U.S. flag fluttering above her new stern. We were complimented continually, yachtsmen begged to buy her, and we were blessed by a priest who made his way down our floating dock with a heavy, garnet-encrusted cross. After all, the summer solstice is the saint day of Ponza's patron of sailors, San Silverio, and mariners, fishermen and boats all seek special blessing and protection.

We spent our days exploring the neighboring Pontine Islands, swimming in the irresistible, clear waters, and shopping on the island. Our nights were filled with fabulous fireworks and a very instructive event. Summer weather is generally tranquil in these waters, but the winter brings huge storms indeed. One of the worst winds that can strike Ponza is the Levante, or east wind. It drives directly into the small harbor, and vessels large and small are forced to flee to a tiny bay on the other side of the island, where they wait for calm to return.

The night before the main events of San Silverio an uncharacteristic east wind pounced upon us suddenly. At midnight we felt our way out of the harbor in the wake of hundreds of yachts. This was a situation to try the expertise of any sailor and we acquitted ourselves well. We used every piece of knowledge we had acquired, maneuvering through unfamiliar, rocky waters in the dark, finding a location to anchor and successfully using the windlass for the first time under duress. Even the hysterical shouts of Italians hailing one another across the dark waters in a Neopolitan dialect foreign to us did not faze us. Again we were reminded of the importance of always having fuel for emergencies and never forgetting that the sea is unpredictable.

Ponza lies 60-odd nautical miles from Rome, and this was the first voyage that I found truly relaxing. Our vessel was repaired, we were legal, and we had good knowledge and experience to fall back on. The entire Ponza trip represented a milestone to us. We had been tested, and we had measured up.

Porto Turistico di Roma is no longer an empty harbor. Most of the slips have been purchased and during the summer months boats from around the world come in and out. In the winter, "cruisers" have found the location an exciting wintering spot. We have become seasonal fixtures at the little café Maremosso and have made many friends of various nationalities at the port and in Ostia. Bill would like to explore by water more; I am happy just being in Rome. For the most part, to date, our exploring has been done by car and train. We have traveled extensively through Italy, France, Switzerland, Spain and Portugal and use *Gatti* much like a waterfront condo. We will be cruising more in the future. We would like to go up the French Riviera and by river and canal make our way through Europe. To tie up at the Bastille certainly has its attraction, not to mention drifting through some of the most beautiful and famous vineyards in the world. Locks are hard on old boats and aging crew, but the difficulties not insurmountable.

Our slip is all that we hoped. Close to the end of the pier, we enjoy our broad view of the busy fairway and the varying moods of the Tyrrhenian Sea beyond. Mega-yachts tie up across the fairway from us and provide constant entertainment. Some are equipped with helicopters, personal submarines, and tenders as big as *Gatti*. We have a new yacht service that is very reasonable and responds to our needs with somewhat less than the average Italian relaxation.

Gatti visits *OceanS* at Palmaria.

A busy day at the port.

Rich boys' toys off *Gatti's* stern.

Alberto Terzi sold his port office at a nice profit and is doing documentation work from offices in Fiumicino and Monte Carlo, but we are still friends. Paola has introduced me to the pleasures of the beach clubs. The *ormeggiatori* and port personal have become friends and watch out for us when there is need. The security systems at the port are excellent, and we have not had any incidents of theft. I haven't even missed cuttings from the much admired pot of basil that sits on the dock when we are in residence.

The posh Roma Yacht Club has opened in the center of the port with panoramic views of the river, sea, ancient towers and the rolling acres of Ostia Antica. The swans apparently found their nesting so successful that they have become permanent residents at the port. One male in particular cruises by every day and stretches up his long neck to take *panettone* from our hands. With the strengthening of the euro and weakening of the dollar, our investment has proved to be an excellent one indeed. More importantly, we need not worry every year about securing a berth at rents that are climbing astronomically throughout the Med. Stretched out on a gently rocking deck with a cold glass of wine, drowsing in a warm sun with the musical flow of Italian washing over me, I feel as though we made a wonderful daydream come true. We have constructed what, for us, is the perfect *pensione*.

Bill's hearing impairment and my heartache over my pet-less life came to a happy, combined resolution. Bill was approved for a hearing dog, which the condominium had to accept under the Americans with Disabilities Act. As you can see, time does not squelch the rebel in us! Sydney is a smart, friendly miniature Australian shepherd that alerts Bill to the telephone, alarms and sirens. The dog travels in the airline cabin with us, where he lies quietly at our feet for the eight to 10 hours our trans-Atlantic trip lasts. On board, he patrols our decks and maintains a sharp lookout. At dock, he has become a favorite and has been known to abandon ship under certain persuasive Italian full moons to run about the deserted port with the night-watch dogs. His Italian is coming along nicely. He has in every way been a gift from the gods.

We visit Lavagna on occasion and find nothing much changed at the port other than dead flowers outside Dominic's office. Even Angelo's window display from 2001 has not been touched. The port is full, but in a state of continuing deterioration. We lunch at the Albatross where the good proprietors hug us well and remember all

248

our favorite foods. Giuseppe represents the only change, and that a small one. At last check, he was involved with a Portuguese girl, and his linguistic interests can be guessed by the reader.

We have no plan to return *Gatti* to U.S. shores. Like us, she started out as a pure American product. Like us, she now is markedly altered. Her wiring and appliances are now European, and she resides in a part of the world where age is respected and great age is venerated. She is as content as we to be an amalgam of many good things.

It remains a fact that our bodies and energies are not what they once were. Bill has had knee replacement surgery, his hearing problem will not get any better, and my hands will never tie a knot that I can be proud of. When *Gatti* had been refurbished at Tecnomar, the Guias' son-in-law, Emiliano, had advised us: "I know she is very sweet on the water, but she is an old lady and should not be overstressed." The same can be said of us. We hope to be able to lead the life we have for many more years, realizing that rashness and speed are not requirements for the enjoyment of sweet blessings.

Enjoyment of sweet blessings.

GLOSSARY OF ITALIAN WORDS AND PHRASES

a bordo – aboard a boat

anello – a ring; the method of mooring at the Port of Rome in which stern lines are tied to a large steel ring set in the side of the jetty rather than a bollard on top

antipasto – hors d'oeuvres

ape – a small three-wheeled motorized vehicle for carrying about small loads. The three-wheeled Vespa is a similar little truck.

Arcipelago Toscano – a string of islands off the coast of Tuscany including Elba

ardesia – slate

Autogrille – small fast food restaurants located near gas stations along state highways

autostrada – turnpikes

barca – a boat of indeterminate dimension

benzina – unleaded gasoline, also called benzina verde

cantiere – a shipyard where boats are constructed or serviced

capitaneria – port authorities and the office in which they are housed

capitano – a ship captain

Carabinieri – the Italian state military police

carnevale – carnival; the period of party-making culminating in Lent

caruggi – streets that are narrow, twisting alleyways, characteristic of towns in Liguria *ceci* – garbanzo beans or chickpeas. In Liguria, especially, they are dried and ground into flour

ciao – an informal hi or goodbye

cima a *terra* – a system of boat mooring whereby the bow is tied to a chain laid on the sea bed

cinghiale – wild boar; a popular Italian meat

comandante – commanding officer, captain

complimenti – congratulations, my compliments

cornetto – brioche, croissant; in Rome the cornetti are usually sweetened or filled with jam, Nutella, or the like.

farinata – a popular Ligurian dish made of ceci flour and olive oil and baked in a wood-fired oven on a large round copper pan. The result is similar to a crepe.

Ferragosta – the 15th of August, which marks the official start of vacation and the Assumption of the Virgin

fiumara – the river entrance to the Tiber River as opposed to the canal entrance

fiume – a river

focaccia – a flatbread such as pizza flavored in many different ways, many as simple as salt and oil. Focaccia in Liguria is considerably thicker than that in Rome.

focaccia a *Recco* – a special local focaccia made with cheese

gasolio – diesel fuel

gelato – the Italian equivalent of ice cream, served with a dollop of whipped cream in Rome

Grande Raccordo Anulare – (G.R.A.) the ring highway that encircles Rome

Guardia Costiera – the Italian Coast Guard

Guardia di Finanza – the Italian tax police involved with smuggling and tax evasion

lavagna – blackboard; the city is so named for the high quality of slate quarried there

Levante – a wind from the NNE-ENE that creates very strong storms especially in the spring and autumn. During cooler seasons, it lowers temperatures and may bring snow to the mountains.

Libeccio – a wind from the W-SW that primarily affects Corsica and the Ligurian coast. It creates wild seas and very high waves. Entrance to the harbor at Lavagna is very dangerous at these times.

lira – the old monetary unit of Italy. At the time of the introduction of the euro in 2002, 1 euro equaled about 1500 lire.

mare – the sea

mare mosso – rough sea; also the name of a café at the port

marinaio – a sailor; crew

moto – a small motor scooter

Mistral – a wind that comes generally from the NW to N. It can be very strong and lasts for several days. Its direction is variable, as it is affected by geographical features such as mountains.

ormeggiatori – port personnel who assist in mooring

palazzo – an Italian palace or very large building. Many old palazzi have been renovated as luxury apartments.

panettone – a traditional Italian Christmas cake made with candied fruit and raisins

passeggiata – a walk or promenade

passerella – a gangway

pesto – a sauce made of basil, olive oil, pine nuts and parmigiano

pesto palermitano – a sauce made in Palermo, Sicily of a number of ingredients including sun-dried tomatoes, peppers, raisins, capers, pine nuts, and other unidentified ingredients. The sauce is quite hot and spicy.

pontile – a bridge; the pier or jetty at which boats moor

posto barca – a boat slip

porto turistico – a pleasure port as opposed to a commercial, fishing, or military port

pranzo – the noontime meal, usually the heaviest of the day and served at 1:00 P.M.

presepe – a nativity scene; a crèche

pronto – literally means "ready"; the traditional answer to a telephone rather than "hello"

prosecco – a light sparkling wine similar to champagne served as an aperitif

rustico – a farmhouse, usually of stone and in a state of disrepair

sagra – a festival or feast, often religious in nature

Sagra del Fuoco – festival of fire held annually in Recco

Scirocco – a south wind that blows from the deserts to the East and North of the Mediterranean. In our part of Italy, is usually a hot, dry wind carrying great quantities of reddish sand but it can also be humid and accompanied by rains. Its sand can be carried as far North as Denmark.

straniere – a stranger or foreigner

torrente – a narrow, steep riverbed that carries water from the mountains to the sea after heavy rains or snow melts

Tramontana – a wind that rises from the NNW-NE. While it can cause storms in the Balerics and Corsica, it frequently brings good weather with calm skies and clear air to Italy and the Tyrrhenian Sea.

villa – a detached house or country house

LIST OF PERSONALITIES

Amerigo – electrician in Lavagna who loves all things American

Andy – the California electrician who rewired *Gatti* and installed inverters

Angelo – junior partner with the yacht service in Lavagna

Bucaccio (Mr.) – carpenter who supposedly repaired *Gatti* in Lavagna

Dominic Asino – owner of the yacht service in Lavagna

Doug Christiansen – the Marina del Rey creator of our mast and davits

Eraldo – an office worker with the Rome yacht service

Frank – the American friend we met at Marina del Rey who maintains a home in Italy

Beppe – employee with the Lavagna yacht service

Giuseppe – talented Lavagna carpenter and Don Juan

Jerry – found and renovated *Gatti*

Lance and Nikki – friends from Monte Carlo who own *OceanS*

Mario – employee at the Rome yacht service

Mary Lou and Phil – friends from New Orleans who own *Marbella*

Massimo – *ormeggiatore* at Porto di Roma

Murphy (Kathy and Don) – American friends from Las Vegas first met in Lavagna, who own *Antipodes*.

Pollino (Mr.) – owner of the slip in Lavagna

Paul – former employee of Doug who now owns the business; actor and model in California

Pino – diver at the Port of Rome

Pino Basilico – yacht broker in Genova

Terzi (Alberto, Paola, Gianluca) – owners of the yacht service in Rome

LIST OF BOAT NAMES

Amerigo Vespucci – Italy's tall ship used in naval training

Antipodes – the Murphy's sailing yacht

Bo Drum – sailing yacht moored to our starboard in Lavagna

Caroline – a neighboring motor yacht in Lavagna

Cielo di San Francisco – the freighter that carried *Gatti* from Long Beach to Genova

Class Action – name given to *Gatti* by Jerry

Freemantle Spirit – name of the new Azimut motor yacht owned by British couple in Lavagna

Gattofelice – sailboat owned by an author in Fiumicino

Gloria – tall ship of Colombia used for naval training; stage for regatta festivities in Cartagena

Hoka Hey – motor yacht in Lavagna

Leone Felice – *Gatti*'s predecessor in Newport Beach

Marbella – Mary Lou and Phil's sailing yacht

Mirande – motor yacht in Lavagna on which lived the Newfoundland dog

OceanS – Sunseeker motor yacht owned by Lance and Nikki

Pietro Micca – steam tug owned by the Giuas in Fiumicino

Rachele – sailing yacht moored to *Gatti's* port side in Lavagna

Shearwater – Frank's sailing yacht moored in Mexico

www.ingramcontent.com/pod-product-compliance
Lightning Source LLC
Chambersburg PA
CBHW031243090426
42742CB00007B/295